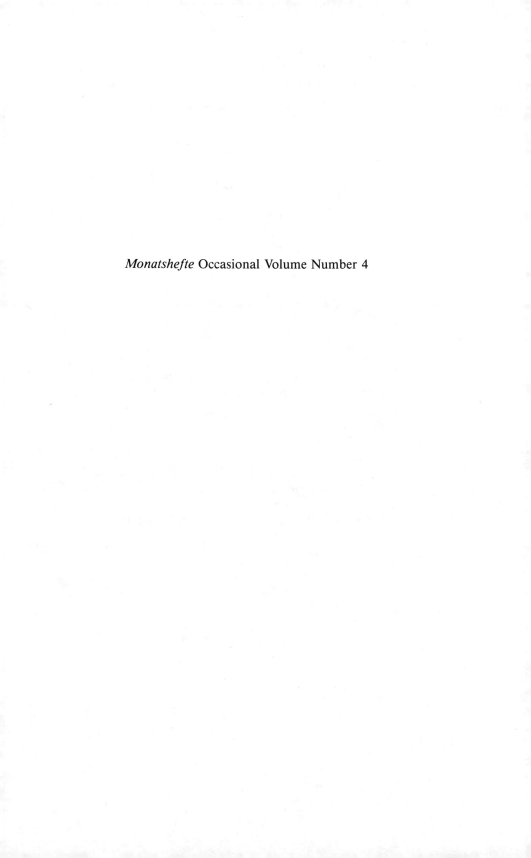

Monatshefte Occasional Volume Number 4

Monatshefte Occasional Volumes

Series Editor
Reinhold Grimm

Walter F. W. Lohnes and Valters Nollendorfs, editors
German Studies in the United States: Assessment and Outlook

Reinhold Grimm, Peter Spycher, and Richard A. Zipser, editors
From Dada and Kafka to Brecht and Beyond

Volker Dürr, Kathy Harms, and Peter Hayes, editors
Imperial Germany

Reinhold Grimm and Jost Hermand, editors
Blacks and German Culture

Blacks and German Culture

Essays Edited by

Reinhold Grimm
and
Jost Hermand

Published for *Monatshefte*
The University of Wisconsin Press

Published 1986

The University of Wisconsin Press
114 North Murray Street
Madison, Wisconsin 53715

The University of Wisconsin Press, Ltd.
1 Gower Street
London WC1E 6HA, England

First printing

Printed in the United States of America

Library of Congress Cataloging-in-Publication Data
Blacks and German culture.
    (Monatshefte occasional volumes; no. 4)
    Revised and enlarged papers read at the 15th
Wisconsin Workshop, held at the University of
Wisconsin—Madison Oct. 5-6, 1984.
    Includes bibliographies.
    1. Arts, German—Congresses. 2. Arts, Modern—20th
century—Germany—Congresses. 3. Blacks in art—
Congresses. 4. Blacks in literature—Congresses.
5. Germany—Civilization—Congresses. I. Grimm,
Reinhold. II. Hermand, Jost. III. Wisconsin
Workshop (15th: 1984: University of Wisconsin-Madison)
IV. Series.
NX550.A1B53   1986   700′.943   86-40051
ISBN 0-299-97017-5

Contents

Preface

The essays assembled in this volume constitute the revised and, in some instances, considerably enlarged versions of the papers that were read and discussed during the Fifteenth Wisconsin Workshop, an interdisciplinary event organized by the Department of German at the University of Wisconsin–Madison, and held in conjunction with its sister Departments of Comparative Literature and of African Languages and Literatures, on October 5 and 6, 1984. The conference, under the title "Blacks and German Culture, Art, and Literature," was further co-sponsored by the Goethe Institute Chicago, the General Consulate of the Federal Republic of Germany, and the Max Kade Foundation, and was attended by African and American as well as German and Afro-American scholars and students.

As will be seen, the nine contributions—by David Bathrick (UW–Madison), Sander L. Gilman (Cornell University), Reinhold Grimm (UW–Madison), Georg M. Gugelberger (University of California–Riverside), Jost Hermand (UW–Madison), Rosemarie K. Lester (University of Maryland, European Division–Frankfurt), Edris Makward (UW–Madison), Marian E. Musgrave (Miami University), and Amadou Booker Sadji (Université de Dakar, Sénégal)—represent a great multitude and variety of facts and findings, analyses and assertions with regard to a possible, indeed posited, if surely debatable "German Blackness of Its Own" (Grimm) or "Blackness without Blacks...in Germany" (Gilman). No attempt has been made at unifying them, either thematically or methodologically, for similar divergences characterize the already sizable amount of previous research as well, bent as it is on exploring and charting what until a few years ago was an almost totally neglected, even widely unknown, area (for a tentative listing of major works, see Grimm's contribution below, especially notes 17–19; for a report on the conference, see Eckhart Kleßmann's pertinent article in *Frankfurter Allgemeine Zeitung* of 22 October 1984). It should also be noted, however, that prejudices or, at least, misconceptions persist not only among the general public but even in the ranks of professionals, as witness views and statements such as those put forth—in an article in *Die Zeit* of 27 July 1984—by the Germanist Leo Kreutzer.

The Fifteenth Wisconsin Workshop has received, as have earlier ones, generous support both for its organization and for the publication of its proceedings. It is most gratefully acknowledged here. Our special thanks are due to the Max Kade Foundation under its director, Dr. Erich Markel, and, once again, to the Vilas Fund of the University of Wisconsin.

Blacks and German Culture

Literary Justifications of Slavery

Marian E. Musgrave

Within three and one-half centuries of the arrival of Europeans in Africa, whole tribes had disappeared or had been decimated, thriving cities and agricultural areas had been laid waste, and from the West Coast of Africa alone, some 20 to 24 million human beings had been carried away into slavery. The cause was sugar. Ceuta, which the Portuguese had captured in 1415, was a terminal port of the trans-Saharan gold trade, but by 1445, slavery, the "black gold" trade, had become the main Portuguese activity, for sugar was king.[1]

Sugar plantations had been established in Madeira, in São Tomé, and in Brazil by the Portuguese. By 1491, the Spanish had begun sugar culture in the Canary Islands and in 1493 introduced the cane into Hispaniola, eventually controlling the Caribbean.[2] Holland, France, and England competed for a share of "the most valuable agricultural commodity in international trade."[3] France established its tropical empire during the second quarter of the 17th century, with important colonies on St. Domingue, Martinique, and Guadeloupe intended to raise sugar in particular and later coffee.[4] By the 1620s, England had begun establishing a chain of West Indian sugar islands and by the end of the century had a sugar empire.

Of all the work done by slave labor, including logging and mining, the sugar industry was the deadliest. Infections of hands and feet received from setting out the cane and from harvesting, crushed fingers, hands, arms, or legs during grinding, burns received during boiling, skimming, and "striking," all could, and often did, prove fatal. Plantation medicine was primitive, often involving amputation or daubing tar on the wound. Inasmuch as the survival time of the average sugar plantation slave was only seven years, regardless of his age at the time of kidnapping, new slaves were always in demand.[5] In fact, a Capuchin missionary was told in 1682 that a black who had survived even seven years was considered to have lived very long.[6]

Planters found it to be cheaper and easier to work one's slaves to death and then purchase more, than it was to set up a "self-reproducing" slave population.[7] "Self-reproducing" is a euphemism for using black women like brood mares, which can both work and foal, and treating black children like crops, to be sold when "ripe," ripeness being interpreted as any age from two or three years old on.[8] This system was widespread only in the United

3

States but obtained to some minor extent in Mexico and Haiti.[9] Black resistance to having children limited the success of the system: men as well as women refused sex, women deliberately aborted, and both men and women committed infanticide.[10] As Voltaire remarked, "A slave who is in another's power has little inclination for marriage."[11]

African blacks had replaced Arawak and other Indians from 1517 on, after the priest Bartolomé de las Casas, filled with horror by the Indians' death rate, pled before Charles V for permission to enslave blacks instead, arguing that domestic slavery already existed in Africa, that the Portuguese were already using blacks to good advantage in Brazil, and that blacks were up to four times stronger than Indians.[12] At the end of his life, Las Casas is said to have regretted what he had done to blacks.

Import data on slaves reveal how the sugar trade consumed manpower. There were, for example, 40,000 slaves in Jamaica in 1690; in 1820, there were about 350,000; but between those two dates, over 800,000 slaves had been imported. Another example: the United States and Brazil entered the 19th century with about 1,000,000 slaves apiece, but importations into Brazil were three times greater than into the United States. By 1861, there were about 4,000,000 slaves in the United States but only 1,500,000 in Brazil. Yet in the 1830s alone, Brazil had imported more than 400,000 Blacks and in 1848 could absorb 60,000 more.[13] French merchants sent more than 3,000 ships to Africa in the 18th century, purchasing over a million men, women, and children, of whom up to 200,000 died before reaching the New World. Of those remaining, Guadeloupe received a large share. In 1656, the slave population there had been 3,000; in 1770, it was only 80,000.[14]

The first justifications of slavery are admissions of the economic value of, and need for, black workers in tropical lands, such as Montesquieu's remark that these countries could not be developed without black slaves, or George Whitefield's opinion that the providence of God had appointed the colony of Georgia "rather for the work of black slaves than for Europeans because of the hot climate to which the Negroes are better used than white people."[15] One finds, too, that writers who are not attempting to justify slavery often betray a vague anti-black sentiment which expresses itself in fantastic travelers' tales (blacks have no language but screech like bats) and in contemptuous anecdotes and poems.[16]

Black characters in drama and in prose narratives are consistently a source of humor because of physical features and speech.[17] Sylvia Wynter points out the early appearance of *negroide,* a comic stage dialect of Portuguese spoken by actors playing black roles. Even a character representing a black king speaks in *negroide.*[18] The form of debased English put into the mouths of black characters in 19th-century American writing rapidly lost any relationship which it might have had to actual black dialects but remained almost unchanged well into the 20th century, since its purpose was to make blacks seem stupid and funny. One writer even put such English into the mouth of black physicians and other professional men.[19]

An Austrian who created a debased German to represent the speech of blacks was Karl Postl, who wrote novels in German about 19th-century America. He says of a slave who had been "transplanted" thirty years ago from Africa to Louisiana that the man could scarcely pronounce ten words of English or French correctly: "But how could he, with those monstrous lips through which every word would have to force its way?"[20]

The blackness of Africans, and their semi- or total nakedness, both fascinated and horrified Europeans, since black had intense emotional meanings and nakedness was perceived as proof of depravity, not of innocence.[21] Richard Baker, describing a meeting with blacks on the African West Coast in 1562, wrote:

> Their captain comes to me
> as naked as my nail;
> Not having wit or honesty
> to cover once his tail.

Such negative portrayals, full of contempt and rejection, helped create the climate in which incredibly sadistic treatment of black men, women, and children was ignored, denied, minimized, and justified for four and one-half centuries.[22]

Using only the justifications which appear to some extent in the belles lettres of slaving countries, I have divided the arguments into five groups. Some justifications did not lend themselves readily to fiction or verse; writers who persevered with philosophical or political-science arguments ended up with tracts, not novels. Cases in point are the fourteen proslavery "novels" which were written to refute Harriet Beecher Stowe's *Uncle Tom's Cabin.*[23]

Arguments were seldom if ever held separate and distinct from one another even in the 16th century. As the abolition movement gained strength, proslavers tended to grasp at any arguments, fusing them and sometimes using mutually contradictory ones—"the work is so exhausting that only Negroes could do it" and "the Negroes do not work hard"—and sometimes blasphemous ones.[24] The arguments to be discussed are the legal, the Biblical, the moral (slavery as a missionary enterprise), the sociological, and the biological.

1

The legal justifications of slavery (and the refutations) probably exercised more great minds of Europe than any other; questions about the right of one man to enslave another had arisen even in ancient Rome and were certainly known to educated Europeans.[25] The theses involved in the legal justification are these:

1. Property rights may be extended to include persons. This thesis became important after proslavers had ceased their attempt to prove that a slave was quite literally a thing. Many ambiguities remained, such as the right of a slave to take his master to court, the legality of seizing slaves as securities for debt, and the listing of slaves in inventories and wills along with other goods and chattels.[26] Still, the fight to define a slave legally as a thing had been lost; even the United States Census Bureau listed slaves as $3/5$ of a man.

In literature, the issue becomes the right of the owner to sell his slaves at will, separating married couples from each other and children from their parents. The proslavery group tried to avoid the subject but sometimes used the arguments that blacks are incapable of love between the sexes and that black mothers have no feelings for their own children but love white children dearly. "Meet a bear robbed of her whelps; but attempt not to tear away the white babes from the black woman's heart! She would rend you as if she were a raving maniac!" writes Bayard Hall in *Frank Freeman's Barbershop.* Of a black woman, all of whose children had been sold except the last one, John P. Kennedy writes: "All before Abe had been successively dismissed from Lucy's cabin, as they reached the age fit to render them serviceable, with the satisfied concern that belongs to a negro mother who trusts to the kindness of her master."[27]

2. Slavery is legal if the parties involved freely consent. Samuel von Pufendorf's Contract Theory, supported by appeals to Hobbes and Grotius, and based upon an actual practice in antiquity, is the source of this thesis. It finds reflection in John Barbot's narrative of his slaving voyages. He declares that in 1682 he saw famine victims in Goree selling themselves and likens the sight to the seven years' famine in old Egypt, when the Canaanites and Egyptians sold themselves to Pharaoh and Joseph.[28] More importantly, it finds seeming approval in Voltaire's dialogue of 1768, *L'ABC,* in which A maintains that a man may sell himself, while B maintains that he cannot, since liberty is priceless. A replies: "Everyone to his price. So much the worse for him if he sells me cheaply something so precious. Say that he is an imbecile, but don't call me a rogue!" In justice to Voltaire, however, it should be noted that he said of Pufendorf's slavery contract: "I would believe Pufendorf only if he showed me the first contract" (cf. Seeber, pp. 65 and 63).

3. It is legitimate to hold as a slave one who was born in slavery. Aristotle, Hobbes, and Grotius had held that human beings are never naturally equal, but that some are born for domination and some for slavery. Seeming to agree, Voltaire wrote that the French are reproached for their commerce in Negro slaves, but "a people which traffics in its own children is more to be

condemned than the buyer. This trade demonstrates our superiority. Whoever takes a master was born to have one" (Seeber, p. 63). Rousseau's contemptuous answer in his *Social Contract* was that everyone born *into* slavery is of course born *for* slavery, but the slaves "love their servitude as Ulysses's men loved their brutish transformation" (ibid., p. 68). A footnote to the controversy is the royal French decree of 15 June 1736 forbidding the freeing of children born in slavery (ibid.).

4. If a purchaser buys in good faith an illegally enslaved person, the purchaser is not obliged to inquire how or where the slave was obtained. This issue became increasingly more important as the slave trade with Africa was declared illegal in more and more countries—1807 in England, 1815 in France, 1828 in the United States, 1850 in Brazil. Slave traders, determined to stay in business, purchased old American ships and papers, flew the American flag, and carried on their trade boldly, since they knew that British ships would not challenge the American flag. Fresh slaves continued to be unloaded in United States ports as well as in Caribbean and Brazilian ports until into the 1850s.[29] Slavers also kidnapped free blacks, whites, and children of whatever race, facts which are reflected more in antislavery literature than in proslavery. Even a German national, Salome Müller, was kidnapped and sold in Louisiana, finally being freed by court order in 1846, according to William Wells Brown.[30]

5. Historically, the Right of War permits prisoners of war to be killed or ransomed. They can therefore be enslaved as a merciful alternative. Thomas More uses this argument in his *Utopia*. Three notorious slave traders who published their log books *cum* reminiscences—John Barbot, William Snelgrave, and Theophilus Conneau—also used this justification.[31] A contemporary of Snelgrave accused him of "a pious attempt to throw an air of charity over the slave trade" by his accounts of rescuing prisoners of war, since it was notorious that slaving nations and traders started tribal wars by bribing chieftains with brandy, rum, cloth, jewelry, and the like.[32] Even the French missionary Labat, a slave holder himself, admitted that the "native wars" were merely pretexts for supplying the slave markets (Seeber, p. 22).

6. Slaves who are bought legally are lawful property which can entail to the purchasers' lawful heirs and to theirs after them. This argument figures strongly in proslavery literature, usually by implication. Proslavery novelists preferred to present slavery as a *fait accompli;* purchase and ownership seemed to be argument enough. George Fox, the Quaker leader, said it clearly: "Let me tell you, it will doubtless be very acceptable to the Lord if so be that masters...would so deal with their Negroes and Blacks, whom they have bought with their own money, as to let them go free after they have served a considerable number of years, be it 30, more or less."[33] Herder's Quaker, who releases his slave on the man's thirtieth birthday, illustrates Fox's advice.[34]

Showing slavery as already peacefully established meant that pro-slavery authors had to dispense with many of the most exciting, suspenseful, and horrible episodes—kidnappings, slave rebellions, slave auctions, rapes, and torture—which antislavery authors could freely use. For this reason, proslavery fiction tends toward sameness and blandness, even when written by fairly competent authors. Three novels which enjoyed popularity in their time will illustrate the point. *Swallow Barn* by John P. Kennedy, *Ein Pflan-zerleben* by Karl Postl, and *María* by Jorge Isaacs show such similarities as untroubled pastoralism, few slaves in evidence, concentration upon whites' love affairs, and "crises" which have nothing to do with slavery. Two of the three—*Pflanzerleben* and *María*—begin with slave "festivals."[35]

Manumission implied the legality of slavery; it also implied the right not to manumit. Postl's spokesman in *Ein Pflanzerleben* declares that Washington, Jefferson, and Patrick Henry did not manumit their slaves "because they were completely convinced that not even the slaves, much less the society, would be benefited by this freedom" (Sealsfield, p. 88).[36] But a few proslavery authors as well as some who are ambivalent about either slavery or blacks do show manumission for exceptional service, usually for saving the life of a white. Such episodes occur in Heinrich von Kleist's novella *Die Verlobung in St. Domingo* and in William Gilmore Simm's *The Yemassee*.[37] In the first, the black "rewards" his master by killing him; in the second, the black indignantly refuses freedom, a scene which became a staple in proslavery literature (one master "punishes" a disobedient slave by forcing him to be free) and was even used by the black poet, Paul Lawrence Dunbar.[38]

2

The Biblical defense of slavery uses Scripture and apocryphal tales to "prove" that blacks are accursed by God, outcasts like Cain, and evil by nature. In the United States, this defense was the first to appear and was used more often than any other. It was invariably linked to color, the black skin being identified as the "mark of Cain" and, at least for Johann Scheffler, a sign of the black's distance from God. "God is...fire and light / Thou art black, dark, cold," he wrote in the *Cherubinische Wanders-Mann*.[39]

Those Biblical passages in which the Hebrews are told whom they may enslave (Leviticus 25:44–46), Paul's words concerning submission to those above us (Romans 13), and the infamous line in Colossians 3:22, "Slaves, obey in all things your masters"—the text most often preached on American plantations—were proof enough to proslavers that God had no objection to slavery.[40] Hagar, Sarah's slave woman, was considered by some to be the female progenitor of blacks. When she bore a child by Abraham, into whose bed she had been sent by her barren mistress, she became so proud that Sarah whipped her and sent her and her son, Ishmael, away. As "Aunt Hagar's Children" blacks are condemned to slavery, to being outcasts, and, a further implication which is seldom mentioned, to bear the children of the enslavers. Mary Chesnut, in her famous *Diary from Dixie* which she kept during the Civil War, wrote that every Southern woman knew that Harriet Beecher Stowe, far from exaggerating the amount of black concubinage in the South, had not gone far enough.[41] The mulattoes and mulattas who thronged the streets and plantations of slaving lands soon filled the pages of fiction and poetry, replacing the heroic 18th-century blacks, whose lineaments had to be so carefully described in order to conform to European standards of beauty—Aphra Behn's Oroonoko and his bride, Imoinda, for example.

Blacks were also linked to Ham, who uncovered Noah as he lay drunk in his tent and was cursed by Noah when he awoke (Genesis 9:26–27). "And in the very second of that curse, Ham's hair curled and his face became black, by which it is plain," says Johann Heinrich Heidegger, "that Negroes are the sons of Ham and damned to eternal slavery."[42] Another sign, evidently bestowed at the same time, was the "enormous size" of black men's organs of generation, "an infallible proof that Blacks are sprung from Ham, who, for uncovering his father's nakedness, had, according to the Schoolmen, a curse laid upon that part."[43]

Ham was alleged also to have broken God's commandment against human sex on the Ark, lest a child then conceived should claim the world through inheritance. When Ham's wife conceived, "God ordained the birth of a son named Chus, who not only himself but all his posterity should be so black and loathsome that it remain a spectacle of disobedience to all the world."[44]

A logical result of God's curses is the sinful, corrupt nature and the tendency to have commerce with evil spirits. John Saffin of Massachusetts wrote:

> Cowardly and cruel are these Blacks innate
> Prone to revenge, imp of inveterate hate;
> He that exasperates them soon espies
> Mischief and murder in their eyes.
> Libidinous, deceitful, false, and rude,
> The spumy issue of ingratitude.[45]

Thomas Grainger, an English physician and author of a long poem, "The Sugar Cane," warned against the purchase of Coromantee slaves because of their implacable, unforgiving nature.[46] Theodor Waitz, a German anthropologist, charged blacks with "coarse sensuality, slothfulness, and unfeeling cruelty"; Karl Postl echoes the charges of sensuality and cruelty and adds that blacks are animallike, instinct-driven, deceitful, natural liars, thievish, and imitative. As for black women, they are incapable of a "high, self-sacrificing love."[47] The Brazilian writer, Loreto Couto, wrote a series of short stories in which various slaves, "into whose heart the devil had introduced himself," told terrible lies to their masters, causing the masters to murder their own wives and daughters.[48]

The linkage of blacks (hellish, devilish, said the *Cherubinischer Wanders–Mann)* to Satan and devils reaches a peak in the *Simplicissimus* and in a colonial Mexican folktale, "The Mulatta of Cordoba." In the first, a beautiful Abyssinian woman floats on a chest to the desert island where Simplicissimus and the young carpenter are languishing. She asks permission to remain as their cook and helper, but suggests to the carpenter that he murder Simplicissimus and marry her. Once they are seated at the dinner table, Simplicissimus says grace and makes the sign of the cross, upon which both lady and chest vanish, leaving behind such a foul stench that the carpenter faints.[49] The Mexican tale concerns a lovely mulatta who had made a pact with the devil. When the elderly mayor of the village cannot win her love with gifts and pleas, he charges her before the Inquisition with witchcraft, has her jailed, and raises a lynch mob. But she is snatched away by a man on a fiery steed. When she reappears, she is seized and condemned to the stake. But the Inquisition judge is so smitten by her that he promises to spare her if she will yield to him. She mocks him, points to a ship painted on the wall, steps aboard, and sails away amid "diabolical" peals of laughter.[50]

Blacks and devils are further linked in the Argentinian *payada* or song contest tradition among the gauchos. Santos Vega, a legendary gaucho *payador,* is said to have roamed the countryside, challenging and defeating all rivals until he met the devil, who was disguised as a black.[51] This tale should remind us that Simplicissimus roamed the German countryside disguised as a black devil in order to extort food from the superstitious peasants.

3

The moral defense of slavery treats slavery as a missionary enterprise to bring a heathen people with little or no moral or ethical sense, to God. Though "generally extremely sensual, knavish, revengeful, impudent, lying, impertinent, gluttonous, extravagant in their expressions, so intemperate that they drink brandy as if it were water, deceitful in their dealings with Europeans...and very lazy," the blacks' nature changes for the better, once they are enslaved.[52] Perhaps the first person to use the moral defense was the chronicler of the voyages of Prince Henry the Navigator, who wrote of the first shipload of blacks brought to Portugal to be slaves in 1441 that "though their bodies were placed in subjection, that fact was of small importance compared with the eternal freedom of their souls" (Sayers, p. 15). According to Mauricio Goulart, Pope Nicholas V agreed with the chronicler, as did subsequent popes, who "rejoiced at the prospect of extending the faith" and reserved all trading privileges in Africa for the Portuguese (ibid.).

The moral defense was important in the United States, where few seemed to doubt the value of religion for a slave—witness Tom in *Uncle Tom's Cabin,* who, surrounded by whites who corrupt, distort, misuse, and ignore Christian teachings, nevertheless perseveres and, on his death bed, brings two more souls to Christ.

Both antislavery and proslavery writers were likely to imply that some special providence had brought blacks to America, God's country. William Grayson, author of a long poem contrasting the miserable lot of the free worker with the privileged lot of the slave, wrote: "Hence is the Negro brought by God's command / For wiser teaching, to a foreign land."[53] Phillis Wheatley, a little genius who was kidnapped at the age of seven, purchased by the Wheatleys in order to save her life, and educated with their daughters, began writing perfect iambic pentameter verse at twelve. She wrote:

> Twas mercy brought me from my native land,
> taught my benighted soul to understand
> that there's a God, that there's a Savior, too...
> Remember, Christians, Negroes black as Cain
> May be refin'd and join th'angelic train.
>
> (from *Poems,* 1802)

Slavery as a missionary enterprise is often linked with attacks on Africa as a sink of evil, a dangerous land full of diseases, fierce animals, and cannibalistic people. This perception of Africa was so powerful that it has persisted to the present, seducing even people of good will. In 1820, Maciel da Costa, who later became president of the Brazilian Constituent Assembly, wrote that he was not opposed to slavery on humanitarian grounds; on the contrary, he agreed with those who believed it to be beneficial to Negroes to be taken away from Africa (Sayers, p. 67). *Anti-Fanaticism,* by Martha Butts, and *The Black Gauntlet,* by Mary Howard Schoolcraft, depict the horrid barbarism of Africa, where naked inhabitants worship snakes and devour one another. The New Orleans *Daily Delta* and the Galveston *Weekly* reminded their readers that the "degraded" inhabitants of a "depraved" continent dined on frogs, redworms, lizards, wasps, bumblebees, and grasshoppers; a European might be invited to supper by a native, "when as a delicacy reserved for him, there is fished up out of the big pot of soup a black head, with the lips drawn back and the white teeth grinning, and such a painful resemblance to the faces around him that for a moment he wonders which of the younger members of the family has been sacrificed to the exigencies of the occasion. But he is reassured and discovers that he is not eating man but monkey."[54]

Writers also harrowed their readers' soul with tales of atrocities perpetrated by African blacks. William Snelgrave strengthened the proslavery side by his frightful stories recounted in an easy, straightforward, colloquial style. One tale, the execution of Testesole, will suffice to show the genre:

They tied him to the ground, where, spreading him on his belly, they with sharp knives cut open his arms, back, thighs, and legs...and filled the wound with a mixture of lime juice, salt, and pepper...having cut off his head, they cut his body in pieces, broiled them on the coals, and ate them. (Grant, *Fortunate Slave,* p. 132)

John Barbot, another slaver, tells of seeing pregnant women's bellies ripped open; both Barbot and Snelgrave make the point that "the worst of Christian slavery" is better than living free in Africa, an opinion seconded by Mrs. D. J. McCord, "perhaps the ablest woman of her day in the South," who wrote: "Christian slavery, in its full development, free from the...galling bitterness of abolition interference, is the brightest sunbeam which Omniscience has destined for the slave's existence."[55]

4

The fourth defense, the sociological, is basically secular; and though it is sometimes bolstered with images from the Bible, writers are more likely to borrow the patriarchal image of slavery from ancient Greece and Rome. The view is that though low on the scale of humanity, blacks are educable under the benevolent guidance of a wise master. Some writers see slavery as a kind of apprenticeship from which the black will eventually graduate; others see slavery as a permanent institution. Gilmore Simms wrote in 1852 that slavery was "an especially wisely devised institution...for the benefit, the improvement, and safety, morally, socially, and physically, of a barbarous and inferior race who would otherwise perish."[56] George Fitzhugh, one of the founders of sociology as a discipline in the United States, wrote: "The Negro slaves of the South are the happiest...and freest [*sic*] people in the world. The children and the aged and infirm work not at all...oppressed neither by care nor labor. The women do little hard work and are protected from the despotism of their husbands by their masters. The Negro men and stout boys work...not more than nine hours a day."[57] Fitzhugh saw Negroes as "improvident children," with the master occupying the place of parent or guardian (ibid., p. 91).

This view of slaves and slavery was by far the favorite one; the perennial popularity of *Gone With the Wind* (the film, not the book) attests to the hold of the sociological justification on the popular imagination. Even some writers who, strictly speaking, were not proslavery, were likely to present slavery in a patriarchal guise, a task which became increasingly more difficult after the Abolitionists began disseminating factual materials and presenting escaped slaves, bodies mutilated and scarred, to tell their stories.[58] Many writers solved the problem by restricting the scene to just one plantation or area. Daniel Defoe, for example, tells us that Crusoe owns plantations in Brazil, but we never see him there with his slaves. Instead, we see

Crusoe with Friday, whose "very affections were tied to" Crusoe "like those of a child to his father."[59] But the first word taught to this child is "master," not "papa." The Colombian novel of unhappy love, *María*, presents a patriarchal form of slavery in the household of the lover, Efraín, but nowhere else. Efraín's father caresses the black children and even dances a few steps with the black bride. The author shows us María reading *Paul et Virginie* by Bernadin de Saint-Pierre, a novel which also presents a pastoral view of slavery, and carefully restricted scenes.[60]

Even black writers could fall into the patriarchal trap. Alexandre Dumas père published the novel *Georges* in 1843, one year before he published *Les Trois Mousquetaires*. Though it does contain some negative scenes, the book is by no means an antislavery novel. The mulatto plantation owner runs a model plantation. When his son Georges returns from his fourteen years of education and travel, the two enlarge the plantation and purchase fifty new slaves from an honorable trader who asks honest prices for good ware. Georges's brother, Pierre, is himself a slave trader, but he never overloads his ship.[61] *The Garies and their Friends,* a novel by Frank J. Webb about free blacks in mid-19th-century Philadelphia, contains a pastoral plantation scene which could have come from any proslavery novel, with its descriptions of the scenic beauty of Georgia, the table laden with food, the happy little black children, and the slaves who love and trust master and his octoroon mistress. The blacks show no anxiety about having a new overseer, nor about master's move to Philadelphia.[62]

The idea of the "natural inferiority" of blacks is not usually a separate argument since inferiority alone could not justify enslavement. Inferiority is implied, however, in the other arguments and is central to the idea of the Great Chain of Being. The black's presumably low place in the Chain is then used to establish or to justify other points which the author wishes to make.

David Hume, the British philosopher who woke Immanuel Kant from his "dogmatic slumber," wrote: "I am apt to suspect the Negroes, and in general all other species of men...to be naturally inferior to the white. There never was a civilized nation of any other complexion than white, nor even any individual eminent either in action or speculation."[63] Hume's remark is the more amazing when one remembers that Chinoiserie was sweeping fashionable England, and that tea was replacing coffee. Hume concludes by saying that a Negro in Jamaica of whom he has heard "is considered as a man of parts and learning, but tis likely he is admired for very slender accomplishments, like a parrot who speaks a few words plainly."

Hume's attitude can be compared with Thomas Jefferson's on the poetry of Phillis Wheatley and on the mathematical skill of Benjamin Banneker, the self-taught son of a freed black and a mulatta (the daughter of an Englishwoman and her slave). Jefferson's harsh evaluation of Wheatley's poetry, which was admired on both continents, might be owing to the poet's favorable reception by the Countess of Huntingdon and her circle during

Wheatley's trip to England in 1773. In 1784, Jefferson wrote that Wheatley's compositions "are below the dignity of criticism."[64] But Banneker was one of the three designers of Washington, D.C. In a letter to Condorcet, then secretary of the Academy of Sciences in Paris, Jefferson in 1791 had mentioned proudly the Negro in the United States "who is a very respectable mathematician."[65] By 1809, Jefferson could write to Joel Barlow that though Banneker knew spherical trigonometry, he, Jefferson, considered him to have a "mind of very common stature, indeed."[66]

5

Since anything which was different about blacks was used to establish the idea of inferiority, Winthrop Jordan believed that it was a "tragic happenstance of nature" that Africa was the habitat of the animal most like humans, the chimpanzee, called orangutan by Europeans. The British had long been using the words "brutish" and "beastly" to describe the behavior and diet of blacks, and the educated had seen the medieval bestiaries, with their pictures and descriptions of creatures which were part man, part animal. Jordan thinks that it was perhaps inevitable that the English should begin to make comparisons between chimpanzees and blacks.[67] The fifth justification of slavery, the biological, was at first an attempt to prove that blacks were not human beings at all, or if human, then of a totally different species than whites. One often finds Negroes and orangutans linked together in the same sentence: Karl Postl wrote that a group of slave women looked like apes or like a troop of clothed orangutans (*Pflanzerleben,* p. 14); Thomas Jefferson wrote that blacks are perhaps intermediate between orangutans and whites, since orangutans prefer Negro women, and blacks prefer whites.[68] Jefferson did not finish his analogy.

Edward Long, author of a history of Jamaica in 1774, wrote that orangutans could learn to eat at dinner tables, had the same mechanical and intellectual capacities as Negroes, and were "equally lascivious"; to prove that Negroes are closer to the animal world than the human world, Long said that Negroes have wool, not hair, and have black lice, not white lice on their bodies.

Jean-Louis Agassiz, the Swiss-born naturalist "who imbibed Negrophobia upon settling in the United States," extended his theories of separate origins of plants and animals to include humans. He wrote that the brain of an adult Negro, "besides other singularities, bears a striking resemblance, in several particulars, to the brain of an orangutan."[69]

Samuel Cartwright, a physician in Louisiana, believed that blacks have two diseases peculiar to them: drapetomania, which is a morbid tendency to run away, and dyaesthesia aethiopica, which causes rascality (Karcher, p. 23).

Alexis de Tocqueville wrote: "We scarcely acknowledge the common features of mankind in this child of debasement...and we are almost inclined to look upon him as being intermediate between man and the brutes." He concluded by saying that Europeans will "never mix with Negroes" (Fishel and Quarles, pp. 106–7). De Toqueville lived from 1805 to 1859; at the time he was writing, Paris had a sizable black and mulatto population, as did in fact other French mainland cities, in spite of efforts of the government to limit the number of Negroes in France.[70] As for attempting to limit mixing, as early as 1662 a law was passed in Virginia providing double the *usual* fine for "any Christian committing fornication with a Negro man or woman." A Maryland law mentions those "shameful matches" between free-born English women "forgetful of their free condition...and Negro slaves" (Gross and Hardy, p. 42 fn.). And Jefferson himself was linked to four of his house slaves, most especially to Sally Hemings, by whom he is alleged to have had several children. Some of her descendants still live in Ohio.

The idea that God or nature had created several species of mankind was called pluralism. It was considered dangerous, even blasphemous, and was originally associated only with such freethinkers and innovators as Paracelsus, who in 1520 wrote that Negroes were not descended from Adam; and Giordano Bruno, who in 1591 wrote: "No sound-thinking person will refer the Ethiopians to the same Protoplast as the Jewish one."[71] For religious persons, pluralism contained intrinsic problems because it contradicted Scripture by its insistence on what could only be called multiple creations and, as a natural consequence, multiple Adams and Eves, all of whom were presumably made perfect, and one pair of whom must have been black.

But pluralists were indifferent to the implications, being quite willing to expel their own ancestors from the Garden of Eden if they could lock blacks up in the Zoological Garden. The physician J. H. Van Evrie began measuring brains in order to prove that whites and blacks were different species. He concluded that the brain of a white "measures 92 cubic inches, with the cerebrum...predominating over the cerebellum...thus it is capable of infinite progression and transmits the knowledge or experience gained in one generation to subsequent generations, the record of which is history." If deluded people wish to improve on the works of the Creator and *elevate* the Negro to the standard of the white, they would have to add 25 or 30 percent to the Negro brain, but "such a brain could no more be born of a Negress than can an elephant pass through the eye of a needle."[72]

Johann Friedrich Blumenbach was not a pluralist but like Van Evrie was interested in skull measurements. The facial angle, that is, a measurement of prognathism derived by looking at the human head in profile, interested him especially. One line was drawn from the meeting of the lips to the most prominent part of the forehead, and another from the opening of the ear to the base of the nose. The crucial angle was formed where those two lines met. The wider the angle, the smaller the degree of prognathism, supposedly, prognathism being suggestive of the head shape of animals. A wide angle was supposed to accompany a higher forehead, greater skull capacity, and greater intelligence. The theory had been introduced by a Dutchman, Pieter Camper, according to whom blacks had the smallest "Camper's facial angle" and therefore were the lowest on the human scale.[73] Blumenbach accepted Camper's theory until he saw the African heads painted by Van Dyck, two of which had wide Camper's Angles, and later met "the beautiful Negress of Yverdon," who was "witty and sensible" and also had a wide Camper's angle. Blumenbach revised his theories, stating that individual Africans differ from each other as much as Europeans differ from one another.[74] Johann Gottfried Herder held a similar opinion, saying that there were "uncounted variations" among African blacks, but Herder insists on arranging these peoples according to their degree of deviation from European standards of beauty.[75]

In literature, blacks are often represented as grotesque in appearance and brutish in behavior. For Francisco de Quevedo, blackness alone constitutes the grotesque. In *Boda de Negros,* the poet reports upon a wedding which he supposedly witnessed, in which everyone and everything is black, including the wedding party, the wedding guests, the feast table, the tablecloth, the food, and the drinks. The bride's face had been "powdered" with soot and coal. The guests, attempting to eat their black food with their black fingers in an underilluminated room, at times bit themselves.[76]

Other writers pick physical features, such as the swollen lips, large, white, protruding eyes, flat nose, double head, long ears, pot belly, and bow legs of Edgar Allen Poe's Toby in *The Journal of Julius Rodman,* or the distorted feet and legs described by John Pendleton Kennedy and James Fenimore Cooper. Lessing writes: "Everyone knows how filthy the Hottentots are and how many things they consider beautiful and elegant and sacred, which with us awaken disgust and aversion. A flattened cartilage of a nose, flabby breasts hanging down to the navel, the whole body smeared with... goat's fat and soot gone rotten in the sun, the hair dripping with grease, arms and legs bound about with fresh entrails."[77] Victor Hugo describes a dwarf with "the agility of a monkey and the submissiveness of a dog," whose ears are so big that some say he wipes his eyes with them when he cries; Alexandre Dumas père creates another dwarf who has tiny legs, huge feet, apelike arms, and a bilious-yellow face. To a European, he would be ugly, writes Dumas, but not to Negroes, "less ardent partisans of the beautiful."[78] (Herder wrote somewhere that Negroes and Greenlanders have no sense of the beautiful.) These dwarfs are both villainous mulattoes, a relatively new kind of character which rapidly became a stereotype as the 19th century advanced, though, to be sure, the beautiful mulatta and handsome mulatto continued to appear.[79]

Like the villainous mulatto, the brute black is also a fairly late development in characterization, since he calls into question the contentedness of slaves and the patriarchal nature of slavery. In American literature, the brute black is a post–Civil War character, but in other literatures, there are earlier examples, of which I intend to use one from German, one from French, and one from Brazilian.

Die Verlobung in St. Domingo, by Heinrich von Kleist, deals with a Gold Coast slave who belongs to a wealthy French planter. As so often happens in slavery stories, Kongo Hoango saves his master's life and is manumitted in return. M. Villeneuve heaps good deeds upon Hoango, giving him a house and a housekeeper, makes him an overseer "against the custom of the country," retires him at sixty with a pension, and even mentions Hoango in his will. Nevertheless, during the great slave rebellion, Hoango is one of the first to seize a gun and put a bullet through his former master's head. In his "inhuman vengefulness," he carries on a deadly guerrilla war against all whites from that time on and is so rejuvenated by his actions that he sires a son, though already "frightfully old."[80]

The second brute black is Tamango, Prosper Merimée's title character. At first glance, he is a comic black, flanked by two wives, drunk from brandy, and wearing cast-off European clothing—an old uniform jacket which is too short, two epaulettes on each shoulder, and shorts made of Guinea cloth, his black belly showing between the bottom of the jacket and the top of the shorts like a broad black belt. But this man is selling Wolofs to Captain Ledoux and casually shoots a slave whom Ledoux has refused to purchase. When Tamango's favorite wife objects to his selling a holy man, Tamango gives her to Ledoux. Tricked aboard the ship and himself put in irons, Tamango hatches a successful mutiny during which he and Ledoux fight to the finish. Both men fall, Ledoux on top; but Tamango strains Ledoux to himself and bites into his throat with such violence that the blood gushes forth as if under a lion's tooth.[81]

The third story is supposedly true and comes from a Brazilian periodical entitled *Museo Universal, Jornal das Familias Brazileiras.* An unfaithful husband stayed out late night after night, to the sorrow and rage of his wife. One night, after she had waited long for him, he returned home and fell immediately asleep. She watched him for awhile, then—"The African woman is wild in her choler, and with her teeth, like a tiger, she throws herself upon her prey. When the unfortunate one awoke with a frantic cry, he was no longer a man."[82] In both proslavery and antislavery fiction, the black is typically represented as not seeking vengeance, regardless of the provocation (Musgrave, pp. 428–29). He is nonviolent, forgiving, ultra-Christian. It is significant, then, that both Kleist and Merimée, as well as the anonymous Brazilian, represent those who do avenge themselves as behaving in inhuman ways.

The dismal materials here examined are tributes to the wicked ingenuity of human beings. They would not be so depressing were it not for the fact that they were refurbished and brought forth again to justify colonialism, peonage, discrimination, and segregation. The only changes have been in the kinds of pseudoscience used to bolster them.

1 C. R. Boxer, *Four Centuries of Portuguese Expansion, 1415–1825* (Johannesburg, 1961), p. 24.
2 Between 1493 and 1508, the Indian population of Hispaniola declined from over 1,000,000 to fewer than 60,000. Edward D. Seeber, *Anti-Slavery Opinion in France During the Second Half of the Eighteenth Century* (Baltimore, 1937), p. 13.
3 Francis Adams and Barry Sanders, *Three Black Writers in Eighteenth Century England* (Belmont/Cal., 1971), p. 2.
4 Robert Louis Stein, *The French Slave Trade in the Eighteenth Century* (Madison, 1979), pp. xiii, xiv.
5 Boxer, p. 68. See also Richard Pares, *A West-India Fortune* (New York, 1968), pp. 116–17. Young male slaves were preferred.
6 David B. Davis, *The Problem of Slavery in Western Culture* (Ithaca, 1966), pp. 232–33.
7 The British, as well as the Spanish and Brazilians, worked slaves to death, too. See Frank W. Pitman, "Slavery on a British West Indies Plantation in the Eighteenth Century," *Journal of Negro History* 11 (1962): 484–668.
8 The "self-reproducing" system was never popular in the sugar plantation economies because of the long period during which children would be simply an extra expense, and women would never reach the work capacity of men, supposedly. The psychological effect of seeing women and girls worked to death might have played a role also.
9 Daniel C. Littlefield, *Rice and Slaves: Ethnicity and the Slave Trade in Colonial South Carolina* (Baton Rouge, 1981), pp. 71–73.
10 The Dominican Nicolson, horrified by the frequency of abortions among black women, indicted whites: "This atrocious crime redounds upon you. You are more barbarous than these homicidal mothers." From the "Essai sur Saint-Domingue," cited in Seeber, p. 79.
11 Seeber, p. 108. Voltaire insisted that God made all animals and vegetation for the specific place on earth where they perpetuate themselves.
12 Adams and Sanders, p. 2. The Indians of Central Mexico, estimated at 25,000,000 in 1519, numbered about 1,075,000 by 1605 because of European-introduced diseases, wars, relocations, ecological changes, and starvation. See Richard Price, *Maroon Societies: Rebel Slave Communities in the Americas* (New York, 1973), pp. 82–83.
13 C. R. Boxer, *The Portuguese Sea-Borne Empire, 1415–1825* (New York, 1969), appendix 5 for table of slave imports from Angola to Benguela, 1710–48. See also Adams and Sanders, p. 3.
14 During those 114 years, however, the French population stayed at 12,000. Cf. Stein, pp. xiii, 1, 92.
15 William S. Jenkins, *Pro-Slavery Thought in the Old South* (Chapel Hill, 1935), pp. 40, 41. Not all whites believed that blacks had high toleration for heat. The Dominican missionary du Tertre wrote that the sun makes the blacks' work unbearable (Seeber, pp. 24–25).
16 E. M. Coulter, *A Short History of Georgia* (Chapel Hill, 1833), p. 12; Reba C. Strickland, *Religion and the State of Georgia in the Eighteenth Century* (New York, 1939), p. 14. Moravians, Scots, Jews, Swiss, Germans, Salzburgers, and Piedmontese were some of the whites encouraged to settle in Georgia, along with 2,500 men from debtors' prisons.
17 Editors of the works of metaphysical poets Henry King and George Herbert have often omitted from the canon such works as "A Blackmoor Maid Wooing a Fair Boy" and "A Fair Nymph Scorning a Black Boy Courting Her." See Elliot H. Tokson, *The Popular Image of the Black Man in English Drama, 1550–1688* (Boston, 1982), pp. 22–35.

18 Miriam de Costa, *Blacks in Hispanic Literature* (Port Washington N.Y., 1977), pp. 16–17.
19 Peter Farb, *Word Play* (New York, 1975), pp. 175–79. See also J. L. Dillard, *Black English* (New York, 1972). According to Sterling Brown, Octavus Roy Cohen, who wrote a number of humorous stories using comic blacks, "found nothing funnier than a Negro doctor or lawyer."
20 Charles Sealsfield (pseud.), *Lebensbilder aus der westlichen Hemisphäre, Teil III: Pflanzerleben I* (Hildesheim, 1976), p. 18. See also Otto Heller, *The Language of Charles Sealsfield: A Study in Atypical Usage* (St. Louis, 1941), pp. 57–58.
21 Whites tended not to distinguish complexion differences among blacks; but Gustav Nachtigal, exploring Africa in the late 19th century, found that from the North Coast to Central Africa, seven grades of complexion were distinguished.
22 Since revisionists are once again trying to deny murder and mistreatment of slaves as being contrary to the interests of their owner, the Code Noir is valuable for correcting such notions. Meant by Louis XIV to regularize and reform punishments administered to slaves, the Code permitted burning alive, breaking on the wheel, hamstringing, hacking off of hands, feet, ears, cutting out the tongue, and branding.
23 Some titles: *Life at the South, or Uncle Tom's Cabin as it is,* by L. G. Smith; *North and South, or Slavery and its Contrasts,* by Caroline Rush; *Aunt Phyllis' Cabin,* by Mary Eastman; *The Planter's Northern Bride,* by Mrs. Hentz; *The Slaveholder Abroad,* by W. T. Thompson; *Uncle Robin in his Cabin in Virginia,* and *Uncle Tom Without One in Boston.*
24 See Thomas Carlyle's peculiar argument, that the white man cannot work in the West Indies, followed by his argument that one-half hour of work per day will supply a Negro with enough food. *The Nigger Question,* ed. by Eugene August (New York, 1971), pp. 6–7.
25 Orlando Patterson, *Slavery and Social Death: A Comparative Study* (Cambridge/Mass., 1982), pp. 31–32.
26 Thomas Stephens listed as agricultural equipment "Negroes, axes, hoes, and other utensils." Cf. Seymour Gross and John E. Hardy, *Images of the Negro in American Literature* (Chicago, 1966), p. 44. For an important court case, that of "Mulatto Louis," see Hans Werner Debrunner, *Presence and Prestige: African in Europe* (Basel, 1979), p. 139.
27 Bayard R. Hall, *Frank Freeman's Barber Shop* (New York, 1852), p. 15; John P. Kennedy, *Swallow Barn* (New York, 1962), p. 466.
28 Douglas Grant, *The Fortunate Slave* (London, 1968), p. 139. In Jean-Pierre Claris de Florian's novel *Sélico,* the hero decides to sell himself in order to feed his refugee family; cf. Seeber, pp. 188–89.
29 Sir Reginald Coupland, *The British Anti-Slavery Movement,* 2d. ed. (London, 1964), pp. 172–73. Some American officials were involved in the illegal trade.
30 William Wells Brown, *Clotel or the President's Daughter* (New York, 1969), pp. 139–42. For other novels dealing with kidnapping whites and free blacks, see *Peculiar* by Epes Sargent; *Sofía* by Martin Maria Delgado; *Twelve Years a Slave* by Solomon Northrup; *Ida May* by Mary Langdon Pike.
31 Theophilis Conneau, *A Slaver's Log Book, or Twenty Years' Residence in Africa* (Englewood Cliffs, 1976), pp. 121–22, 173. Grant, *The Fortunate Slave,* pp. 134–39. For the many voices exposing the falsity of the Droit de Guerre argument, see Seeber, pp. 68–70.
32 Grant, *The Fortunate Slave,* pp. 104–5.
33 William Goodell, *Slavery and Anti-Slavery: A History of the Great Struggle* (New York, 1853), p. 33.
34 In the "Negeridyllen," five versified stories of slavery found in Letter 114 of Herder's *Briefe zur Beförderung der Humanität.*
35 A wedding and a lying-in party are shown. Proslavery works seldom show slaves doing the work of a plantation, preferring to concentrate on evening cabin scenes and on holidays.
36 Large-scale manumission was almost never practiced because of the monetary worth of slaves after the outlawing of the trade with Africa. See Patterson, *Slavery and Social Death,* pp. 219, 264.
37 The black who saves a white's life at the risk of his own appears in many works, attesting to the popularity of the theme. Examples: *Uncle Tom's Cabin* by Stowe; *Bug-Jargal* by Victor Hugo; *Sab* by Gertrudis de Avellaneda; *Georges* by Dumas père; *Maria ou a Menina Roubada* by Teixeira e Sousa. Compare stories in which a poor man saves a rich man or his daughter—one's worth is measured by the worth of the life saved.

38 William Gilmore Simms, *The Yemassee,* ed. by C.H. Holman (Boston, 1961), p. 355. Dunbar, writing dialect verse in the postslavery period, was a northern black who had imbibed the plantation myth. One of his contented slaves exclaims: "You can jes' tell Massa Lincoln to take his freedom back!"

39 Cited by Willfried Feuser in "Das Bild des Afrikaners in der deutschen Literatur," *Akten des V. Internationalen Germanisten-Kongresses, Cambridge 1975* (Bern, 1976), pp. 306–15.

40 Many slaves testified that slave holders with religion were the worst. Cf. Frederick Douglass, *Narrative of the Life of Frederick Douglass* (New York, 1963), pp. 55–57.

41 Mary Boykin Chesnut, *A Diary from Dixie,* ed. by Ben Ames Williams (Boston, 1949), pp. 121–22. Black concubinage was psychologically destructive to white women, since black women already cooked, kept house, and cared for the children. See Joel Krovel, *White Racism: A Psychohistory* (New York, 1971).

42 Feuser, p. 307. S. A. Cartwright used the tale to justify the theft of the Americas from the Indians and the enslavement of blacks, who, he said, appeared spontaneously upon the beach of Africa to get passage to America "to fulfill [their] destiny of becoming Japheth's servant"; cf. Jenkins, p. 205.

43 Thomas Astley, *A New General Collection of Voyages and Travels, 1745–47* (London, 1749), vol. 2, p. 268.

44 Paul Edwards and James Walvin, *Black Personalities in the Era of the Slave Trade* (Baton Rouge, 1983), p. 8.

45 Seymour Gross and John Hardy, *Images of the Black in American Literature* (Chicago, 1966), p. 39.

46 Cited in W. R. Akyroyd, *Sweet Malefactor* (London, 1967), p. 66.

47 Joachim S. Hohmann, *Schon auf den ersten Blick* (Darmstadt, 1981), p. 202; Milosch Djordjewitsch, *Charles Sealsfields Auffassung des Amerikanertums und seine literarhistorische Stellung* (Hildesheim, 1978), p. 40.

48 Raymond S. Sayers, *The Negro in Brazilian Literature* (New York, 1956), pp. 57–58.

49 Grimmelshausen, *The Simplicius Simplicissimus,* trans. and ed. by George Schulz-Behrend (New York, 1965), pp. 340–42.

50 John F. Matheus, "African Footprints in Hispanic-American Literature," in *Blacks in Hispanic Literature,* p. 59.

51 Nancy Vogeley, "The Figure of the Black Payador in Martín Fierro," *CLA Journal* 26 (Sept. 1982): 41.

52 Thomas Phillips, *Journal of a Slaving Voyage,* in Churchill's *Voyages* (London, 1732), p. 78.

53 Grayson's argument has considerable popularity. Thompson, author of *The Slaveholder Abroad,* expresses his indignation at the plight of English workingmen as compared with the happy lot of slaves; the anonymous author of *The Yankee Slave Dealer* has pity for white northern workers and for northern prostitutes, who, he thinks, would be better off in "humane southern slavery." Charles Sealsfield wrote that "though slaves are forced to labor by the master's iron will, they are happy...and share in the fruits of their labor to an extent which would be envied by thousands of needy Europeans," in *Der Legitime und die Republikaner,* vol. 3, p. 7.

54 Ronald T. Takaki, *A Pro-Slavery Crusade* (New York, 1971), p. 82.

55 This remarkable passage was Mrs. McCord's "refutation" of *Uncle Tom's Cabin.*

56 William P. Trent, *William Gilmore Simms* (Boston, 1892), p. 173.

57 Leslie H. Fishel and Benjamin Quarles, *The Black American,* rev. ed. (Glenview, Ill., 1970), p. 92.

58 The proslavers had no weapon so powerful—they simply tried to deny the existence of cruelty. See Marian E. Musgrave, "Patterns of Violence and Non-Violence in Pro-Slavery and Anti-Slavery Fiction," *CLA Journal* 16, 4 (June 1973): 430–32.

59 Daniel Defoe, *Robinson Crusoe,* ed. by Michael Shinagel (New York, 1975), p. 163.

60 Instead of seeing the evil in the entire system of slavery, readers were likely to contrast the "good" master with the "bad" master, to think in terms of a "kindlier face of slavery" (Friedrich Gerstäcker's term) and of amelioration.

61 Alexandre Dumas père, *Georges* (New York, 1975), pp. 147–48.

62 Frank J. Webb, *The Garies and Their Friends* (New York, 1969), pp. 1–2, 52, 60, 103–5.

63 David Hume, *Essays and Treatises* (London, 1768), vol. 1, p. 235. Goethe, in the *Farbenlehre,* also considers white to be the superior complexion.

64 Louis Ruchames, *Racial Thought in America* (New York, 1969), p. 165.

65 *Black Heroes in World History* (New York, 1969), p. 45.

66 Jefferson's letters to Benjamin Banneker, Joel Barlow, and to Bishop Gregoire all contain a sentence to the effect that no one could wish more sincerely than Jefferson to have proof of the intelligence of Negroes, though it seems plain that no amount of proof would have sufficed. Gilbert Imlay, an officer in the American army during the Revolution, was "ashamed" to read Jefferson's "disgraceful prejudices." Cf. Ruchames, p. 171.

67 Winthrop Jordan, *White Over Black* (Baltimore, 1969), pp. 31–32.

68 Thomas Jefferson, *Notes on the State of Virginia* (Boston, 1829), p. 145.

69 Carolyn R. Karcher, *Shadow Over the Promised Land* (Baton Rouge, 1980), p. 23; George Sawyer, *Southern Institutes* (Philadelphia, 1858), p. 195.

70 Sein, pp. 115–16; see also Debrunner, pp. 138–40.

71 Robin W. Winks, *Slavery: A Comparative Perspective* (New York, 1972), p. 20. See also Thomas F. Gossett, *Race: the History of an Idea in America* (Dallas, 1963), p. 15.

72 Van Evrie probably was unaware of the stunning sexual image in his statement. See Fishel and Quarles.

73 Debrunner, pp. 141–42. Blumenbach, who has written a description of the typical "Ethiopian" which reads like a caricature, nevertheless was able to let the spirit of science win out over ethnocentrism.

74 The beauty was Pauline Hyppolite Buisson of Saint-Domingue, the daughter of Congo slaves.

75 *Deutsche National-Literatur*, ed. by Joseph Kürschner (Stuttgart, n.d.), vol. 77, p. 219.

76 Donald W. Bleznick, *Francisco de Quevedo* (New York, 1972), pp. 110–11.

77 G. E. Lessing, *Laocoön*, ed. by William A. Steel (London, 1961), pp. 93–94. Note that the idea of love between two Hottentots seems ridiculous to Lessing.

78 Victor Hugo, *Bug-Jargal* (Paris, 1832), p. 18; Dumas, pp. 72–73.

79 The character of mixed blood had already been presented negatively during the Spanish "Golden Age" by Juan Eugenio Hartzenbusch, himself a mixture of Spanish and German. His popular drama *Los Amantes de Teruel* contains a sultana of black and Arabic blood whose color and passion disgust the hero. In Brazilian Romantic drama, mulattoes are often traitors, while dark-skinned blacks are shown as patriotic and self-sacrificing. In the Argentinian novel *Amalia,* a mulatta maid helps to betray the hero to his death. In the United States, the evil mulatto appears after the Civil War, as for example in *The Birth of a Nation,* as a partial justification of segregation and Jim Crow.

80 Heinrich von Kleist, "Die Verlobung in St. Domingo," in *Sämtliche Werke* (München, 1952), pp. 731–32, 757.

81 Prosper Merimée, "Tamango," in *Romans et Nouvelles* (Paris, 1951), pp. 223, 225–26, 234.

82 Cited in Sayers, pp. 81–82. Compare the author's belief that "the vehemence of Negro love is proverbial" with the general denial and mockery of Negro love in the United States media.

African Nature and German Culture: Colonial Women Writers on Africa

AMADOU BOOKER SADJI

Precisely one hundred years ago, from November 15, 1884, to January 26, 1885, the European powers convened at the famous Berlin Congress—also called the Congo Conference—in order to organize the imperialistic division of Africa. Somewhat belatedly in comparison with other European countries, Germany emerged in the following years as an effective colonial power, a role it played only from 1884 until 1918. At the end of the First World War, pursuant to Germany's defeat, its colonies were stripped away by the victors.

The 100th anniversary of that historic event in 1884 prompts us to take up various aspects of Germany's brief and largely unknown colonial history. Literary scholarship—and, more particularly, Germanistics—has the task of sifting through colonial literature; and this task is all the more important because of the widely held belief that the brief history of German colonialism resulted only in literature which is so meager—at least in comparison with British and French sources—that it is scarcely worth examining.

Yet the bulk of German colonial literature is virtually unlimited. Non-fiction writing—reports and narratives, mostly autobiographical travel accounts—developed into an extensive literature: diaries, stories, novels, small dramatic essays, colonial plays, and poems. All these works offer diverse and detailed images of Black Africa and the Black African.

The contribution of colonial women writers to German colonial literature is most important, both quantitatively and qualitatively. The fact that works by writing housewives are so numerous has to do with both the objective and subjective conditions that shaped the emergence of German colonial writing.

The literary products of the initial stage of colonization are relatively scanty, for the German colonial pioneers, who joined with missionaries in conquering the land, had to fight first and foremost for sheer survival. The absence of a centrally guided, firm colonial policy from Berlin hindered early settlement. Only toward the end of the 19th century, after the official occupation of German "protectorates" in Black Africa, were the prerequisites given for the emergence of a literature about these regions. With the general growth of interest in the colonies, especially among the settlers, a completely new type of German colonizer emerged, one who was distinguished from historical antecedents by having attended a university or school of higher learning, and who subsequently continued to cultivate intellectual and cultural pursuits, even in Africa.

Turning to colonial authors, we find that these were not only the sons but also the daughters of respected families, both with equal education and the same intellectual capabilities. Two chief categories of women can be distinguished: first, the wives of settlers, missionaries, officers, civil servants, merchants, or physicians; second (and more rarely), women who were themselves in the intellectual professions.

In the "better" society of that period, it was quite rare for a married German woman to continue to practice a profession, if indeed she ever had one at all. Obviously, this also held true for women who lived in the colonies with their husbands. They tended to be housewives because of the additional factor that it was a risky and demanding adventure for a single woman to attempt to master life abroad. The well-known writer Clara Brockmann had actually gone through this experience and warned her countrywomen about it. If we exclude the Catholic mission sister, who in any case constituted a special category of colonial woman, we find that the few instances of single women who sought "to create a position on their own in foreign parts"[1] were mostly teachers or private tutors and domestic governesses.

Apart from this purely quantitative factor, the key position occupied by housewives' writings within colonial literature can further be explained on the basis of additional objective and subjective factors. Housewives had sufficient prior education and leisure to involve themselves with literature, both actively and passively. They could, on the one hand, allow their fantasy about the country and its inhabitants free rein, far more so than their professionally occupied husbands or working single women. On the other hand, direct and personal contact on a daily basis—shared, incidentally, only by the missionaries—with the Black African people, especially with servants, offered an optimal basis for observing with the aim of literary reproduction. They were also devoted to observing and describing nature, as were hunters, soldiers, physicians, and civil servants—to name only those professional groups.

The complex ensemble of motifs concerning Black African nature and landscape is thus among the most important topics within German colonial literature altogether, not just that written by housewives and settlers. Given the particular historical circumstances, this presented an opportunity to express "that longing, so distinctively German since time immemorial, to glimpse distant places."[2] So much has been written about nature and landscape in this connection that even making an exemplary selection is difficult.

Generally speaking, a positive, exotic-romantic image predominates in all pertinent writings, corresponding to the proverbial German longing for the sunny South, for ideal distant lands. By contrast, realistic presentations in a neutral vein are not very numerous, and negative ones are almost nonexistent. The latter, however, are concerned less with nature as landscape than with the "murderous" fever-climate. The portrayal of such a climate occurs principally in works produced, predictably enough, by colonial physicians.

Among the women writers to be cited here, place of pride must surely go to Frieda von Bülow, whose colonial novels and diaries are exemplary in every respect. Her *Travel Sketches and Diaries from East Africa*,[3] for example, portray actively experienced nature and the landscape of the East African coast in an almost consistently neutral tone. At the beginning of her novel *Tropical Choler*,[4] too, the author initially draws a largely neutral and distanced image of this same area—almost a photograph, so passively and objectively are nature and landscape experienced. Then, however, apropos of the infinitude of the ocean, she switches to a completely different narrative tone, allowing her to be simultaneously critical and rhapsodic about Africa's "loneliness, freedom, and grandeur,"[5] thus valorizing the typical tropical midday heat. African nature is deployed in its entirety; images of European Nordic landscapes are matched by Africa's "enormous, wild, lonely, sun-sated park landscape" experienced in all its particular characteristics.[6]

After comparing *Tropical Choler* with works of this sort by other writers, it is evident that Frieda von Bülow distances herself from any uncritical enthusiasm for the exotic; in fact she writes rather realistically by conceding "the poetic charm of Nordic landscapes."[7] This novel eschews a one-sided poetic glorification of the foreign landscape and nature of Africa. Bülow's tendency to realism is strengthened by the fact that nature is described from the divergent perspectives of various figures, landscape and climate thus being treated in a differentiated way. Drake, for example, the director of a colonial export company, speaks in such dithyrambic paeans as: "Otherwise, the land would be splendid. This externally cheerful sky!...And the marvelous vegetation, pure paradise!"[8] His antagonist, the company commander Rosen, advances a contrary view point:

> This stretch of coastline is not at all paradise for the European: the enervating climate makes us nervous and choleric, we suffer from the lack of leisure activities, recreation, intellectual nourishment, etc. Our life here seems to be easy enough, but to lead it with dignity is not at all easy, not at all![9]

In her novel entitled *In the Land of the Promise* (1889),[10] Bülow's effort to offer a balanced portrayal is even more evident. Negative and positive, that is, romantic, images of the black African landscape are evenly matched here: difficult living allegedly filled with sacrifice is balanced against a longing for ideal southern climes fulfilled. The negative image is captured especially well in a passage describing the first night spent in Africa by a German colonial wife, Maleen Dietlas. The "creeping, crawling animal life"[11] of luxuriant tropical nature, plus the flies and rats, keep her awake in her bedroom until dawn. The positive stereotype—a romantic, exotic and idealistic, enthusiastic image of Black African nature and landscape—undergoes a heightening and simultaneous relativizing in this novel. Whereas positive and negative images of Africa had been represented and enunciated by one figure each in *Tropical Choler,* here one and the same person is not bound exclusively to a single viewpoint, but instead varies in outlook depending on the situation at hand. Maleen's shifting attitude offers a clearcut example. Although her first night in the tropics was so horrific, in another context she sees black Africa as "a sort of Shangrila [or paradise on earth]."[12]

This term [*Schlaraffenland*] is used for the first time when her brother Rainer lets her discover coconuts; the entire image draws on the typically exotic mood to which some Europeans are prone when they imagine breaking out of technical industrial civilization. Maleen and her brother are handed the freshly cut coconuts:

> He drank the half liter of nut juice in long draughts, as if it were Munich Hofbräu... Maleen thought of all the baked goods and desserts she would later make from these giant nut kernels. Truly, this land seemed to be a kind of paradise on earth.[13]

At another point, the paradisiacal impression is confirmed: Maleen meets the old Africa-hand, Krome, who draws a comparison between Africa and the Garden of Eden based on his own experiences. In this instance, however, the glorification of black African nature aims not at an abstract, dreamy exoticism but instead focuses soberly on Africa as a rich field for colonization:

> Just imagine what all this soil would produce if managed properly! Why, it's gold! We will create a German India here. The millions that Germany spends abroad for tropical foodstuff will stay in the country in the future.[14]

The highpoint in the reciprocal relationship between exoticism and colonialism in Frieda von Bülow's *In the Land of Promise* occurs when the novel's narrator alludes to the story of Paul and Virginie by Bernardin de Saint-Pierre and then turns directly to the "sobriety of the industrious Europeanism"[15] in the colonies. This time, it is Maleen and her husband Georg who take a walk through East African nature and landscape:

> Under the giant trees... [stood] a few palm straw-covered huts that nearly disappeared among the gigantic leaves surrounding them, and looked as if they belonged in the story of Paul and Virginie. Maleen forgot her tiredness and the heat because of the romanticism of this splendid wilderness... "Now, open your eyes wide!" called Dietlas. "What you now see before you is our plantation." She had to give herself a sharp nudge to find her way back all at once from the... fairytale world to the sobriety of industrious Europeanism.[16]

In comparison with Frieda von Bülow's mode of portrayal, Magdalena Prince consistently deals with African nature and landscape matter-of-factly, without any link to either rhapsodic exoticism or calculating colonialism. Thanks to Prince's success at sober realism, her texts offer some of the most valuable images of black African—or, to be more precise, East African—nature and landscape. The following vivid image is cited as an example:

> Collected many butterflies, of which there are more now, subsequent to the rainy season (especially in damp places), and many strange-looking animals, salamanders, snakes, and a peculiar caterpillar, spiny like our hedgehog, except that the spines stick to your fingers like our burs and then itch horribly. These unpleasant burs also exist here, by the way, and they make their presence felt most uncomfortably on treks. One type of grass with little thorns is pesky while trekking.
>
> In the realm of flowers, too, nature shows many European varieties: for example, bindweed in the most diverse colors—yellow, red, blue, violet. Of trees, I noted especially the wealth of acacias.[17]

In Margarethe von Eckenbrecher's *My Give and Take with Africa,*[18] on the other hand, enthusiasm for the exotic predominates, and nowhere does the book explicitly link nature and landscape with colonial profitability. The entire portrayal derives from the exotic postulate combined with a longing for beautiful, ideal, distant places, as formulated by the writer in her foreword:

> Love for Africa can be followed like a red thread through my entire life, from childhood on. My oldest brother Hans and my cousin Themis—my present husband—described Africa to me in the most glowing colors: Africa, the land of my dreams...
>
> A starker contrast is scarcely possible: Berlin, the center of German culture and science, versus an isolated farm in Damaraland. And yet, when I think back now: If I were placed before the choice again, I would make exactly the same decision all over again.[19]

At the very beginning of her memoir, Eckenbrecher describes with poetic accents her experience of Liberian nature and landscape at sunrise. With her arrival in Southwest Africa, she rises to an almost rhapsodic pathos, particularly when depicting the rocky and sandy desert of Namib and its environs:

> The Namib offered a most glorious view, veiled in a blue haze, above which rested, rosy in the gleam of the sun, the enormous mass of the Brandberg. It is among the most beautiful things I have ever glimpsed in my life, so splendidly exalted and yet so desolate and lonely...I felt it with all my senses...Heavy tears streamed down my face. I could have clasped my hands and said: "Dear God, I thank Thee for vouchsafing to me that I might see Thy beauty in the wilderness. I will gladly endure hunger and thirst and privation, but let me enjoy the wonder of Thy creation far from the hustle and bustle of mankind."[20]

Similar exotic and romantic accents are to be found, surprisingly enough, in the descriptions of Southwest African landscape and nature penned by Clara Brockmann, a woman writer otherwise oriented strongly towards practical colonial profitability. Especially in the chapter "My Home in Windhoek" in her early work *The German Woman in Southwest Africa*,[21] there are traces of various romantic motifs, such as yearning for distant parts, the desire to escape the industrialized European world, and, above all, the wish to escape Germany's crowdedness. The reader learns how Brockmann conquered unknown nature on an excursion with her woman friend, and this during one of those famous moonlit African nights always celebrated in European literature. Simultaneously, the thought surfaces in these lines that while new domestic happiness is possible here, far from industrial Europe, an early death looms as the price to be paid:

> We look at the moon and feel that it alone is where our feelings meet with those of our loves in Germany; it is the meeting point of our recollections. And suddenly I become aware of how far, how infinitely far from home we really are. . . How many moved to this land in the bloom of youth, brimming with hope, and now sleep in the steppes of the Herero country.[22]

Quite as surprising as Brockmann's grasp and depiction of African landscape are the nature descriptions offered by Lydia Höpker, and not merely because she is otherwise unambiguously interested in colonial economics, but also because she otherwise has virtually nothing positive to say about black Africa and its inhabitants. Despite all this, her quest for exotic adventure, isolation, and fairytale enchantment leads her to such gushy glorifications of virgin nature and landscape as the following:

> Everything was so dewy fresh and untouched, round about loneliness and quiet, only from afar did the call of a bird resound now and again. We hiked silently through this beautiful morning. A dreamlike feeling enveloped me, and I felt enchanted, as if in another world.[23]

Among the relatively few poems that occur in German colonial literature, those of Charlotte Deppe, a physician's wife, deserve mention here. In the book *About East Africa*,[24] which she published jointly with her husband Ludwig Deppe, she sketches an enthusiastic picture revealing her basically positive attitude toward Africa, yet cautions that her portrayal draws on her purely personal perspective, and that Africa can be experienced in relatively diverse ways. With this caveat Deppe demonstrates a dialectical way of thinking far superior to that of most colonial writers:

> The charm of Africa is apparent only to someone who has spent considerable time there; but the longer the time, the greater it becomes. . . The degree to which one feels the charm of Africa of course varies, depending on the uniqueness of each individual. I personally have experienced a feeling of being at home there in a way that I never had back in Germany.[25]

Under the title "Africa, Thou Land of Great Strength!" Deppe includes this romantic verse:

> Gigantically great thoughts
> hover
> over the exalted loneliness
> of thy immeasurable wilderness
> with its mountains, steppes, rivers, and forests,
> and in this great experience
> thou givest great thoughts
> to the wanderer in your infinitude.
>
> O Africa,
> my soul has remained in thee,
> and the rest of my self
> thirsts
> for thee,
> for thy nature and thy human children,
> for thy wide distances,
> and for thy peace.

A second motif ensemble of considerable significance to the image of the black African and of black Africa in the literature of German housewives and settlers concerns the matter of home life and eating habits, which is closely linked to the relationship between service personnel and their employers.

Concern with orderliness and cleanliness plays a central role in these matters. Frieda von Bülow again was among the first and most representative German colonial women writers whose works handled these issues in an exemplary way. As early as 1896, her novel *Tropical Choler* portrayed the basic concern of many German or European settler families in the black African colonies regarding eating and living habits. Most were seeking to transplant Germany to Africa, as it were—an attitude demonstrated particularly clearly by one of the major European figures in Bülow's novel, Countess Leontine. As a typical woman settler, she is quite unwilling to adjust to the conditions and the associated lifestyle in the tropics. Of and by itself, German housekeeping is something completely sacred to her—an outlook which the writer herself by no means shares completely:

> Conservative in outlook...she clung almost fanatically to accustomed ways and rejected anything new or foreign without allowing it to challenge her thinking. She therefore lapsed into the error, not uncommon among her compatriots, of immediately wanting to transform everything she found abroad according to models from home...Had she been on the moon she would have tried to introduce German housekeeping.[26]

Whenever the "uncultivated" circumstances in black Africa receive emphasis, the motif of general cleanliness cannot be far behind, and with it comes the image of service personnel. Although real events from everyday life are portrayed from the perspective of the countess, that is, in a stereotyped manner, the writer herself seems to adopt a critical and detached attitude toward her, expressed by the practical Eva.

The tendency of German housewives to pass judgment on circumstances they find abroad, without considering special conditions, and to want to change them is criticized even more strongly in Bülow's novel *In the Land of Promise*. The following thought occurs to Maleen Dietlas, the protagonist:

> How unwise we are...when we replace with German customs, without any further ado, whatever we encounter here! The Negroes know quite well why they place their cooking fires in free air, under just a little protective roof...But we build an enclosed little room in the German manner, and whenever the stove is hot it's sheer hell.[27]

Similar sentiments are expressed in other German colonial works, for example in Johanna Wittum's report *Under the Red Cross in Cameroon*[28] or in the book *A German Woman in the Interior of East Africa* by Magdalena Prince.[29] Economic factors and social status play a decisive role in both the emergence of modern living habits and the acquisition of a "middle-class" lifestyle, as emphasized by Prince when she portrays how the Sultan Mpangire and his brothers are guests in her home. The private behavior of these highly placed allies of the colonial power demonstrates an unusually keen sense for adaptation in the area of lifestyle and living habits. The book also documents, however, the nearly racist Eurocentrism typical of virtually all European colonial literature, in that Prince is unable to grasp or depict the sociopolitical reasons for Mpangire's conformity. In the absence of a dialectical mode of portrayal, we are ultimately left with stereotyped thinking capable only of regarding the behavior of Mpangire and his brothers as an exception. Whenever the behavior of a black African can be viewed positively from a Eurocentric perspective, any manifestation of orderly and clean living is interpreted not as normal outcome of a certain economic and social constellation, but instead constantly yields to the no less racist view that "it really doesn't feel" as if one is "dealing with a black,"[30] since the black African in question is an exception.

As the problem of the relationship between German households and black African service personnel is one of the most frequently exercised themes in German colonial literature, it seems obvious that it should be portrayed in the most exemplary manner by German housewives and women settlers, for they had the most to do with service personnel. In the chapter "Housewife's Worries," Margarethe von Eckenbrecher draws a series of miniature portraits of her domestic servants, each of whom is introduced by name in the manner of a realistic, individualized portrayal. In keeping with the general tendency of German colonial literature about black Africa, this type of portrayal cannot conceal the fact that the writer offers precisely those images which cast a negative light on the black African; yet they do not even bear the stamp of militant colonial thinking. In their simplicity and candid openness, they convey the impression that on a formal level the writer is seeking to provide harmless, cheerful entertainment for the average reader. Such systematically selected negative or ridiculous images as those offered by Margarethe von Eckenbrecher appeared in widely read works, contributing decisively to the persistence and power of German clichés about the black African.

Even so, these Eckenbrecher portraits may well appear relatively harmless in comparison with those offered by Clara Brockmann. In her first published work, *The German Woman in Southwest Africa,* for example, the chapter "The Service Personnel Question" begins thus:

> One . . . field of activity that one is reluctant to leave to the blacks is the kitchen. The food may be of a splendid appearance when it arrives on the table, and it may taste so, too; but I can never completely suppress a feeling of disgust when I think of the notorious state of cleanliness among the natives.[31]

After this remark, the writer reports a hodgepodge of examples on the practical methods she used in black Africa to ensure hygiene and cleanliness in the area of eating, and also on the reasons that prompted her to such methods. In the process, carefully selected instances of extreme trespasses against hygiene and cleanliness are portrayed with the propagandistic intent of "strengthening the extreme difference between white colonizers and the 'vrais nègres' "[32] and of legitimating colonialism as an absolutely necessary and beneficent task of civilization.

The same tendency also predominates in Lydia Höpker's book *For Soil and Life—Destiny of a German Woman Farmer in Southwest Africa,* despite her attempt at a more objective, less emotional mode of portrayal. She offers a sort of mosaic displaying all instances of disorder and dirt in living room, dining room, and bedroom. In contrast to Brockmann's strictly ideological and propagandistic mode of portrayal, however, Höpker's narrative is largely entertaining. The humorous tone arises from objectively portraying European colonizers who are by no means devoid of an inclination to go native, as it were, because they live under the same conditions of material and technological underdevelopment as do the blacks. Thus, by carrying ad absurdum the racial or, rather, racist view generally emphasized in colonial literature, Höpker paradoxically arrives at a relevant standpoint.

Whereas the stereotyped idealization of the white woman is not presented by Höpker as an overtly racist component, racism is completely foregrounded in works such as the ones by Brockmann which glorify the white farm woman in an uncritical way. The contrast to ideal figures is provided by black African women portrayed as incapable of striving for higher culture or running a household. Their condemnation occurs especially in connection with the touchy area of mixed marriage between black and white:

> It is an old, sad, established fact that the black woman has never made the slightest effort to climb to a higher cultural level; on the contrary, the [white] man approximates the level of his colored life companion and not rarely sinks down to it.[33]

Only quite occasionally do German colonial works carry stereotypical thinking ad absurdum in the process of simply reporting positive experiences, without intending any colonial, paternalistic demagogy. Among the handful of such works is a narrative already mentioned, *About East Africa—Memoirs,* by Charlotte and Ludwig Deppe. They offer the following pertinent remark:

> Managing a youngster...was all the easier because the boys were generally quite clean. It would never occur to the cook, for example, to touch foodstuffs while cooking other than with a fork. Thus we could enjoy our meals with appetite undiminished.[34]

The process of colonization often entails a sweeping nonidealization of one's own culture and compatriots, which in turn leads in most cases to a complex, differentiated portrayal of the colonized black African. This is suggested in an exemplary way by the closing words of the chapter "The First Time Spent in Africa" from the Deppes' memoirs:

> So there was much work waiting to be done by me at home and in the hospital ...It was, to be sure, necessary to know how to adjust and acclimatize in this new and surprising setting, and I praised the day when I finally learned to do so.[35]

In concluding our remarks on the motif of orderliness and cleanliness in the home life and kitchen, and on the related image of black African servants, we can summarize our findings as follows: The mode of portrayal, the spectrum of more or less clichéd or differentiated narrative perspectives used to treat this motif, is itself connected with what Frieda von Bülow termed general behavior vis-à-vis the new and foreign. And the latter is directly linked to the critical or uncritical attitude of the German colonial writer toward his or her own national "master race mission" to the colonies as portrayed in literature.

If we seek to draw an overall conclusion from our analysis of works by the major representatives of German colonial women's literature, we must observe that they can ultimately be fitted into a well-known tradition, namely that of the dominance of the epic form. The typical colonial narrative in the form of a colonial novel must also be associated with the development of the so-called anthropological novel, as has done Hans Plischke quite correctly in his study *From Cooper to Karl May—A History of the Anthropological Travel and Adventure Novel.*[36]

Yet this should by no means lead us to overlook the fact that the impulses colonial literature received from the anthropological novel cannot be separated from more complicated phenomena, for example, from Romantic literature with its tendency to transport the reader into the past and into nature. With the enormous growth of the reading public during the 19th century, didactic and entertaining literature also asserted an ever stronger presence. These trends, in combination with the aforementioned factors, provided the historical and literary context for the emergence and particularly strong development of a German colonial narrative genre—a process in which women writers played a role of the first rank.

Translated from the German by James Steakley

Notes

1 Clara Brockmann, *Die deutsche Frau in Südwestafrika: Ein Beitrag zur Frauenfrage in unseren Kolonien* (Berlin, 1910), p. 36.
2 J. Trümpelmann, *Das deutsche schöngeistige Schrifttum über Südwestafrika* (Windhoek, 1933), p. 121.
3 Frieda von Bülow, *Reiseskizzen und Tagebücher aus Ostafrika* (Berlin, 1887 and 1889).
4 Bülow, *Tropenkoller* (Berlin, 1896).
5 Ibid., p. 2.
6 Ibid., p. 214.
7 Ibid., p. 215.
8 Ibid., p. 63.
9 Ibid., p. 137.
10 Bülow, *Im Lande der Verheißung: Ein deutscher Kolonialroman* (Dresden, 1889, 1907, and 1908).
11 Ibid., p. 13.
12 Ibid., p. 18.
13 Ibid., p. 16.
14 Ibid., p. 32.
15 Ibid., p. 91.
16 Ibid.
17 Magdalena Prince, *Eine deutsche Frau im Innern Deutsch-Ostafrikas* (Berlin, 1903), p. 12.
18 Margarethe von Eckenbrecher, *Was Afrika mir gab und nahm: Erlebnisse einer deutschen Ansiedlerfrau in Südwestafrika* (Berlin, 1904).
19 Ibid., p. v.
20 Ibid., p. 146.
21 Clara Brockmann, *Die deutsche Frau in Südwestafrika: Ein Beitrag zur Frauenfrage in unseren Kolonien* (Berlin, 1910).
22 Ibid., pp. 47f.
23 Lydia Höpker, *Um Scholle und Leben: Schicksale einer deutschen Farmerin in Südwest-Afrika* (Minden in Westfalen, 1927), p. 21.
24 Charlotte und Ludwig Deppe, *Um Ostafrika: Erinnerungen* (Dresden, 1925).
25 Ibid., p. 24.
26 Bülow, *Tropenkoller*, pp. 29f.
27 Bülow, *Im Lande der Verheißung*, pp. 350f.
28 Johanna Wittum, *Unterm Roten Kreuz in Kamerun* (Heidelberg, 1899).

29 Prince, *Eine deutsche Frau im Innern Deutsch-Ostafrikas* (see n. 17 above).
30 Ibid., p. 60.
31 Brockmann, *Die deutsche Frau in Südwestafrika,* p. 24.
32 Martin Steins, *Das Bild des Schwarzen in der europäischen Kolonialliteratur* (Frankfurt, 1972), p. 53.
33 Brockmann, *Die deutsche Frau in Südwestafrika,* pp. 5f.
34 Charlotte und Ludwig Deppe, *Um Ostafrika,* p. 10.
35 Ibid., p. 16.
36 Hans Plischke, *Von Cooper bis Karl May: Eine Geschichte des völkerkundlichen Reise- und Abenteuerromans* (Düsseldorf, 1951). He points out that "the impulses for the novellistic portrayal of the cultural conditions of an exotic people" came "from abroad, more specifically from North America, where since the beginning of the 17th century...the struggle between redskin and paleface occurred" (p. 15).

Bibliography

Primary Sources

Borke, Helene von. *Ostafrikanische Erinnerungen einer freiwilligen Krankenpflegerin.* Berlin, 1891.
Brockmann, Clara. *Briefe eines deutschen Mädchens aus Südwest.* Berlin, 1912.
Brockmann, Clara. *Die deutsche Frau in Südwestafrika: Ein Beitrag zur Frauenfrage in unseren Kolonien.* Berlin, 1910.
Bülow, Frieda Freiin von. *Deutschostafrikanische Novellen.* Berlin-Dahlem, n.d.
Bülow, Frieda Freiin von. *Drei Jahre im Lande Hendrik Witbois, 1891-1894.* 2d ed. Berlin, 1897.
Bülow, Frieda Freiin von. *Im Lande der Verheißung: Ein deutscher Kolonialroman.* Dresden 1889, 1907, and 1908.
Bülow, Frieda Freiin von. *Reiseskizzen und Tagebücher aus Ostafrika.* Berlin, 1887 and 1889.
Bülow, Frieda Freiin von. *Tropenkoller.* Berlin, 1896.
Busse-Lange, Erika. *Afrikanisches Pflanzerleben: Aus den Briefen einer deutschen Pflanzersfrau in Deutsch-Ostafrika.* 2d ed. Berlin und Leipzig, 1925.
Cramer, Ada. *Weiß und Schwarz: Lehr- und Leidensjahre eines Farmers in Südwest im Lichte des Rassenhasses.* Berlin, 1913.
Deppe, Charlotte und Ludwig. *Um Ostafrika: Erinnerungen.* Dresden, 1925.
Eckenbrecher, Margarethe von, et al. *Deutsch-Südwest-afrikanische Kriegs- und Friedensbilder: Selbsterlebnisse.* Leipzig, 1907.
Eckenbrecher, Margarethe von. *Im dichten Ton: Reise- und Jagdbilder aus Deutsch-Ostafrika.* Berlin, 1912.
Eckenbrecher, Margarethe von. *Was Afrika mir gab und nahm: Erlebnisse einer deutschen Ansiedlerfrau in Südwestafrika.* Berlin, 1904, 1906, 1908, 1911, and 1940.
Etzel, Gisela. *Aus Junte und Kraal.* Stuttgart, 1911.
Falkenhausen, Helene von. *Ansiedlerschicksale: Elf Jahre Deutsch-Südwestafrika 1893-1904.* Berlin 1904 and 1908.
Frobenius, Else. *Dreißig Jahre koloniale Frauenarbeit.* Berlin, 1936.
Funke, Luise. *Im Banne der Furcht: Blicke in das afrikanische Heidentum Togo.* Bremen, 1935.
Grunicke, Helene. *Nach Deutsch-Ost-Afrika—Reise-Erlebnisse.* Dresden, 1916.
Haas, Thea de. *Urwaldhaus und Steppenzelt: Ostafrikanische Erlebnisse.* Leipzig, 1926.
Haase, Lene. *Durchs unbekannte Kamerun: Beiträge zur deutschen Kulturarbeit in Afrika.* Berlin, 1915.
Haase, Lene. *Raggys Fahrt nach Südwest 1908.* Berlin, 1910.
Höpker, Lydia. *Als Farmerin in Deutsch-Südwest: Was ich in Afrika erlebte.* Minden, 1936.
Höpker, Lydia. *Um Scholle und Leben: Schicksale einer deutschen Farmerin in Südwest-Afrika.* Minden in Westfalen, 1927.
Irle, Hedwig. *Unsere schwarzen Landsleute in Südwestafrika.* Gütersloh, 1911.
Jentzsch, Frieda. *In Ostafrika: Ein Tagewerk unter meinen schwarzen Kranken.* Leipzig, 1938.
Karow, Maria. *Wo sonst der Fuß des Kriegers trat: Farmersleben in Südwest nach dem Kriege.* Berlin, 1909; 2d ed. 1911.

Karsten, Paula. *Wer ist mein Nächster? Negertypen aus Deutschwestafrika.* Berlin, 1903.

Kayser, Alwine. *Aus den Anfängen unserer Kolonien: Meine Erlebnisse als Begleiterin meines Gatten. . . auf Inspektionsreise in Deutsch-Ostafrika 1892.* Berlin, 1912.

Kühne, Käthe. *Tagebuchblätter, geschrieben während der Jahre 1891 bis 1895 in Südafrika.* Berlin, n.d.

Liliencron, Adda von, ed. *Reiterbriefe aus Südwest—Briefe und Gedichte aus dem Feldzuge in Südwest-Afrika in den Jahren 1904–1906.* Oldenburg und Leipzig, 1906; 2d ed. 1907.

Mathuschka, Maria Gräfin von, geb. Gräfin Strachwitz. *Meine Erinnerungen aus Deutsch-Ostafrika: Von 1911–1919.* Leipzig, 1923.

Prince, Magdalena [von]. *Eine deutsche Frau im Innern Deutsch-Ostafrikas.* Berlin, 1903; 3d ed. 1905.

Reck, Ina, geb. von Grubkow. *Auf einsamen Märschen im Norden von Deutsch-Ostafrika: Reiseskizzen.* Berlin, 1925.

Reck, Ina, geb. von Grubkow. *Mit der Terdagurn-Expedition im Süden von Deutsch-Ostafrika: Reiseskizzen.* Berlin, 1924.

Rein-Wuhrmann, Anna. *Liebes und Leides aus Kamerun: Erlebnisse im Missionsdienst.* Stuttgart und Basel, 1931.

Rein-Wuhrmann, Anna. *Lydia: Ein Frauenleben im Grasland von Kamerun. Der Wirklichkeit nacherzählt.* Stuttgart, 1927.

Rein-Wuhrmann, Anna. *Mein Baumvolk im Grasland von Kamerun.* Stuttgart, 1925.

Rein-Wuhrmann, Anna. *Vier Jahre im Grasland von Kamerun.* Basel, 1917.

Seeck, Eva. *Um Südwest.* Baden-Baden, 1926.

Wittum, Johanna. *Unterm Roten Kreuz in Kamerun und Togo.* Heidelberg, 1899.

Zeeb, Anna. *Nach Deutsch-Ostafrika: Reisebriefe.* Herrnhut, 1899.

Ziemann, Grete. *Mola Koko: Grüße aus Kamerun. Tagebuchblätter.* Berlin, 1907.

Secondary Sources

Plischke, Hans. *Von Cooper bis Karl May: Eine Geschichte des völkerkundlichen Reise- und Abenteuerromans.* Düsseldorf, 1951.

Steins, Martin. *Das Bild des Schwarzen in der europäischen Kolonialliteratur 1870–1918: Ein Beitrag zur literarischen Imagologie.* Frankfurt am Main, 1972.

Trümpelmann, J. *Das deutsche schöngeistige Schrifttum über Südwestafrika.* Windhoek, 1933.

Black Sexuality and Modern Consciousness

SANDER L. GILMAN

1

Amos Oz, one of the most insightful of contemporary Hebrew novelists, paints an extraordinary portrait of the *yeke,* the German Jew in Israel, in his epistolary novella "Longing." In this tale, Dr. Emanuel Nussbaum remembers a moment in prewar Vienna, "a summer's day," when, while walking through the city, he saw "a pair of Negro beggars":

> I stop and linger, watching them from a short distance away. Not long ago I took a course in anthropology, yet I believe that these are the first Negroes I have ever seen. Outside the circus, of course. Yes, they are woolly-haired. Coffee-skinned, not cocoa-colored. A slight shudder ripples through me. I brush aside a fleeting mental image of the shape of their sexual organs.[1]

Oz's evocation of pre-Holocaust Vienna contains this epiphany which associates the German image of the black with the fantasy of black sexuality. But even more directly it associates the act of seeing the black with a fantasy of the genitalia. Seeing the black evokes the genitalia in a direct and unmitigated manner. For Oz, this association reveals the attitude of the German Jew to the sexuality of that exotic which he will become once transplanted into the Near East. The German Jew becomes the object of his own sexual fantasy. Amos Oz's literary portrayal of this association enables me to state my own thesis most directly. During the rise of modernism, from the *fin de siècle* to the collapse of the Nazi state (and beyond), the black, whether male or female, came to represent the genitalia through a series of analogies. It is this series of mental associations which must be unraveled in order to understand the epiphany which typifies for Amos Oz the nature of the Viennese fantasy of black sexuality.

Let us begin with an aside in cultural history, one which will help place Amos Oz's image of the fantasy of the black. Let us remove ourselves to the German or Austrian zoological garden before World War I. If we cast our eye back into time, to turn-of-the-century Vienna, and see with the eye of the Viennese of the period, we would be seeing a zoological garden quite different from that perceived if we found ourselves in our contemporary "zoo." We would be struck by the fact that animals were on display. And that "animal," in its accurate biological usage, would include specimens of the genus *Homo sapiens.* Indeed, the European zoological garden of the late 19th century provided "ethnological" exhibitions, representations of "exotic" cultures, eating what were viewed as appropriate foods, living in appropriate housing, and undertaking appropriate tasks for "primitives." Replaced in the late 1920s by the film travelogue, the "ethnological" exhibition was a natural extension of the ethnological museum, placing living "exotics" within the daily experience of the European. Vienna was certainly no exception to this. In the Prater, the major city park, imported exotics served as the focus for the fascination of the masses. Here were "noble" exotics whose presence countered the malignant "ignobility" of the local exotics, Eastern Jews; but they shared many of the same stereotyped sexual characteristics.

It is important to understand that just as the Jews, especially the Eastern Jews, represented a specific type of perverse sexuality—in their case, incest—within the stereotypes of *fin de siècle* perception, so, too, did the black represent another type of damaged sexuality.[2] This sexuality, like that of the Jews, was presented within the systems of Western perception as a disease. This pathology, like that ascribed to the Eastern Jews, was one which articulated many of the fantasies of the publicly repressed sexual discourse of the turn of the century. The signifier of black sexual pathology was tied to the form of the genitalia of the blacks.

This is not to deny that the black was perceived as an attractive sexual object in *fin de siècle* Vienna. Magnus Hirschfeld reports in a rather jaundiced tone (quite unusual for this great sexual liberal) about the "queer predilection for Ashantis that for a while raged in Vienna" among the women of that city, who would "approach these Negroes under different pretexts" for sexual encounters.[3] The Ashantis became the sexual icon for the "royal and imperial" monarchy, being exhibited in Budapest as well as Vienna. But it is important to understand that the Ashantis were simply representative of the "black" as an abstraction, just as the "black" as an abstraction signified the diseased but attractive Other for the Viennese. The attraction of the black was coupled with the sense of danger lurking within the pathological, as we shall see.

2

After an exhibition of a group of Ashantis in 1896, Peter Altenberg published his *Ashantee* (1897), a work which was then anthologized, but always in extract, in his later collections.[4] Altenberg was the master of the sketch, the creation of an intense, evocative literary image; in *Ashantee* he provided an interlocking series of such sketches—with, however, an overall literary structure lacking in his other works. *Ashantee* is a record of Altenberg's internalized fascination with the young Ashanti women and girls exhibited in the Prater. The structure which Altenberg superimposed upon the sketches included in the volume reveals the overt ideology of his public position as well as the hidden dimension of his perception of the black. On the surface, the book serves as a liberal protest against the exploitation of the blacks by the European public's taste for the exotic. But there is a powerful subtext which presents the author's association between his "seeing" of the black and his fantasy about human genitalia.

The work opens with a long quotation from *Meyer's Encyclopedia,* placing the Ashanti into the ethnology of Africa (3–4). Following the general view of the most influential geographer of the late 19th century, Friedrich Ratzel, the anonymous author of the encyclopedia article begins by placing the Ashantis within the geography of the West Coast of Africa, as the central determining qualifier for all of the following description.[5] The author observes that the Ashanti are "true, woolly-headed blacks," whose priests have the function of exorcising evil spirits through "hysterical" dances. These two qualities, the "true" nature of the Ashanti as a race and the "hysterical" quality of their religion, begin Altenberg's text. The reader is presented with the black within the encyclopedia, a textual ethnological museum, but one which exhibits the black within the context of scientific discourse, rather than the sideshow of the Prater. In citing this passage as our opening into the text, Altenberg draws upon the scientific status of ethnology, or at least upon the power of a "scientific" text to counter or undermine the popular tone of the Prater exhibition of the black. Yet the citation also begins to document, no matter how subtly, the analogy he will present between the black and the genitalia.

Altenberg's opening vignette provides the expected liberal condemnation of the Ashanti exhibition in the Prater (5–13). In the zoological garden, there stands a cage inhabited by two exotic beasts from the Amazon, two pampas hares, sitting quite humanlike on their haunches nibbling the sweets tossed to them by the crowd. Next to this cage are the Ashantis, seen performing a native dance. We, the readers, find ourselves viewing the scene in the company of two employees of the zoo, who discuss the Ashantis, or at least one of the young Ashanti women, in much the same tone as they had spoken about the pampas hares. What is striking about the point of view created by the author for his figures is that it mirrors Peter Altenberg's own lifelong fascination with prepubescent females, for our narrative perspective throughout the work permits us to see only the young females present among the Ashantis. It excludes from our vision the males present. The first vignette documents this exclusion and provides the reader with the appropriate liberal perspective: how horrible it is to have human beings exhibited and gawked at like pampas hares. This ideological message is completed in the closing sketch which frames the collection. The volume concludes with one of the employees commenting to the director of the zoo about someone who had just left the abandoned huts of the Ashantis in tears. The director's response is: "By the way, these huts have to be demolished tomorrow to make way for the tightrope walkers and a tethered balloon ride" (72). Thus, on its surface, Altenberg's most sustained work serves as a condemnation of Viennese society for having turned the Ashanti into a source of amusement. This overtly ideological frame, however, contains within it a complex set of textual references to the sexual nature of the black, references which are the direct result of the observations by the narrative "I/eye" who is called "Peter A." These references are a hidden code which, once deciphered, reveals to us the function of the black within the fantasy world of Peter Altenberg, but also within the world of the modernist text.

Our first introduction to the consciousness of this "eye" occurs in the second vignette. The structure of this vignette is typical for all of the following sketches— a dialogue (with or without the other partner actually being present and responding) with one of the young females in the mock village of the Ashantis. It is programmatically labeled "Dialogue" and begins with a discourse by "Peter A." on the nakedness of the young girls:

> "It is cold and very damp, Tioko. There are puddles everywhere. You all are naked. What are these thin linen things? You have cold hands, Tioko. I will warm them. You need at least cotton flannel, not this smooth cloth." (14)

She responds by stressing the fact that it is the exhibitioners who demand that the Ashantis appear "naked." Tioko observes that the Ashantis would never dress this way in Africa, nor would they live in huts which are only fit for dogs. "They want us to represent animals," she comments. The organizer of the exhibition told her that there are enough clothed females in Europe, and what they need is for them to be "naked." The word *naked* is Altenberg's label for the state of dress in which the Ashanti women are exhibited. It is clear that they are dressed in the traditional garment in which blacks were exhibited in Europe from the beginning of the 19th century, a garment which was thin enough to be quite revealing. When Sarah Bartman, the "Hottentot Venus," was exhibited in London in 1810, her presentation caused a public scandal, not only because of the British antislavery feeling but because she was exhibited "to the public in a manner offensive to decency. She exhibits all the shape and frame of her body as if naked."[6] Such garments seem to be standard for the black female, if a print of a ball given by the Duchess du Barry in Paris during 1827 is any indicator. But exactly what was the signification of the nakedness of the black female, a nakedness which Peter Altenberg deplores?

The "Hottentot Venus" served as the emblem of black sexuality during the entire first half of the 19th century. She represented a sexuality inherently different from that of the European—not merely in its "voluptuousness," to quote the French biologist J. J. Virey, but in the form of their sexual organs. Virey further associated the physiology of the black female (her "hideous form") with her physiognomy (her "horribly flattened nose").[7] Thus there was an attempt to differentiate between the races, based on a Western perception of the appearance of the black and the analogy between that appearance and the sexual difference of the black. The view that the races were inherently different rested to no little extent on the sexual difference of the black. The iconography of the "Hottentot Venus" was a means of differentiating the black female from her white counterpart as a representative of a separate and distinct species. The proof for early 19th-century ethnologists and biologists was to be found in two very specific physical attributes of the black: the steatopygia, or protruding buttocks, which served as the "public" sign for that hidden sign of her unique sexuality, and the "Hottentot apron," a hypertrophy of the labia and nymphae. When 19th-century Europeans "saw" the black female, they looked at her buttocks and fantasized about her genitalia, as can be seen in a mid-19th-century German caricature of the "Hottentot Venus."[8] What is of interest is that while the scientific discourse concerning the "Hottentot Venus" makes much of both her buttocks and her genitalia, its impact on the "popular" consciousness subsumes the discourse about the genitalia into the fantasy about the buttocks. By the late 19th century, this fantasy has found a specific locus. For the idea of the sexual anomalies of the black female were linked with fears of sexually transmitted disease. The genitalia of the black were perceived as analogous to those of the infected prostitute, as in an essay written by Adrien Charpy in 1870 on the external form of the genitalia of the prostitute, or in Cesare Lombroso's standard work on prostitution published in 1893.[9] Sexually transmitted illness and the pathology of the black genitalia were associated, and the fear (and fascination) accompanying the one became associated with the Other. Thus by the time Peter Altenberg begins to write his *Ashantee,* the idea of black sexuality as a sign of pathology was well implanted in the consciousness of the European. The double sign of the unapproachability of the black woman—her difference as a member of an inherently different race—and her pathological character became a signifier for the European. As we shall see, its function within the structure of the literary discourse assumed a most surprising dimension.

By the late 19th century, seeing the black meant fantasizing about the human genitalia. Following "Dialogue," the next paradigmatic sketch in Peter Altenberg's *Ashantee* is labeled "Culture" and presents the reader with an account of a dinner party in Vienna to which two of the Ashanti women were invited (28–29). The dinner party chit-chat revolves about the fact that the guests perceive a real difference between the "childlike" nature of the black woman and the "adult" (although the word never falls) nature of Western women. Our eye in the tale, "Peter A.," comments quite directly that "blacks are children." Here is a further marker of difference, the roots of which can be found in classical antiquity. The Other is like the child, different from the mature and sensible adult. But in the *fin de siècle* the very idea of the analogy between "child" and "adult" assumes a sexual dimension. Indeed, when Josephine Baker appeared in Vienna in 1929—or at least tried to appear, for the city council found her costumes much too lascivious—she was glorified, totally without irony, by her supporters in Vienna as "that beautiful black child."[10] The implications of the child as sexual object become evident later in the course of the dinner party when the younger of the two Ashantis is given a "wonderful French doll," to which she begins to sing. The older of the two "suddenly bared her perfect upper body and began to nurse the doll from her magnificent breasts." The audience to this spectacle is awed by the naturalness of her action, moving one of the guests to comment that this was one of the "holiest" moments in her life. The bared breast has a function as a sexual sign of physical maturity, but is given here an association with "childishness," an association which is clearly contradictory. It has a quite different signification than (to take a well-known example) the function of the iconography of the breasts in Theodor de Bry's illustrations of the early reports of the explorers of North America, where, as Bernadette Bucher has shown, the shift from the "classic," that is, firm, breasts to sagging breasts has major structural significance in representing the general shift in attitude toward the "exotic."[11] Here the sign of the breast is that of the "girl-woman": the child with the physical characteristics of the adult.

The power of this association within the world of Peter Altenberg can be judged by the central sexually referential vignette, entitled "A Letter from Africa" (32–35). This, the eleventh vignette in the book, begins on a somber note. The brother of one of the young women has died in Accra and this news is received by all with an act of communal mourning. This opening leads, however, to a further moment in this natural history of Altenberg's perception of the black. Suddenly it is nine at night:

> I enter the hut. On the ground lie Monabo, Akole, the wonderful one, and Akoschia. Not a pillow, not a blanket. Their perfect upper bodies are naked. The air is filled with the odor of pure, noble young bodies. I lightly touch the wonderful Akole.

The sexual overtones to this passage are unmistakable. What is striking is the association of the concept of racial purity, such as is mentioned in the selection from *Meyer's Encyclopedia,* and the "purity" ascribed to the "odor" of the black. Olfactory qualities had long been used to label the Other as different. Indeed, the mephitic odor of difference had been one of the central markers for the Jew in the biology of race in late 19th-century Germany.[12] The function which the "pure" odor of the "noble young bodies" of the black women has is to reverse the association of odor and difference. Yet the deep structure associates the two within the system of sexual discourse in the late 19th century. We have already remarked on Altenberg's use of the absence of "shame" as an indicator of the childlike "nobility" of the Ashanti. Lombroso provided a reading of the origin of this sense of shame in the "primitive." He remarked that in the Romance languages the term for shame is taken from the root *putere,* which he interprets as indicating that the origin of the sense of shame lies in the disgust for body smells. This he "proves" by observing that prostitutes show a "primitive pseudo-shame," a fear of being repulsive to the male, since they are loath to having their genitalia inspected when they are menstruating. Altenberg's "pure odor" and absence of shame (the exposed upper bodies of the Ashantis serving as an icon of their unselfconsciousness) are signs of their sexual availability. Shame has, for the late 19th century, only one major function as the organizing principle of that which the male conceives as desirable in the woman.[13] Shame thus has the function of making the Other sexually attractive.

The next moment in the vignette makes the covert reference to the sexuality of the black overt. "Peter A." is told by Akole, whom he has touched in her sleep, to go to Tioko. Monambo, awakened, turns to him and asks:

> "Sir, tomorrow can you bring us a 'piss-pot'? It is too cold to leave the hut at night. It must be blue outside and white inside. We will pay you what it costs. You would give Tioko one! What might it cost?!"

"Peter A." replies:

> "Monambo, I have never bought a 'piss-pot.' I don't know how much it will cost. Between 50 Kreuzer and 500 Gulden. Queens use golden ones."

Monambo then repeats her first speech to him and the vignette has "Peter A." leaving the hut as dawn comes.

Altenberg's fantasy of consummation with the black is cast in a literary mold. His seduction takes place within the safe confines of the text. But it is a fantasy of seduction which equates the black women with her genitalia, which makes her into the representation of sexuality *per se.* Altenberg's literary encoding of this is uncomplicated. Without a doubt, the most blatant sign is the conclusion of the vignette, the lover departing at the crack of dawn. This time, that of the *aube,* is part of the standard literary repertoire of seduction. It is an image whose associations are self-evident. Consummation has been accomplished and the male leaves, walking into the new day. The act of coitus is part of the nightside of fantasy. The dawn song serves as an extended metaphor for the postcoital depression of the male. But Altenberg has peppered his text with further sexual associations, which lead the reader to expect the final "dawn song," rather than be startled by it. Central to them is Monambo's request for a "piss-pot."

The sexual association of the image of the female genitalia with urination has a long textual history. Indeed, the first major text in the Western literary tradition which associates these two images relates them also to the figure of the black. *The Song of Songs* (7:2) sings of the "navel [that] is like a round goblet, which wanteth not liquor." But it is with the further, post-

Enlightenment association of urination and shame within a literary context
that the fascination of the 19th-century male for the genitalia of the female
is made overt. Goethe's *Wilhelm Meister's Apprenticeship* describes Wilhelm's seduction by the actress Marianne's overt unselfconsciousness:

> It seemed to him when he had here to remove her stays in order to reach the
> harpsichord, there to lay her skirt on the bed before he could set himself, when
> she herself with unembarrassed frankness would make no attempt to conceal
> from him many natural acts which people are accustomed to hide from others
> out of decency—it seemed to him, I say, that he became bound to her by invisi-
> ble bonds.[14]

The act of observing excretion destroys the illusion of "shame," just as the
nakedness of the Ashantis and their request for a "piss-pot" removes the
veil of social practice and bind the observer, schooled in those practices, to
the one whom he has designated as the exhibitionist. The power of this passage from *Wilhelm Meister's Apprenticeship* can be judged in a report of
William Wordsworth's response. He read the novel until "he came to the
scene where the hero, in his mistress's bedroom, becomes sentimental over
her dirty towels, etc., which struck him with such disgust that he flung the
book out of his hand, would never look at it again, and declared that surely
no English lady would ever read such a work."[15] It was clearly the "etc."
which caused Wordsworth's agitation. For the observing of Marianne's act
of exposure revealed the power which the perception of sexuality has on the
male. Altenberg picks up this theme and links it to the fantasy of "seeing"
the black, a black of "pure" race and "pure" sexuality. It results, however,
in a seduction which takes place only within the text, only through the association of perceiving the black and fantasizing about their genitalia. The
movement from talking about the act of urination to the fantasy of coitus is
buried in a nest of ellipses in the text, ellipses which herald the introduction
of the trope of the parting lovers. Again, Altenberg uses a "liberal" overlay
to rationalize his projection concerning the sexuality and genitalia of the
black. Altenberg's use of the anglicized term "piss-pot" leads the reader
back to a colonial world where, according to the women, "piss-pots" would
not be used by blacks. The blacks need the "piss-pot" because they are being
housed in kennels and clothed in thin, revealing garments. The covert association comes about through speaking about urination, for urination in the
late 19th-century mind leads to a fantasy of the buttocks.

In one of Havelock Ellis's case studies, which, as Phyllis Grosskurth has
shown, are themselves fantasies on sexual themes, a "firsthand" account of
this association between the act of urination and the buttocks is given:

> Flossie herself, who became so acute an analyst of her own experience, pointed
> out the significant fact that in a woman there is invariably a mental
> association—an association which has no existence in a man's mind—between

the nates and the act of urination. The little girl's drawers must be unfastened behind to permit of the act being accomplished and the grown women must raise her clothes behind for the same act; even when, as is now so often the custom, she adopts the standing attitude in private, she usually raises the clothes behind, though, as the stream tends to take a forward direction, it would be more convenient to raise them in front. Thus, throughout life, in a women's mind there is an association between urination and bared prominent nates. Custom, as Flossie emphasizes, compels a women to bare and protrude the nates and sit for the purpose of urination, and when there is nothing to sit upon to squat, although, she adds, "as far as decency goes, it might be much more modest to turn one's back to any stray passerby, and raise the skirts in front, towards a protective bush; but this would be contrary to habit—and savour of a man!" Even when, as we have seen to be the case with Flossie, the practice of urination in the open without raising of the skirts is adopted, the prominence of the nates may still be asserted, for, as Flossie discovered, the act is best performed in this attitude when bending forward slightly and so protruding the nates.[16]

Present in Ellis's text are the associations of childhood, of exhibitionism, with the act of urination and the baring of the buttocks. The powerful association of the buttocks with the primitive, with the buttocks of the black in the 19th century, thus leads the reader back to Altenberg and the bodies of the young Ashanti women on display in the Prater.

Havelock Ellis's case study of Flossie is a tale of the growth of a perversion. The analogy which Flossie sees among the image of the buttocks, the act of urination and her eventual flagellist fetish documents a representative course of associations for the *fin de siècle* perception of the sexual act. The distancing effect of presenting these analogies as the central focus for the image of the black stresses the strong historical associations of the black with the pathological, especially the sexually pathological. The fascination of *fin de siècle* writers such as Altenberg is the mirror image of the Victorian image of the sexualized being found in works such as George Gissing's *The Whirlpool* (1897). Bernard Meyer has commented that "when one of the characters is killed off by bad street drains, it is tempting to suspect that this annihilating instrument of public plumbing was a symbolic representation of the devouring female genital, an awful image of that cloacal anatomy that appears to have become for Gissing an emblem of all ugliness. The very streets of London appear to partake in the mephitic attributes of the women who roam them."[17] It is the association of fantasies about pathology and excretion which Meyer associates, quite correctly, with the image of the genitals. It is the reversal of this image, maintaining its association with pathology, which appears in the association of the excretory act with the genitals among the moderns.

The "piss-pot" serves as a marker in the text of a shift from the accepted exoticism of the breasts of the black to the hidden sexuality of the black female. This, too, has a parallel in the text from the *Meyer's Encyclo-*

pedia cited at the very beginning of *Ashantee*. For the quotation stressed the fetishistic nature of the religion of the Ashantis and the "hysterical" dances of the priests. By 1896, the term *hysterical* had a specific female context which was used in analogy to the repressed sexuality of the clergy.[18] To describe the priests of the Ashanti as "hysterical" meant to classify them with the Bacchanti and other groups of "hysterical" females. The German makes this overt, since the masculine form of priest *(Priester)* is used, excluding the female from this now feminized category, the fetishistic priest. The Ashanti females are thus portrayed as the antithesis of the hysteric. They are not hysterical *even in their shared grief.* They are users of objects in their non-fetishistic function: the "piss-pot" is to be used as a "piss-pot." This places them in the antithetical category to the "hysterical" men who are the priests of the Ashanti. Altenberg has confused two categories which can quite easily be unraveled. The first is that of the adult, sexualized exotic, whether male or female. These are the priests, the male blacks who disappear from within the text and are banished to the margins, appearing only in the opening passage and in our knowledge of the historical structure of the exhibition held in the Prater. The second is that of the child, the unconsciously sexualized exotic, the black as child, which he can approach in his fantasy.

Manambo knows Altenberg's fantasy when she asks him to buy her a "piss-pot," and observes that she would most probably give one to Tioko. Altenberg approaches a fantasy of physical intimacy only hinted at in the description of Baudelaire's "Vénus noire." It is indeed a detailed fantasy of the difference of the black based on the ethnologists' discussions of the inherent difference between black female sexual structure and that of the non-black. Again, it is in Friedrich Ratzel's ethnology that this sexual difference, perceived in the structure of the "Hottentot apron," becomes one of the central markers for the polygenetic difference of the races. For Ratzel, this sexual anomaly is present in many of the African races and makes the woman into a "perfect monster."[19] For Altenberg, the difference perceived between the clothed, demure prepubescent Austrian "Mädel" such as the thirteen-year-old Bertha Lecker, whose photograph he ornamented with a lover's heart, and the bare-breasted "young Egyptian," whose photograph he described in a letter to Arthur Schnitzler as "my black friend Nahbaduh,...the last madness of my soul," is the fact of approachability.[20] It is the difference between health and pathology. When Altenberg sees the black, it is as the approachable exotic, with the bared breast functioning as a signifier in analogy to the beckoning genitalia. In another context, I have discussed how the image of the childwoman in *fin de siècle* Vienna became closely linked with the sexual license through the distancing effects of projection.[21] It is indeed the pure child as sexual object, the child free from the curse of adult sexuality (with all of its pathological associations for the 19th century), which is projected onto the exotic as sexual object. In that essay, I stressed the importance of class as well as age as the matrix into which the projections of sexuality, the creation of the permissible object of desire, are made. With Altenberg, the exotic is not merely class- and age-determined, she is also race-determined. Part of this is the patriarchal attitude of the West toward the black, mirrored in the liberalism of "Peter A." as well as in the conservatism of the entrepreneur in the Prater. But there is a hidden agenda in Altenberg's projection. For there is yet another group viewed as a "pure" race, speaking a different tongue, whose males are portrayed as possessing feminine characteristics. It is, of course, the Jews. At the same time that Altenberg was publishing *Ashantee* (1897), Walter Rathenau published his *"Hear, O Israel,"* which was one of the most widely discussed self-critical texts of the day.[22] In it, Rathenau described the Jews as a tribe much like the Ashantis, except stressing the negative aspects of such attitudes and behavior in the context of Western culture. Rathenau's views, which included the description of the male Jew as possessing all of the qualities usually ascribed to the woman (or indeed the homosexual), were part of the discourse on race which dominated the 19th century. The two major examples for theories of race in the 19th century were the blacks and the Jews. Altenberg identifies with the Ashanti as part of his distancing and projection of the conflicts he perceived in his own Jewish identity. Altenberg, who will convert to Catholicism three years after *Ashantee* is published, sees the young black females as the antithesis of the racial stereotype of the Jew. The Jew is a male who acts like a female, one who belongs to the category of the "hysteric" like the Ashanti male priests. The Jew belongs to a "pure" race, the sign of which is degenerative sexual selectivity. The Ashantis are females who act like children, who do not belong to the category of the "hysteric." They are a "pure" race who, however, permit the sexual attention of the outsider. This is Altenberg's reaction to the criticism of Jewish sexual selectivity. For 19th-century psychiatry saw *all* blacks as especially prone to hysteria, whether male or female.[23] Like all Jews, the blacks were at risk because of the racial association. Altenberg has created an acceptable projection of his own internalization of the charges brought against the Jews because of the sexual selectivity. He has incorporated this into his own fantasy about the sexuality of the child and has thus created his own image of the accessible black child.

Altenberg's *fin de siècle* fantasy of the black is not unique. His mentor, Karl Kraus, makes numerous references to the prejudiced attitudes of German and Austrian society toward the black, but refers only to incidents concerning the depiction of black sexuality.[24] Kraus's fascination is with the German and Austrian interest in black sexuality, but this focus reveals his own preoccupation with black sexuality. Austrian liberalism focuses on the question of an alternative, perhaps even utopian, sense of human sexuality as perceived within the sexual difference of the black. The sense of difference dominates this discourse, as it does the discourse of other writers, writers whose views of human nature stresses the biological aspects of human nature over the social conventions.

3

The role of the black as the icon of sexuality, the fascination which Kraus shares with conservative critics whom he rebuts, permeates the entire liberal discussion of the black during the early 20th century. The black's identity is as surrogate genitals—often, but not always, of the other sex. If we move from Vienna to Paris during this same period, what is striking is that even though the ideology of the writers we shall examine is diametrically opposed to the "liberal" ideology of Altenberg and Kraus, they share the same perception of the black. If Viennese modernism condemned the exploitation of the black as sexual object, and used the condemnation to explore the author's own fascination with the sexual difference of the black, authors in Paris during the 1930s had no such compunction. For them, black sexuality served as the untrammeled expression of sexual power unlimited by the repressive conventions of European society, or so it was supposed to appear. The complexity of a conservative, vitalistic image of the Black as sexual object can be judged by an aside Mellors makes to Connie in D. H. Lawrence's *Lady Chatterley's Lover:* "I was really getting bitter. I thought there was no sex left: never a woman who'd really 'come' naturally with a man: except black women, and somehow, well, we're white men: and they're a bit like mud."[25] Fantasies of black sexuality are usually linked, as in Lawrence, to some negative qualification of black sexuality as pathological. Henry Miller in his *Tropic of Capricorn* (1938) presented a world which, like that of Lawrence, centers about the sexual act as the image of natural force.[26] His black figure, Valeska, had one "sad thing about" her. "She had nigger blood in her veins. It was depressing for everybody around her" (57). She also possessed the mephitic odor still associated in the 1930s with blacks and Jews (113). These flawed black sexual objects evoke the association of the black as the image of human sexuality, but only as peripheral figures (or metaphoric asides) in modernist literary works.

Henry Miller's novel stood as the inspiration of the first major work by one of modernism's most widely read authors, Lawrence Durrell. His novel *The Black Book,* while not his first work of fiction, was viewed by the author as well as his readers as his first "original" work. Published in 1938 under Henry Miller's influence (and in a series edited by him), the novel is a sexual adventure tale drawing heavily on Miller and James Joyce for its inspiration. It is a *Bildungsroman,* a tale of the education of an author into the complexities of the world. This world is represented by the womb (as it is in Miller's *Tropic of Capricorn*) and the novel uses the image of the womb as one of its central metaphors. None is more revealing, because of its high modernist language, than the protagonist Lawrence Lucifer's evocation of the black. It functions as an aside in the novel, presenting a contrast to the image of the central female figure, Hilda, who, following Otto Weininger's precept, is both mother and whore, and whose presence, while dying of venereal disease, links fecundity and Thanatos. At the close of the novel, Hilda is sterile, her ovaries having been removed, and yet she remains the womb incarnate, a diseased, nonproductive womb, but a womb nevertheless. In contrast to her accessibility is the figure of the black: "Miss Smith's red coon slit, her conk, her poll, her carnivorous ant-eating laughter, her Chaucerian Africa with Freudian fauna and flora...more coon slits and coon slatted laughter."[27] So ran Henry Miller's response to the manuscript of Durrell's novel. Here the circle is closed and the black female literally becomes her genitalia.

Lawrence Durrell introduces the black "Miss Smith" as a student of Lawrence Lucifer, a student to whom he is to teach Chaucer's language and with whom he is warned not to "muck about." Miss Smith is inarticulate, responding to all questions with "a snigger, laughing behind her hand." Lawrence Lucifer looks at her, seeing her as a work of art, as an aesthetic object:

> She will laugh in her sleeves. Her eyeballs will incandesce. Her red Euro-African mouth will begin to laugh again. It becomes impossible to walk hand in hand with Chaucer on the first Monday morning of the world. The laughter penetrates us, soaks us, winds us in spools of damp humorous macaroni. Beads of Nubian sweat break from the chocolate skin, powdered into a matt surface. Miss Smith sits forever at the centre of a laughing universe, her large languid tits rotating on their own axes—the whizzing omphaloi of locomotion. African worlds of totem and trauma. The shingle deserts, the animals, the arks, the floods, carved in fanatical rictus of the dark face, bent hair, and the long steady pissing noise under the lid of teeth.[28]

Laughter is the mark of the black, as in Sherwood Anderson's *Dark Laughter* of 1925, where the sexual ineptitude of the white world evokes "dark laughter," the laughter of "Negro women [who] have an instinctive understanding. They say nothing, being wise in women-lore" (233). Anderson, like Durrell, has written a novel which contains numerous references (both overt and covert) to Joyce's *Ulysses* (1922). As in the later *Black Book,* the interior monologue, especially that of Molly Bloom, structured the discourse of the novel.[29] Thus the inner monologue becomes part of an exploration of the internalized world of sexuality for the moderns. Here, too, Anderson incorporates the idea of the sexuality of the black as an ambiguous marker for the nature of white sexuality:

> "Such a strange feeling in me—something primitive like a nigger woman in an African dance. That was what they were after when they got up the show. You strip all away, no pretense. If I'd been a nigger woman—good night—something exotic. No chance then—that's sure." (184)

Lawrence Lucifer's interior monologue begins with the laughter of the black and the author's perception of the black as aesthetic object, much as does

Peter Altenberg. As in Altenberg, there is the hidden contamination of the image, the breath of sexual pathology. For in listening to Miss Smith's laughter, the sound of laughter reverberates:

> All she can do is laugh in her sleeve and powder that blank conk of hers jutting from the heavy helmet of her head; when she pisses, pressed down, squashed over the sound-box, from the laughter spurt jets of hideous darkness, a storm of Zanzibar, like black treacle.[30]

What begins as the hidden laughter of the black ends with the equation of laughter and "pissing." Urination becomes the focus for the internalized image of the black, but, unlike Altenberg's fantasy, it does not remain with urination. Lawrence moves from urination to sexuality as the all-consuming force:

> That focus which attracts us all so much is centred, like a cyclone, over sex. You may think you are looking at her, looking at the idea of her, but really, seeking under her cheap European dress, you are looking at her fertility. The potential stirring of something alive, palpitating, under her dress. The strange stream of sex which beats in the heavy arteries, faster and faster, until the world is shaken to pieces about one's ears, and you are left with an indeterminate vision of the warm African fissure, opened as tenderly as surgery, a red-lipped coon grin... to swallow all the white races and their enervate creeds, their arks, their olive branches.[31]

All the world is the womb, according to Lawrence, Miller, and Durrell, but the black womb is quite different. In Miller's *Tropic of Capricorn,* the reader is given the fantasy of the womb as the microcosm, the womb belonging to a languageless, mute woman; Durrell's image is quite directly parallel. Miss Smith's inarticulateness is paralleled by the extraordinary nature of her sexual parts, which contain, not the world, but the blackness of the world, Africa, the essence of Thanatos:

> Always I find myself turning from the pages of Geography, of flora and fauna, of geological surveys, to these studies in ethos. The creeds and mores of a continent, clothed in an iridescent tunic of oil. I turn always to those rivers running between black thighs for ever and for ever. A cathartic Zambesi which never freezes over, fighting its way through, but flowing as chastely as if it were clothed in an iridescent tunic of oil. I turn always to those exquisite horrors, the mutilations and deformations, which cobble the history of the dark continent in little ulcers of madness. Strange streaks here and there you will find: hair-trigger insanities, barely showing, like flaws in ice, but running in a steady, heavy river, the endless tributary of sex. They feed those fecundating rivers of seed which flow between the cool thighs of the Nubian, stiffen in his arteries, and escape in steaming laughter down his sleeve. Look, if you dare, and see the plate-mouthed women of the Congo Basin, more delectable than the pelican. Vaginas turning blue and exploding in dark flowers. The penis slit like a ripe banana. Seed spurting like a million comets. The menstrual catharsis swerving

down from the loins, dyeing the black carpets of flesh in the sweet smell, the rich urao of blood. The world of sensation that hums, dynamically, behind the walls of the belly. The slit lips of the vagina opening like a whale for the Jonahs of civilization. The vegetable rites. The prepucophagous family man: the foreskin eater. All this lives in the wool of Miss Smith, plainly visible, but dying.[32]

The black womb becomes the world of blackness, in which the black becomes the genitalia. But the black womb encompasses not only the "vagina" but also the "penis." What was the gender-specific image which equated "blackness" with female sexuality reveals itself, through its association with rites of circumcision, with the power of sexuality in general, as but a damaged, corrupted, and corrupting sexuality.

James Joyce had introduced the association of urination, sexuality, and stream-of-consciousness discourse in Molly Bloom's closing monologue.[33] Her sole act during this monologue so redolent with the fantasies and memories of her own sexuality is to urinate. Joyce's cloacal obsession is but a further variation on the Biblical model of the association of the sexual object's genitalia with the act of urination. These images haunt his work, from the chamberpot fantasies of *Chamber Music* to the "potting the po to shambe" of *Finnegans Wake.*[34] Note merely the literary reflection of some infantile fixation at the urethral stage. Joyce's use of the positive associations of sexuality, fantasy, and the act of writing reflects the modernist preoccupation with an association of the female with the image of creative (but also potentially destructive) sexuality. Durrell is quite unique in his presentation of "Miss Smith." His vocabulary is that of pathology as well as geography. Henry Miller was struck by the exoticism of this vocabulary, even imagining that Durrell had invented the medical vocabulary which he uses in this passage. Later critics have seen in this passage Durrell's fancied flirtation with the study of medicine.[35] What Durrell is undertaking in it is to further the associations found in the *fin de siècle* between black sexuality and the pathological. For Miss Smith's genitalia represent Thanatos. Keyed by his evocation of her urination, an act which is associated with her laughter, Durrell presents a fantasy of corruption and death. Like the dinner party in *Ashantee,* the laughter of the black evokes the unselfconsciousness attributed to black sexuality by writers such as Lawrence. But it is a corrupted and corrupting sexuality. Like Altenberg, Durrell's British colonial fantasy (paralleled to Miller's racist American one) placed the black and her genitalia in the world of the pathological and unapproachable. Blackness evokes sexuality, and sexuality (*pace* the late Freud) evokes death:

> It is this aura of death which seems exciting to experience, to speculate on, as I watch her sitting in this attic room, surrounded by charts of the prehistoric world in which Chaucer still farts and micturates debonairly. The black and white latitudes gathered together in one septic focus. Hush! She has no idea of the disease of which she is the victim. Her face is so beautiful among the medie-

val castles, the hunchbacks, the swans, that even Tarquin is dimly affected by her. From his diary he read me the immortal phrase in which he put down (in clean light Chinese brush strokes) the essence of her. *"Like a black saucer her mind is, shattered among a million white saucers."* And reading it, walked gravely up and down, fingering his temporal lobes. "Hum. Hum. Yes. To judge by the shape of the cranium I am a man of sudden terrible rages. Hum. Hum. I think," he said at last, "I would marry her perhaps, what? Do you know anything about her? Would she marry an Englishman of good family? It would be decorative even if I never fucked her, what?"[36]

Durrell presents a fantasy of the black as the literal representation of the genitalia. This extraordinary passage reflects precisely the same fear and fascination as was found in Altenberg's *Ashantee*. The black is the embodiment of sexuality, her genitalia are the sign of decay and destruction, a marker against which the Western world can judge its own degeneracy and decline. Durrell loads this interior monologue, the monologue of the white male observing the black female, with a level of medical discourse which was evidently confusing even to sympathetic readers. The overtly medical vocabulary, with its images of ripening and decay, point toward the same pathological image as underlies Altenberg's text. Altenberg used a literary topos to carry his approach to the fantasy of fulfillment. He consummates his fantasy within the world of the text through the use of a literary topos. Durrell, in a novel saturated with sexual encounters, a novel built upon the sexuality of its character, has this character make his fantasy explicit only within the interiorized monologue of the character. The very use of the interior monologue is as a sign of the absence of action on the part of the character. The reason for this difference may lie in the difference between Altenberg's Vienna and Durrell's background in India and colonialist Britain. For Altenberg the black was exotic, polluted in many ways, but still the exotic; for Durrell, stemming from a colonial tradition which viewed sexual contact with the "native" as debasing, the very idea of the black, as mirrored in D. H. Lawrence's aside, is linked to the untouchable. Both use the idea of blackness with its link to pathology as a means of exploring the idea of difference. The genitalia, diseased yet attractive, poisoning yet potent, become the confused double of the black.

4

The analogy of the black with sexuality can be one of the touchstones to any examination of the problem of consciousness among the moderns. The Viennese *fin de siècle* writer, such as Peter Altenberg, shares his overtly literary patterning of such awareness with vitalist writers such as Lawrence Durrell. More than merely "substit[uting] for the mouldering and over-stuffed capitalism of late Victorian life the mystique and promise of some intense and heightened, more authentic existence," so writes Frederic Jameson on Wyndham Lewis, the "liberal" as well as the "conservative" writers, in theme as well as form, incorporate the myth of black difference in the deep structure of their world of words.[37] For both Altenberg's and Durrell's images of the black are embedded in the image of the education of the author, a figure who uses the sexualized figure of the black, the outsider, as an alter ego. But it is of course a crude alter ego, for the sexual pathology ascribed to the black, the reduction of the black to the genitalia, is in no way parallel to the distance perceived by the author in isolation from society. Altenberg may have been labeled as an outsider because of his Jewish identity, but he had to create a persona for himself, that of the mad poet, to see himself truly as the outsider. Durrell, removed to Greece from Britain, educated in the finer points of British colonial attitudes toward the natives (attitudes which reappear with variation in *The Alexandria Quartet*), creates himself as the writer *manqué* under Henry Miller's tutelage. Both use the image of the genitalia of the black as markers for difference, but a difference more profound than that which they perceive in themselves.

The best psychological analogy which can be drawn to the creation of the consciousness of these literary figures, these authors *manqués,* and their fascination with the sexuality of difference can be found in the borderline syndrome. As Otto Kernberg has pointed out, the sexual fantasies of these patients parallel those of patients with sexual perversions.[38] Their fantasies are aggressive. Sexual contact becomes the equivalent to filling the body cavities with excrement. Oral, anal and genital fantasies merge and are condensed. They simultaneously express impulses and threats from all levels of psychosexual development, not merely the urethral stage. The typical dedifferentiation of sexual characteristics in such patients mingles homosexual and heterosexual impulses chaotically. All external objects merge. The consciousness of the writer, as mirrored in the literary representations of Altenberg and Durrell, stands at this confused and undifferentiated state. Not that this is necessarily the consciousness of the author, but it mirrors his confusions. The image of the black thus serves a number of functions. First, it serves as a mirror of the idea of difference which the modernist author can adapt. Second, it mirrors the confusions associated with the developmental structures which these writers project onto such figures in search of themselves. The association of the figure of the black with an undifferentiated sexual drive and with the incomplete internalization of the object points toward the necessary association of the black (as a surrogate for the self) with the sense of incompleteness, of the undifferentiated world of power and sexuality perceived as separate from the self. While this pattern has a basis in the creation of a sense of consciousness in the writer, it incorporates the black as the best analogy to this sense of incompleteness, of undifferentiated, pure sexuality, because of the ideological implications of the image of the black in the late 19th and early 20th centuries.

Any number of literary works from either end of the political spectrum could have made our point as well as those by Altenberg and Durrell. George Bernard Shaw's agnostic broadside *The Adventures of the Black Girl in Her Search for God* (1932) concludes with the "black girl" married and the mother of a number of "coffee-colored piccaninnies." John Farleigh's illustrations for the volume stress precisely the iconography of sexual difference I have discussed. Klaus Mann's image of his protagonist's black mistress in *Mephisto* (1936) reflects much the same preoccupation with the black as the object and source of sexual perversity. The fascist science fiction novel *Patrol against Death* (1939) by Rudolf Heinrich Daumann plays with the image of the black as sexual object while embedding this concept in an Africa of the future racked with plague.[39] Saul Bellow's evocation of the corruption and pathology of upper Broadway in *Mr. Sammler's Planet* (1970) uses the exposed member of the black pickpocket as a sign for the potency of those pathological forces which claim the city for themselves. All of these images are part of an internalized search for the "authentic projected onto the image of the sexuality of the black." Giacomo Leopardi stated it quite correctly in 1832:

> In the present century, black people are believed to be totally different from whites in race and origin, yet totally equal to them with regard to human right. In the 16th century, when blacks were thought to come from the same roots and to be of the same family as whites, it was held, most of all by Spanish theologians, that with regard to rights blacks were by nature and Divine Will greatly inferior to us. In both centuries, blacks have been bought and sold and made to work in chains under the ship. Such is ethics; and such is the extent to which moral beliefs have anything to do with actions.[40]

Ideology, whether liberal or conservative, employed the image of the black as a reflex of difference within the world of the literary text. Political ideology can thus be formed as much by stereotypes as it forms them.

1 Amos Oz, *The Hill of Evil Counsel* (London, 1980), p. 189.
2 See my "Jews and Mental Illness: Medical Metaphors, Anti-Semitism and the Jewish Response," *Journal of the History of the Behavioral Sciences* 29 (1984): 150–59.
3 Magnus Hirschfeld, *The Sexual History of the World War* (New York, 1941), p. 47.
4 Peter Altenberg, *Ashantee* (Berlin, 1897). All citations are to this edition. On Altenberg, the best overviews are Camillo Schaefer, *Peter Altenberg: Ein biographischer Essay* (Wien, 1980) and Hans Christian Kosler, ed., *Peter Altenberg: Leben und Werke in Texten und Bildern* (München, 1981).
5 Friedrich Ratzel, *The History of Mankind,* trans. A. J. Butler (London, 1898), vol. 2, pp. 352–57; vol. 3, pp. 125–43.
6 Cited by Paul Edwards and James Walvin, eds., *Black Personalities in the Era of the Slave Trade* (London, 1983), pp. 171–83.
7 J. J. Virey, *Histoire naturelle du genre humain* (Paris, 1824), vol. 2, p. 151.

8 John Grand-Carteret, *Die Erotik in der französischen Karikatur* (Wien, 1909), p. 195.
9 Adrien Charpy, "Des organs génitaux externes chez les prostituées," *Annales de Dermatologie* 3 (1870-71): 271-79, and Cesare Lombroso and Guillaume Ferraro, *La donna delinquente: La prostituta e la donna normale* (Torino, 1893). For a more detailed discussion of these questions, see my essay "Black Bodies, White Bodies: Toward an Iconography of Female Sexuality," *Critical Inquiry* 12, No. 1 (Autumn 1985): 204-42.
10 *Die Fackel* 806-9 (May, 1929), pp. 46ff.
11 Bernadette Bucher, *La sauvage aux seins pendants* (Paris, 1977). An older study, which is, however, quite valuable in this context, is Gustave-Jules Witkowski, *Tetoniana: Curiosités médicales, littéraires et artistiques sur les seins et l'allaitement* (Paris, 1898).
12 Gustav Jaeger, *Die Entdeckung der Seele* (Leipzig, 1880), pp. 106-9.
13 Iwan Bloch, *Das Sexualleben unserer Zeit in seiner Beziehung zur modernen Kultur* (Berlin, 1907). Typical for the resonance of this theme in the philosophical literature of the period is Paul Rée, *Der Ursprung der moralischen Empfindungen* (Chemnitz, 1877), pp. 74-77.
14 Johann Wolfgang Goethe, *Wilhelm Meister's Apprenticeship,* trans. Thomas Carlyle (Boston, 1884), p. 60.
15 John Ritchie Findlay, *Personal Recollections of Thomas De Quincey* (Edinburgh, 1886), p. 36.
16 Havelock Ellis, *Studies in the Psychology of Sex* (Philadelphia, 1928), vol. 7, pp. 171-72. See Phyllis Grosskurth, *Havelock Ellis: A Biography* (New York, 1980).
17 Bernard C. Meyer, "Some Observations on the Rescue of Fallen Women," *Psychoanalytic Quarterly* 53 (1984): 224. Compare the discussion in Nina Auerbach, *Woman and the Demon: The Life of a Victorian Myth* (Cambridge, Mass., 1982), pp. 150-84.
18 Jan Goldstein, "The Hysteria Diagnosis and the Politics of Anticlericalism in Late Nineteenth-Century France," *Journal of Modern History* 54 (1982): 209-39.
19 Ratzel, vol. 2, p. 283.
20 Cited in Schaefer, plate 2.
21 See my essay "Freud and the Prostitute: Male Stereotypes of Female Sexuality in fin-de-siècle Vienna," *Journal of the American Academy of Psychoanalysis* 9 (1981): 337-60. On the merging of the concepts of difference and the forbidden which link sex and race, see Gordon W. Allport, *The Nature of Prejudice* (New York, 1958), pp. 351ff.
22 Walter Rathenau, "Höre, Israel!," *Die Zukunft* 18 (1897): 454-62.
23 Alexander Pilcz, *Beitrag zur vergleichenden Rassen-Psychiatrie* (Leipzig und Wien, 1906), pp. 40-41.
24 See, for example, the essays reprinted in the volume *Untergang der Welt durch schwarze Magie* (München, 1960), pp. 308-11, 327-30.
25 D. H. Lawrence, *Lady Chatterley's Lover* (Paris, 1935), p. 240.
26 Henry Miller, *Tropic of Capricorn* (New York, 1961).
27 George Wickes, ed., *Lawrence Durrell and Henry Miller: A Private Correspondence* (New York, 1963), p. 80.
28 Lawrence Durrell, *The Black Book* (London, 1973), p. 123.
29 Sherwood Anderson, *Dark Laughter* (New York, 1925).
30 Durrell, p. 123.
31 Ibid., p. 124.
32 Ibid., pp. 124-25.
33 James Joyce, *Ulysses* (New York, 1961), pp. 738-68.
34 Id., *Finnegans Wake* (New York, 1947), p. 622. For more general information, see the detailed discussion of this image in William York Tindall, ed., James Joyce, *Chamber Music* (New York, 1954), pp. 71ff.
35 G. S. Fraser, *Lawrence Durrell: A Study* (London, 1973), pp. 46ff.
36 Durrell, p. 125.
37 Frederic Jameson, *Fables of Aggression: Wyndham Lewis, the Modernist As Fascist* (Berkeley, 1979), p. 134.
38 Otto Kernberg, "Paranoid Regression and Malignant Narcissism," in his *Psychotherapeutic Strategies for Severe Personality Disorders* (New Haven, forthcoming).
39 See my *On Blackness without Blacks: Essays on the Image of the Black in Germany* (Boston, 1982), pp. 125ff.
40 Giacomo Leopardi, *Pensieri,* trans. W. S. Di Piero (Baton Rouge, 1981), p. 111.

Two "African Travelers" from Germany:
Leo Frobenius and Janheinz Jahn

Edris Makward

In 1973, the City and the University of Frankfurt celebrated the centenary of Leo Frobenius's (1873–1938) birth. One significant item in these well-deserved celebrations was the production and publication of an anthology[1] of excerpts from his major works, edited by Eike Haberland. And it was, naturally, quite appropriate that Léopold Sédar Senghor, the world-famous poet of *négritude* and former President of the Republic of Sénégal, would be asked to write the foreword to the Frobenius Centennial Anthology. Coincidentally, the year 1973 was also the year of Janheinz Jahn's death in his home near Frankfurt. A very significant coincidence, indeed. Just a few months before his death, Jahn had completed an iconoclastic essay[2] entitled "Leo Frobenius: The Demonic Child," in which—to paraphrase Bernth Lindfors' accurate words—he called Leo Frobenius "names" that could indeed be used by some of Jahn's own more virulent critics to describe the author of the famous *Muntu: An Outline of the New African Culture* (1958) himself. On the basis of just a few of the superlatives listed by Lindfors—"a fascist," "a pseudo-scholar," "a post-Wilhelminian barroom philosopher"— one could but readily agree that the "Demonic Child" was Janheinz Jahn himself; for, instead of participating in the collective commemoration of a great predecessor and inspirer, he was, in fact, literally defacing the shrine of a worthy and highly admired elder. Yet, as if to indicate that all the virulent "names" of the world could not sever the umbilical cord that linked together our two "African travelers" from Germany, fate had it that the last German television interview conducted by Janheinz Jahn was to take place two days before his death on October 20, 1973, and his guest was none other than Léopold Senghor himself.

The three names of Frobenius, Senghor, and Jahn do indeed form a symbolic triangle which has always both intrigued and fascinated me in my attempts to analyze and comment on intellectual attitudes and concerns in contemporary Africa. I am therefore very grateful for this unique opportunity to attempt and pursue a coherent examination of the intricate itineraries of these three remarkable "travelers," with a special focus on Jahn and Frobenius. I shall, in effect, limit myself to the itineraries of our two "travelers" from Germany, but it goes without saying that Senghor is also a "traveler" in the same sense—that is, both intellectually and physically. And his journeys have taken him to faraway shores, thousands and thousands of miles away from his native Sénégal in West Africa, from the quiet and peaceful Joal, the Serer village of his birth in the first decade of this century. For their part, Frobenius and Jahn also journeyed thousands of miles away from their places of birth in Germany, in search of an Africa that would correspond closely to the Africa that they had already conceptualized and "reconstructed" for themselves and for their countrymen before ever setting foot on African soil. It is their "discoveries" during these journeys, the impact of their reflexions on these "discoveries," and above all the beneficent influence of their contributions for a true understanding of Africa and Africans that will constitute the subject matter of the following remarks. I shall refer to Senghor only with reference to his role as a link between our two travelers. It must be noted, however, that while calling both Frobenius and Jahn his friends, and doing so with genuine pride and affection, Senghor does not seem to have ever been really aware of the importance and significance of his role as a link between the two controversial German Africanist scholars.

In his foreword to the Haberland anthology, Senghor begins with the strong statement that "No one did more than Frobenius to reveal Africa to the world and to *Africans themselves.*" [3] Indeed, for Senghor and his fellow black students from French Africa and the French Caribbean then studying in the Paris of the early 1930s, one French translation of Frobenius's numerous works that was most influential was the 1936 edition of *Histoire de la Civilisation Africaine,* a translation by Dr. H. Bach and D. Ermont of *Kulturgeschichte Afrikas* (Gallimard: Paris, 1936). Senghor had by then already started taking advanced courses at the Ecole d'Ethnologie and at the Ecole Pratique des Hautes Etudes of Paris, and he was thus well acquainted with the works of some of the most prominent French and European ethnologists and Africanist scholars of the time. But in his own words, Frobenius was just stunning to his friends and to him, for indeed no one had ever, to their knowledge, put in print such statements as: "The idea of the 'barbarous Negro' is a European invention, which in turn dominated Europe until the beginning of this century." [4]

Senghor's was a generation of black students passionately involved in an intense search for their cultural identity, and this search involved above all a passionate quest for genuine and convincing assurances that while their "ancestors could never have been Gauls" as their textbooks blatantly asserted, the former, however, did create flourishing civilizations and cultures that they and their generation could and should be proud of. And the assurances that they were looking for so passionately and almost desperately were indeed on many pages of this and other books by Frobenius that came into their hands. Thus it was not surprising that, for Senghor and his friends,

Frobenius's *History of African Civilization* would become a new Bible from which passages would be memorized by heart ("Nous connaissions par cœur le chapitre II de livre premier *d'Histoire,* intitulé 'Que signifie pour nous l'Afrique' " [Haberland's *Anthologie,* p. vii]).

For this generation of young African and black intellectuals and students, often referred to as the generation of *négritude,* it was profoundly reassuring to read in a book written by an eminent—if controversial—and established European scholar that Africa, particularly Black Africa, was not a complete *tabula rasa.* And while they had already developed the concept and the idea of *négritude,* it was Frobenius who, in Senghor's words, "helped them give the word [*négritude*] its strongest and, at the same time, most humane significance."[5] Above all, we are told that this German professor, who was by then Honorary Professor at the University of Frankfurt and Director of the Frankfurt African Institute and the Frankfurt Museum of Ethnography, supplemented the teachings of the traditional African masters by teaching a whole generation of African and black scholars how "to see in their traditional myths both works of art and the values of *négritude.*" [6] Suffice it to state that the word was being used here to signify and represent what made the "Negro-African," "the black African" and his descendants, special and unique as producers of culture and civilization.

Now, who was this man, this Herr Professor who could be raised to the stars and be called the ultimate "Master"[7] by one of Africa's most renowned living scholars, creative writers, and statesmen and yet be called "names" by a fellow German student of Africa on the occasion of the centenary of his birth—the same German scholar who had always treated Léopold Senghor himself as his own "Master" for being the initiator of his passionate and prolific involvement in the study of Africa, its culture, and its literature for the last twenty-one years of his life?

One first important point that these two German Africanists had in common was that they traveled to Africa, the continent to the study of which they would devote most of their active lives, not just after a thorough academic preparation supplemented by extensive readings—which is what one would consider today as the most obvious norm—but also after having stunned their contemporaries in their own country and abroad with the impact of several pacesetting and controversial opera on their subject of interest: that is, Africa. Thus they were indeed very different from most other Africanist travelers before and after them. They were "Africanists before having ever traveled to Africa."

Leo Frobenius was born in Berlin in 1873. His father was a retired Prussian army officer. Both his passionate interest in the study of non-Western cultures and, in particular, African cultures and his penchant for unorthodox approaches and conclusions were demonstrated at the age of twenty-one when he produced a weighty volume on "Secret Societies in Africa." He was an independent mind and also a compulsive reader and worker. Thus, when his doctoral thesis on *The Origins of African Cultures* was rejected by the university, he continued to work independently and outside the university structure.

It was after the publication of his famous opus *The Origins of African Cultures* in 1898, as well as of many articles and pamphlets, that he would make his first trip to the African continent. Between 1904 and 1935, he would organize and lead twelve expeditions for ethnographic surveys and studies (in Central Africa, West Africa, North Africa, the Sahara, Egypt, Sudan, and Southern Africa) and he returned with a staggering wealth of notes, index cards, diagrams, drawings, photographs, and artifacts. By the time of his death in 1938, he had published sixty books and hundreds of pamphlets and was then considered one of the greatest authorities of his time for the study of prehistoric art and for African ethnology.

He would later receive recognition for his work, and his African Institute, until then financed and supported independently through his own resources, would subsequently come under the sponsorship of the City of Frankfurt, and he would be appointed Honorary Professor and Director of the Frankfurt Museum of Ethnography.

It is important to note that when he set foot on African soil for the first time, his goal and endeavor were already all too clear to him: namely, to provide a historical background for the civilizations of peoples who had so far been regarded as having no history, because of the absence of written records, and thus to incorporate them into the current of old world history.

In the short 1933 preface to *Histoire de la Civilisation Africaine,* which had such an impact on Senghor and his friends, Frobenius denounced the principle of oversimplification and of exaggerated compartmentalization of scientific research in his day. He found this highly destructive, and preferred to search for "unity rather than immerse [himself] in an ocean of details."[8] With this new approach of seeking to apprehend the whole rather than the parts, not only did he see the necessity of laying down the civilization of a whole continent impose itself on him naturally, but he also felt the need to identify and lay down "the principles of a morphological history of civilization."

In the opening chapter of *Histoire de la Civilisation Africaine,* Frobenius will again and again denounce with indignation the legendary belief of a dark continent where "the vast empires and the great cities of Western Sudan can only be the work of Arabs and Islam,"[9] and where there are only forests, jungles, savannas filled with huge trees, lianas and cannibal natives. But, fortunately, he could rejoice that while this erroneous view prevailed in Europe in the last century, "an admirable group of heroes would brave contempt, fever,"[10] and all sorts of dangers to unveil "Africa's real visage." And these men—intrepid travelers and explorers—who knew "that the vulgar concept was erroneous," were indeed young Frobenius's favorite heroes, and they were responsible for his enthusiasm for Africa (and his conviction that Africa was far from being the *tabula rasa* described in those earlier pamphlets) by succeeding "in laying their eyes on these prodigious splendors; an unknown magnificence appeared to them. But one had to wait another generation before the soul of Europe would be ready to accept this new knowledge."[11]

Also, Frobenius will insist that the first European sailors who landed on the African coasts at the end of the Middle Ages did find these marvels in front of them. He will further admit that, while these brilliant civilizations would be ultimately destroyed by the slave traders, those 19th-century pioneer explorers—his heroes—when penetrating into the remote areas of the continent, far away from the coasts now polluted by "European civilization, would still find the same wonders that the 17th-century sea captains had found on the coasts."[12] For Frobenius, there was no doubt that the European promoters of the slave trade in tropical Africa needed a moral justification for their dreadful and inhuman actions, and they found it by simply describing the black man as subhuman, as merchandise; by inventing the idea of the fetish (from the Portuguese *feticeiro*) as symbol of an African religion. And he will proclaim with passion that "As for me, I have not seen anywhere in Black Africa natives worshiping fetishes." Indeed he would even add that when he first visited the "Kassai–Sankuru" territory (in Central Africa) in 1906, he found "villages with long and wide streets lined with palm trees on each side and for miles and miles,"[13] that were reminiscent of the glorious times of the African past.

In the opening chapter of volume 1 of *Voice of Africa,* Frobenius quotes from a Berlin newspaper article of 1891:

> With regard to its Negro population, Africa, in contemporary opinion, offers no historical enigma which calls for solution, because from all the information supplied by our explorers and ethnologists, the history of civilization proper in this continent begins, as far as concerns its inhabitants, only with the Mohammedan invasion [islamite would be more correct!].

And:

> If the soil of Africa is turned up today by the colonist's ploughshare, no ancient weapon will lie in the furrow; if the virgin soil be cut by a canal, its excavation will reveal no ancient tomb; and if the axe effects a clearance in the primeval forest, it will nowhere ring upon the foundations of an old-world palace. Africa is poorer in recorded history than can be imagined. Black Africa is a continent which has no mystery, no history![14]

Frobenius was profoundly disturbed by such readings. But after cutting the passage with "his scissors by the light of the midnight oil in his tiny study," he tells us that he was able to turn to "his friendly bookshelves" where in-

deed another Africa was described, an Africa that was naturally very different from the one depicted in this 1891 Berlin newspaper article. That other
Africa was the Africa which would fascinate young Frobenius intensely and
would occupy him almost exclusively for the rest of his life. It was the Africa
of King Munsa's court as described by the German Botanist and traveler
Georg Schweinfurth (1836–1925) who had traveled to the West Nile Basin in
the 1860s, the Africa of Heinrich Barth (1821–65), of Mungo Park (1771–
1806), of René Caillé (1799–1838).

Thus the first important conclusion that impressed so vividly Senghor
and his friends in the Paris of the 1930s where they were all students from
Afrique Occidentale Française and from the Antilles Françaises was that
Black Africa possessed an original ancient civilization that they could be
proud of. To understand the nature and the intensity of the enthusiasm of
these young black students we have to situate them in the context of the
movement of *négritude,* that is, at a time when, confronted with the inherent
contradictions of the French assimilation policy in their colonies of origin,
they were but timidly attempting to turn to the African sources—or to their
"roots," to use a more contemporary term made popular by the Alex Haley
odyssey—for confidence in themselves and their future as Africans and as
black people of African descent. And I deliberately qualify their attitude—
at least in the first stages of their movement—as "timid," for that is what it
was! And how could it be otherwise if we remember how unassailable the
forces of colonialism and all its implications must have appeared at the time,
in the eyes of the colonized peoples? It is with that context in mind that I
would humbly wish to reverse Senghor's statement cited above, by saying
that, rather than being "supplementary" to the teachings of their traditional
African masters, the teachings of Professor Frobenius were indeed central
and more important in the first place, since in the eyes of these alienated
young students, the credibility of Professor Frobenius of the University of
Frankfurt was unquestionable and more definitely convincing in comparison to that of the traditional masters, or "masters of initiation," to use
Senghor's own words. For theirs was indeed an almost desperate search by
an already alienated group, a group that badly needed to rediscover the true
Africa, an Africa that would inspire confidence and hope in them and their
generation. And in their timid attempts, which naturally contradicted
openly most of the teachings acquired in the prestigious *lycées,* universities,
and *grandes écoles* of France, the appearance of an explorer and scientist of
Frobenius's caliber and reputation would be naturally invaluable and most
effective. Thus it was thanks to the words of Frobenius that they acquired
the confidence to listen again to the traditional teachers and to consider the
latter's teachings as relevant in the modern context.

The second conclusion in Frobenius's work that was strongly to influence the *négritude* generation and, particularly, Senghor was the concept of
the unity and oneness of African civilization. Frobenius recognized an iden-

tical "spirit" and essence in all the African art objects scattered all over Europe in museums, such as the Trocadéro (now the Museé de l'homme) in Paris, the British Museum in London, the museums in Brussels, in Holland, in Germany, in Italy, and in private collections: "And wherever we can still encounter this civilization [i.e., the Black African Civilization] it carries the same stamp.... Whatever the place of origin on the continent of these objects, they unite to speak the same language."[15]

The third point that Frobenius made and that had a considerable influence on Senghor and his contemporaries was to state explicitly the distinct nature of the common African trait. Comparing the African art objects with art objects and collections from Asia, he concluded:

> Everything has a precise, stern, severe, tectonic goal. That is what characterizes the African style. Whoever gets close enough to it in order to understand it really will soon recognize that it prevails *all over Africa* as the very expression of its being. It permeates the gestures of all the Black peoples, even into their figure; it speaks in their dances as well as in their masks, in their religions as well as in their life styles, in their state organizations and in their destiny as nations. It is alive in their narratives, in their tales, their legends, their myths.[16]

Reading again these lines, one cannot fail to take note of the sometimes harsh criticism made by such younger African scholars as Stanilas Adotévi, author of *Négritude et négrologues* (Paris, 1971), when they point their fingers at Frobenius as the "principal culprit" for what they see as lyrical exaggerations in some of the writings of Senghor and in his vain attempts at defining with precision the specificity of the Negro-African man—the other Western "culprit" being Lucien Lévy-Bruhl (1857–1939). The word "culprit" is used here with indulgence because the critics in question—Adotévi and others—are very clear about their target and they certainly do not exonerate the latter of using the theories and the conclusions of the former to support their own pronouncements, particularly when they do this by distorting or by pretending to ignore the final conclusions of their sources. Naturally, the case in point here is Senghor's famous statement about "the Negro-African mind [being] intuitive through participation and the white mind, analytical through utilization,"[17] or the unforgettable "l'émotion est nègre comme la raison est héllène." This seems to imply that Senghor chose to ignore that Lévy-Bruhl had corrected his own record by stating at the end of his life, in his *Carnets:*

> Pour la loi de participation j'affirmerai une fois de plus que la structure logique de l'esprit est la même chez tous les hommes et que, par conséquent, les primitifs tout comme nous rejettent la contradiction quant ils l'aperçoivent.[18]

Through these works that were like Bibles for young Senghor and his friends, through ten volumes of oral narratives and tales collected in the field, Frobenius maintained basically the same line of thinking regarding the richness and the coherence of African civilization, for, as far as he was concerned, the evidence he found in the field in twelve expeditions and thirty-one years of painstaking and indefatigable analytical work only served to confirm his early convictions. His passion was indeed mankind's past and, more specifically, Africa's past.

Janheinz Jahn was born in Frankfurt in 1918, that is twenty years before Frobenius's death. He started his college education at the University of Munich where he studied several foreign languages including Arabic. He interrupted his studies during World War II and became an interpreter in the German army. At the end of the war, he started writing for a living, instead of returning to the university, and in fact never completed his formal college education. An avid reader and a well-organized compiler, he assembled around him, in his rural home, a very impressive African library in the course of the latter twenty-one years of his life, most of which were spent in that small village near Frankfurt. By the time of his death in October 1973, at the age of fifty-five, he had published 54 books and about 300 articles and radio essays, all dealing with the literature and culture of blacks from Africa and the Americas.

Jahn's passion was indeed the study of the literature and the culture of the Black African and American continuum. But while Frobenius's passion and concern for Africa were exclusively with its past, one can say that Jahn's interest in Africa was primarily with its present and its future. Thus he coined in 1957 the term "Neo-African Literature." Jahn preferred this term to the expression "Modern African Literature," which he found too narrow; for he wanted to include under the same umbrella the new writing from Black Africa as well as the writing of blacks in the New World.

Like Frobenius, Jahn made his first extensive visit to the African continent only after the publication of some of his most momentous contributions; and he was also equally unorthodox and independent-minded throughout his life. 1952 was an important year in Jahn's life, for it was then that he made his first important encounter with Africa—and, in his case, this encounter, which was to play a decisive role in the orientation of his life, did not come initially through "friendly books" as in the case of Frobenius. It was an encounter with Léopold Sédar Senghor, then député of Sénégal in Paris. Senghor had come to Frankfurt to give a public lecture and Jahn was in the audience. By then, Senghor had already published several volumes of poetry and his momentous *Anthologie de la nouvelle poésie nègre et malgache de langue française* (1948). It was with this encounter with Africa through Senghor that Jahn's African "journey" started. He immediately set out to translate into German the works of this new literature. Before this, however, he wanted to acquaint himself with the African background through reading. Thus, in a few months, he read Lévy-Bruhl, Frobenius, the Rev. Placide Tempels, the author of *Bantu Philosophy* (1945), and the works of a number of other black writers from Africa, the Caribbean, and the

United States. His first anthology, *Schwarzer Orpheus* ("Black Orpheus"), appeared in 1954. This anthology was to meet with a remarkable success in Germany and was to be reprinted several times in just a few years.

Jahn's most outstanding and controversial book is without doubt *Muntu: An Outline of Neo-African Culture* published in 1958. It was the result of a remarkable work of synthesis in which concepts that had been extricated from the thorough studies of individual African cultures by such scholars and authors as Marcel Griaule, Alexis Kagame, and Placide Tempels were used to describe and analyze African, Afro-American, and Afro-Caribbean culture and art as a whole and in a unified context. First published in German, the book was quickly available in most European languages, and while the number of critical—sometimes harsh—reviews abounded on either side of the Atlantic, there were a number of readers who found it a very useful tool for understanding the complexities of contemporary African thought in the midst of the important changes that were taking place in Africa in the late 1950s and early 1960s.

Naturally, many scholars found Jahn's sweeping generalizations unacceptable; for many others, however, *Muntu* was indeed the first key, and a very stimulating one, to African philosophy. And just as Frobenius's *History of African Civilization* was a highly stimulating revelation for Léopold Senghor and his generation, Jahn's *Muntu* was indeed a Bible of sorts for a number of young black scholars on this side of the Atlantic.

Jahn's other major contributions include yet another controversial but highly commendable effort, namely, *A History of Neo-African Literature: Writing in Two Continents (Geschichte der Neoafrikanischen Literatur* [Düsseldorf, 1966]) as well as his ground-breaking bibliographical achievements, *A Bibliography of Neo-African Literature from Africa, America and the Caribbean* (1965), *Bibliography of Neo-African Literature* (with Claus Peter Dressler, 1971), and *Who's Who in African Literature: Biographies, Works, Commentaries* (1972).

In 1958–59, Jahn took his first extensive trip to West Africa and visited Nigeria, Dahomey (now the Republic of Benin), and Ghana. He published a candid and insightful account of his experiences during this visit to the "new" Africa in *Through African Doors* (1960). This visit was like a second "initiation" to Africa, his first one having taken place in the studious privacy of his library at Frankfurt. Jahn's library was subsequently acquired by the University of Mainz and named the Janheinz Jahn African Library.

It is appropriate to point out before concluding that iconoclasts do not come only from the banks of the Main or the Rhine rivers but also from those of the river Niger. Yambo Ouologuem, the author of the controversial and skillfully written novel, *Le Devoir de violence* (Paris, 1968; *Bound to Violence* [New York, 1971]), drew a satirical portrait of the famous German ethnographer in both cruel and sympathetic tones. Ouologuem's ambiguity in his fictional depiction of our "African traveler" is comparable to Jahn's in his 1974 essay, *Leo Frobenius: The Demonic Child*. He refers to the author of *Origins of African Cultures* and of *Histoire de la Civilisation Africaine* as "a salesman and manufacturer of ideology who assumed in the manner of a sphinx to impose his riddles, to justify his caprices and past turnabouts." Hardly disguising the name of his model, he introduced him as "secreting his own myth," adding that "Shrobenius molded his personality: brilliant but easygoing, waggish but pessimistic, attentive to his publicity, but scoffing at a society that had given him everything."[19] Yet it is this same Ouologuem who will express with genuine sadness his disapproval of the shameless way in which *négritude* was given a dressing down "as if for a final burial"—at the 1969 First Pan-African Festival of the Arts in Algiers. This opinion of Ouologuem appeared in an interview he gave to the correspondent of the Parisian daily *Le Monde* at the 1969 Algiers Festival.

In conclusion, Leo Frobenius and Janheinz Jahn were indeed remarkable and unusual African travelers. They traveled to Africa to meet Africans in order to confirm on the spot what they thought, what they believed that they knew about Africa; and they both returned with the confirmation that they had been seeking. The thorough and comprehensive way in which they both prepared for their first journey to that continent that they never saw or thought of as "the Dark Continent" was definitely a common denominator between them.

Enfants terribles they both were indeed; but their mischief did not turn out so badly after all. First, while one had his doctorate thesis rejected by the university but later ended up as a result of his phenomenal achievements an Honorary Professor and Director of a prestigious Museum of Ethnology, the other, who never completed a college degree, did end up lecturing at many great universities near his native country and elsewhere and gave his name to a University African Library in his native Frankfurt. Second, in spite of all the reservations and the criticisms that have been directed against them from different quarters, Africa, Africans, and blacks in general will remember them always for having raised their passionate and stubborn voices against the misconceptions and distortions of their contemporaries with regard to a whole continent and its peoples. They will indeed be remembered for having made the world aware of the dignity, pride, and the beauty of African cultures, of African civilizations. And this even though their vision could be said to be warped or distorted by their respective obsessions— one by his obsession with the past to the point of detaching himself completely from the problems of colonialism, from the struggle for emancipation and liberation which was entering its early phase on the continent, the other by his fascination with the "new" Africa, the Africa of the future, to the point of not seeing or feeling that the harmony was only apparent, and that the synthesis of the "old" and "new" was far from perfect. Yet they were neither "demonic children," nor "Wilhelminian barroom philosophers," nor "pseudo-scholars"; and both will indeed be remembered for having helped Africans and blacks "find a new consciousness of themselves within the African heritage"[20] at a time when they needed it most.

And the position of Senghor between our two "travelers" is remarkable, for he was the disciple of one while the other considered him his teacher. Leaving aside the exaggerations, the inconsistencies, and the far-fetched speculations regarding the so-called affinities between Germans and Ethiopians, or the specific peculiarities of the "intuitive Negro-African mind that participates" versus the "analytical white mind that utilizes," we cannot but agree that these three men, Frobenius, Senghor, and Jahn, do indeed form a remarkable and symbolically important triangle in the study and understanding of Africa, its peoples, and its cultures, in the last eighty years.

1 *Leo Frobenius 1873/1973: Une Anthologie,* ed. by Eike Haberland (Wiesbaden, 1973).
2 Janheinz Jahn, *Leo Frobenius: The Demonic Child* (Austin, 1974).
3 *Leo Frobenius 1873/1973,* p. vii (my emphasis).
4 Leo Frobenius, *Histoire de la Civilisation Africaine,* trans. by Dr. H. Bach et D. Ermont. 3d ed. (Paris, 1952), p. 15.
5 *Leo Frobenius 1873/1973,* p. viii.
6 Ibid., p. x.
7 Ibid., p. xiii.
8 Frobenius, *Histoire de la Civilisation Africaine,* p. 8.
9 Ibid., p. 13.
10 Ibid., p. 14.
11 Ibid., p. 15.
12 Ibid.
13 Ibid.
14 Leo Frobenius, *Voice of Africa* (London 1913), vol. 1, pp. 1–2. Original German edition: *Und Afrika sprach,* 3 vols. (Berlin, 1910–1912).
15 Frobenius, *Histoire,* p. 16.
16 Ibid. p. 18.
17 Senghor has said this repeatedly but sometimes with different wording. For instance, more recently in an interview with Armand Guibert: "La raison blanche est analytique par utilisation, la raison nègre, intuitive par participation."
18 Quoted by Stanilas Adotévi in his *Négritude et négrologues* (Paris, 1971), p. 52.
19 Yambo Ouologuem, *Bound to Violence,* trans. by Ralph Manheim (New York, 1971), p. 95. (Note the allusion in the name Shrobenius, for German *verschroben* means eccentric, odd, slightly crazy.)
20 Cf. Jahn, *Leo Frobenius,* p. 20.

Artificial Atavism: German Expressionism and Blacks

JOST HERMAND

1

When the exhibition entitled "Degenerate Art" was mounted in 1937 by the National Socialists in Munich, works by German Jews and Communists appeared next to black-influenced pieces as clear examples of the debased, primitive, subhuman—in short, 'degenerate,' which had allegedly given Expressionism its specifically 'anti-Aryan' touch.[1] Using what has been termed the conspiracy theory or string-puller ideology, the Nazis claimed that leading circles within world Jewry, the so-called Elders of Zion, had quite consciously used Expressionist art to present a wickedly tempting image of the inferior black race. This art, so the conspiracy theory continued, was to bring about a state of universal licentiousness, uninhibited instinctuality, and, finally, miscegenation, enabling the Elders of Zion to achieve their long-held goal of world control. The official *Exhibit Guidebook* actually opens with an Expressionistic, black-inspired, fetish on its title page and goes on to claim that Expressionism represents a "broad-scale attack on German art" and furthers the aim of killing "the final remnants of any racial awareness."[2] The "racial ideal of modern art," the booklet explained, was especially "Negroes and South Sea Islanders," apart from 'white' prostitutes, sex slayers, psychopaths, and other "cretins" (see plate 1). The entire Expressionist movement amounted only to "Nigger art," out to degrade and even deprave superior Aryan morality by conjuring up the atavistic and downright barbaric.[3] Thus Hitler could intone at the opening of the Munich exhibition: "These prehistoric cavemen and atavistic art stutterers are welcome to go back to their ancestral caverns and to scrawl their cosmopolitan graffiti there."[4] In Germany, he continued, the art of the future should be informed exclusively by the beautiful, the spiritual, and the emphatically Nordic. And all German newspapers agreed enthusiastically. *Der Ruhrarbeiter,* for example, wrote on July 20, 1937, that people were generally portrayed in Expressionist paintings as "half-apes."[5] A week later, the *Westdeutscher Beobachter* declared that viewing this exhibition revealed just how persistently the Jews had tried to make "the Negro into the racial ideal of a degenerate art in Germany," indeed even to degrade the "German mother" into a black "primal woman."[6]

Such vitriolic outbursts against the deliberate 'Niggerization' of German art had, of course, long been prepared ideologically, first by *volkish* cir-

Plate 1. A page reprinted from the guide book for the exhibition Degenerate Art (Munich, 1937).

cles and later by fascists. Especially after the French had occupied the Rhineland with Senegalese and Moroccan troops in 1919, and once the 'Americanization' of the Weimar Republic was in full swing by the mid-1920s (as manifested in the jazz of the "Chocolate Kiddies" and the dances of Josephine Baker), right-wingers branded any trends toward the non-German as 'Niggerization' or 'Jewification.'[7] This sort of response took on a specifically fascist quality for the first time in *Art and Race* (1928) by Paul Schultze-Naumburg. The same views reappeared, now as an authoritative expression of Nazi ideology, in Alfred Rosenberg's *The Myth of the Twentieth Century* (1930), a book dominated by the conspiracy theory or string-puller ideology already mentioned. Rosenberg condemns Expressionist artworks as "bastardized mongrels" of depraved "mestizoism." The *"foetor judaicus,"* he writes, "mingles [in this art] with the scum of the earth. Bastards have become the 'heroes' of the hour," while "nude dance shows and whore acts under Nigger direction" are the latest rage of the "new culture."[8] Berlin has been conquered not just by "Jews," but by "mulattos and Negroes, too."[9] When state power was yielded to the National Socialists on January 30, 1933, Rosenberg's views were embraced by ever widening circles of the German cultural establishment. In the first years of the Nazi era, the greatest attention was stirred up by Kurt Karl Eberlein's book entitled *What Is German in German Art?* (1934). Here, in the company of "village idiots, schizophrenics, whores, pimps, godless criminal Jews who try to pass themselves off as Jesus, consumptive welfare sluts who come on as the Mother of Christ," we again encounter the aforementioned "wooden idols and South Sea Islanders," completing the spectrum of the subhuman, from the "insane to the Negroid," that gave Expressionist art its "African stoop-worker" character.[10] And in the following years, many fascists other than Eberlein assailed the black, and thus racially threatening, elements of Expressionist art. Invariably, they involved Rosenberg's Jewish conspiracy theory, pointing to such prominent cultural thinkers as Carl Einstein, Max Jacob, Carl Sternheim, Herwarth Walden, Alfred Knoblauch, and André Salmon as the instigators of Expressionism.

The terrible thing about these Nazi condemnations is that, even with all their racist paranoia and colonialistic rhetoric, it is difficult to deny that they contain a grain of truth. Not unlike certain voices within the Marxist "Expressionism Debate" of the same era, the Nazis stressed Expressionist art's extremeness, distortion, irrationalism, and savagery. What the Nazis correctly recognized was the central role played by the so-called primitive, exotic, and Negroid in Expressionism, which they then went on to interpret, largely or entirely, in terms of their racist conspiracy theory. And they either ignored or skillfully repressed the fact that, within the sphere of Expressionism, the intentionally "primitive" had been regarded as a highly positive value, even as the highest value altogether. Upon closer examination, this artificial atavism clearly seems to have been a revived, somewhat radicalized, variant of older Rousseauian, Romantic, anticivilizational responses to the rising tide of "alienation" within our modern, bourgeois, utilitarian society. Without any sinister hidden agendas or conspiratorial schemes, the Expressionists sought to emphasize what they perceived as the simplicity, authenticity, and natural highs enjoyed by so-called savages. The real intention underlying this forced primitivism was therefore that of protest, rebellion, contradiction. As in so many revolts of artistic elites against the philistine masses, the bourgeois-antibourgeois outsiders of the Expressionist movement intentionally turned to the completely "different" and drew attention to themselves by means of the unusual, the loud, clashing, shocking—in a word, the extraordinary.[11]

It is evident that this Expressionistic primitivism, precisely when it made use of black elements, had from the outset a twofold function. It contained on the one hand a genuine longing for a truly livable society, for more spontaneity among people, for warmth and sensuality, for a sense of community. In its artistic expression, however, this longing made a radical leap into the savage, barbaric, atavistic, exotic, and black. Thus the Expressionists ended by transfiguring the primitive, instead of trying to face the given situation and master it with dialectical means, i.e., by taking into account the prevailing political, social, and economic conditions. In the Expressionist context, then, artists turned to the primitive because it seemed to embody authenticity in the purest possible form. Whether the Eskimos, the Laplanders, the Bushmen, Australian aborigines, Indios of the Amazon basin, or black Africans: any and everything still unspoiled by European civilization was regarded as appealing. Thus the pursuit of the primitive came to be regarded as the basic principle of living a full life, of the liberalistic, vitalistic, youthful, and erotic lifestyle—as is so often true of purely cultural, nonpolitical, pubertal protest movements.[12]

On the other hand, the intentional primitivism of Expressionist art points simultaneously to a specifically aesthetic concern of that era, the steadily growing desire for "simple forms." The black, savage, and exotic were primarily regarded as a means to simplification and reduction. Shortly after 1900, this desire for the simple came to be expressed not just in terms of content, but also formally, i.e., as a trend to the linear, simplified, or geometric (see plate 2). For even the art of these years could no longer remain untouched by the trend toward the technological and industrially produced that was becoming evident in other products of this era.[13] But let us ignore this purely aesthetic aspect for the time being. Instead, let us take up the more fundamental question as to the ways of seeing the exotic and the black that predominated in European and, especially, German art of the late 19th century, and then go on to define more precisely the specifically "Expressionistic" variant of this trend.

Plate 2. *Argument* by Max Pechstein, woodcut, 1917.

2

Until far into the 19th century, blacks played a role in German art that, while marginal, was significant and clearly defined. One might recall the Oriental King Balthasar and St. Mauritius within Christian iconography, the role of the black in the framework of Dürer's early humanistic interest in the individual and characteristic, the role of the sinister Moor in the so-called drama of intrigue (such as *The Magic Flute, The Conspiracy of Fiesco at Genoa, Duke Theodor von Gothland*), as well as the stock character of the "noble savage" in utopian novels and genrelike idylls of the 18th and early 19th centuries. A thoroughgoing shift in the relationship to the black did not get underway in German art until the late 19th century. Then blacks acquired an entirely different reality, both as the objects of investigations and as subjects, following German exploratory journeys in Africa and the founding of a colonial empire including German East Africa, German Southwest Africa, Togo, and Cameroon. In the cultural sector, a highly complex process ensued: whereas blacks had heretofore been found interesting primarily as figures or as allegories, now it was black African art which moved increasingly to the center of interest. The principal groundwork for this was carried out by the German ethnologist and explorer of Africa, Leo Frobenius. Previous positivistic study of African arts and crafts had been confined largely to mere collection building and had derived art from purely utilitarian forms (as defined by the Semper school). Frobenius, however, moved rapidly into the historical and aesthetic. This was evident as early as 1898, when his book *The Origin of African Cultures* laid the cornerstone for the cultural morphology he later developed fully.[14] In the years up to 1912, he sketched out the image of five black African cultural regions whose art—in contrast to the notion of a crude, uncultured Africa—stood up well in comparison with that of other early cultures.

Thanks to works like these, "exotic" art was suddenly accorded far more respect. Native arts and crafts had heretofore been exhibited alongside bizarre mineral formations or stuffed animals in ethnologic collections and museums of natural history, but now their religious and aesthetic character came under scrutiny. Apart from Frobenius, it was especially Ernst Grosse who achieved distinction in this area. His studies emphasized repeatedly that the artwork of Australian aborigines, Bushmen, Eskimos, North American Indians, and central African tribes could not simply be lumped together as "primitive"; rather, each had to be seen in its aesthetic uniqueness.[15] The *fin-de-siècle* mood of weariness with European civilization, the satiation with Western art, and the rejection of Wilhelminian values by cultural thinkers led in the following years to the demand finally to take exotic art, including that of black Africa, out of the ethnologic exhibit cases and to grant it the recognition it had always deserved.[16]

Of decisive importance for the heightened esteem rendered exotic art—be it Far Eastern, Australian, Arctic, or African—was, apart from Frobenius, the influence of Paul Gauguin, the first major artist who cherished "primitive" art, collected it, even sought to imitate it in his own art—and that out of not just anthropological, but also religious and aesthetic, interest. Aside from the art of the Malagasies, Incas, and Malayans, Gauguin valued especially highly the instinctlike imagination and nonverbal communication in the art of the Polynesians. Like many Europeans, he simply equated Polynesian religious forms with Buddhist and Hindu ones in a theosophical way.[17] Gauguin lived in the South Seas between 1891 and 1903, and sent to Paris the paintings he produced there. On them, he sought to depict religious visions full of depth, beauty, and symbolism. In contrast to the colonial devastation which had long since begun even on Tahiti, his paintings portray holy, quiet people still totally in harmony with themselves and with nature, appearing to live in a dream world devoid of any inner danger.

But by about 1905, this image of the "noble savage" was pushed aside by a new image that was considerably wilder and more barbaric. In the place of Gauguin's Romantic dream landscapes, the imagery in paintings now came to be inspired by the wildest works in the ethnological collections, which is to say by Africa.[18] The first impulses for this came from Paris, where writers such as Apollinaire, Max Jacob, and André Salmon spoke out on behalf of the exemplary character of *art nègre*. Among the artists at work around 1905, these motifs were taken up by the "Fauves" (the "Wild Animals") such as Matisse, Vlaminck, and Derain, and then, starting in 1907, by the early Cubists around Picasso and Braque.[19] As we can see in old photographs, these painters tended to surround themselves in their studios with black African masks and figurines.[20] At this time, Picasso began to be interested not just in Congolese masks but also, at the urging of Apollinaire and Max Jacob, in Canadian totem poles and pre-Roman Iberian art. In May or June of 1907, he visited the Palais Trocadéro in order to examine the African sculptures there.[21] The result of these studies was his celebrated picture, *Les Demoiselles d'Avignon* (1907–8),[22] a bordello picture with slightly black features which introduced his *période nègre*.[23] This picture is rightly regarded as a milestone in modern art, since it expresses in a particularly vivid fashion the stimulating ambivalence of simultaneous tendencies toward the savage and toward the simplified and technological. Viewed in terms of content, this picture both protests against the depravity of prostitution and transfigures woman as a natural being in the sense of black atavism and savagery. Viewed on a formal level, it continues and advances all the avant-garde techniques developed since Cézanne while simultaneously tending to an almost brutal reduction. This painting raises several questions: What is ecstatic here, and what is calculated? How much is uninhibited passion, how much formal-analytical intellectuality? To what extent is this an avowal of primitivism, to what extent modernistic cubism? Are we confronted here—as in a bordello—with unrestrained sexuality or with mere technique? Picasso himself answered all questions pertaining to the function of black elements in this painting with the cryptic response: "Discovering these statues matched what we were searching for at that time."[24] But what exactly was a painter like Picasso looking for around 1907: the cubistic and technological or authentic savagery, a new avant-garde form for pictures or a return to nature? In contrast to other cubists such as Delauney or La Fresnaye, Picasso did not attempt to give this contradiction a simple solution favoring the technical and avant-garde.[25] Instead, he simply let the contradiction stand; and this is what continues to make up this picture's provocative riddle.

3

Much the same contradiction is to be found in the work of nearly all German Expressionists, who by 1907–8 were endeavoring to depict motifs with a new vividness and to create modernistically reduced formal qualities. Like the French, the Germans espoused both a liberalistic freedom from constraint and a clear technical simplification of artistic means of expression. In Germany, as in France, there was a discernible trend away from the view of the exotic shaped by Gauguin's preoccupation with the "noble savage," especially his vision of the profound, sacred, spiritual, and ontological. This was increasingly superseded by a concept of savagery that emphasized the intoxicated, uninhibited, ecstatic, and sexual.[26] The inspiring image of the wild, atavistic, prehistoric, Polynesian, or African stood in opposition to all aspects of bourgeois normalcy and tended increasingly to the utopian. An earlier generation might have permitted itself to be whipped into line, but the Expressionists countered the bureaucratization and specialization so typical of modern "overcivilization," as Eckart von Sydow wrote, with the principle of "primitivism."[27]

But when this intentional primitivism appeared in German art, it was not at all "primitively" expressed—as we have already seen in the work of Picasso. Following the painterly refinement of Impressionism and the decorative exuberance of Art Nouveau, Expressionist primitivism merged with avant-garde form concepts that leaned toward the "abstract." Ultimately, Expressionist art—in contrast to the art of the blacks—served neither everyday use nor any mytho-religious purposes, but was instead purely aesthetic in character. Lacking both cultic and functional dimensions, Expressionism was confined to a highly subjective, confessional, character. The violent reduction of its means of expression, however, forces it into abstraction and even emptiness. While the chief works of Expressionism do express a life intensity raised to the highest point, on the level of content they are ideologically largely uncategorizable and thus interchangeable.

As one might expect, black elements were used in the three arts in rather diverse ways beginning in 1910. African influence remained marginal in the realm of Expressionist music, for although it did incline toward certain forms of neo-primitivism,[28] Expressionist music tended largely to the elitist and exclusive, particularly in the "Viennese School" around Schönberg. The only black musical form that did crop up in European concert music of this era was the ragtime, used by Satie in *Parade* (1917) and by Stravinsky in *Histoire du soldat* (1918). The linkage of African music and ragtime is only indirect, for the latter derives from jazz, an American form of music that employs almost exclusively what might be termed "white" melodies while its black elements are discernible only in rhythms and certain modes of presentation.

In Expressionist literature, on the other hand, the black element is far more in evidence (although here, too—in comparison with Expressionist painting and sculpture—it still seems rather secondary). The black presence in literature is found, not in the formal aspect but as an element of content, be it as a motif, a figure, or a background. The lack of black influence on the formal level is due to the fact that in the Germany of that era virtually none of the poetry of the black Africans was known or familiar—apart from a few translations by Carl Einstein that appeared in *Die Aktion* in 1916–17.[29] But Expressionist writers apparently felt no need for any such models, since they themselves had sufficient fantasy to fill in this blank with vivid images of a wildly agitated, primitive black life. Some indeed proceeded in the most clichéd manner imaginable, emphasizing solely the sensual, instinctual, animal side of blackness. In the German literature of the 18th and 19th centuries, Blacks had appeared primarily as idyllic, natural humans (in the works of Herder and Claudius) or as pitiable slaves (in Heine's work)—apart from a few conventional intriguers (in the works of Schiller and Grabbe).[30] In Expressionist literature, on the other hand, blacks almost always appear as oversexed, in heat, constantly in motion, emitting yowls of lust, or at least casting steamy glances about. The Expressionistic black is almost invariably the savage, the madman, the animal given over entirely to his or her sex drive.

This is quite evident in Expressionist poetry, if we briefly ignore Iwan Goll's *Panama Canal* (1919), in which blacks figure as "holy proletarians."[31] In Albert Ehrenstein's poetry, we read about a black likened to the "lion from the rushing river";[32] in the poetry of Theodor Däubler, about the "Moor" who sees slavery as an "obstacle to lust";[33] in the poetry of Gottfried Benn, about a dead "Nigger," two of whose toes "of his dirty left foot" are stuck in the ear of a white woman's corpse;[34] in the poetry of Hugo Ball, about a "steer-headed Negro" with a bulging neck, flaring nostrils, and a broad stride";[35] in the poetry of Richard Huelsenbeck, about a black whose huge "thighs" are his most striking feature.[36] All in all, Africa is the continent where naked instinct reigns, blood sets the tone, and "no one ever thinks," in the words of Gottfried Benn.[37]

In the area of Expressionist drama, the primary symbol of the "primitive," at least initially, is the South Sea Islands. Thus at the end of Carl Sternheim's *Tabula rasa* (1916), the protagonist, Wilhelm Ständer, wants to depart for the "South Seas" in order finally to encounter "true humanity." The *South Sea Play* (1917) by Alfred Brust is indebted to Gauguin's vision and takes place among the "savages" of Palau, whose lives seem to be totally bound up in the cycle of procreation, birth, and death.[38] In Reinhard Goering's *Naval Battle* (1917), the sailors stuck in their turret can be raised to a frenzy by the single word "Samoa." They babble that the women on Samoa were like "the fruit of date palms"; that there was true happiness; that there was "living."[39] Things are quite as wild in *Medea* (1926) by Hans Henny Jahnn, whose title figure is not the famous woman from Colchis but instead a black, a woman of "savage ghastliness" regarded by all the Greek men as an "animal" because of her boundless lust.[40] In his play *Matumbo* (1925), Rolf Lauckner goes even further, describing a protagonist who strikes most Europeans as a "jungle muscle-machine," has supple limbs of "rubber," and slinks along like a "panther."[41] Indeed, a few ladies of white "higher" society are so awed by his overwhelming sex appeal that they wish only to be "taken" by him.

The black is coupled with the erotic and orgiastic just as frequently in Expressionist prose. Here, too, the scenery teems with love-hungry bodies, with incests and rapes, as soon as the topic of primitiveness is broached. Alfred Knoblauch wrote in 1919 that by emphasizing the "frenzy of sexual intercourse," many Expressionist novellas seem like an "archeological museum of curious sex customs" or an "eroticon and folklore of all sexual cults."[42] Nonetheless, a number of variants can be distinguished. The tale "Island Girl" (1919) by Robert Müller, for example, is characterized by a nostalgic quality since it is set in a Polynesia where the magical unity of nature, instinct, and life has been fractured by white colonial masters. In the realm of sensual daydreams, on the other hand, the black and exotic are primarily used as a means of enhancing sexual stimulation. Thus in the context of Mediterranean fantasies, Gottfried Benn in his sketch "The Birthday" (1916) repeatedly turns to what he terms the "licentious lip of Africa."[43] But the prize in this category is clearly taken by the tale "Ulrike" (1918) by Carl Sternheim, in which a refined young Prussian noblewoman from the arch-conservative Uckermark falls in love with the Jewish painter Posinsky, who is clearly based on the figure of Carl Einstein.[44] Out of love for this man, who constantly talks about his African journeys and who owns "Sudanese figurines of wood and ivory," she finally consents to become his model, allowing herself to be tatooed, dyeing her hair black, accenting her nipples with gleaming cinnabar red, and, finally, even building a round hut out of lion skins in her living room. All this she does in order to give herself to her Posinsky, her "meaty chieftain," her "hairy animal," like a "polished maiden" or a "frenzied ape." And then—and this is stated quite insinuatingly—there "was Kilimanjaro, no time, and hot wind."[45] Despite some parodistic elements, this "transformation" is presented as the fulfillment of deepest, heretofore suppressed, desires. "Ulrike peeled away evolution, it dripped off, freeing her," we read toward the end of this tale, "she was scraping down to her authentic core, long since buried under descent and lineage, until she was gleaming and became her most concentrated self. She had turned back through millennia, and could not wish a more glorious, if belated, paradise."[46]

4

Intentional primitivism shapes Expressionist painting in a far more complex way, since here it is not just a theme, a motif, or a key ideological concept, but simultaneously a question of style and form. But let us remain for the moment at the level of the thematic, which is to say at the point of congruence between figurative art and literature. As mentioned before, individual blacks had already appeared in German painting, first in the context of medieval Christian iconology and then in the universalizing portraiture of the 16th century—in both eras, it might be added, in a highly dignified manner.[47] Later on, blacks appeared in German painting as "noble savages" or as allegorical representatives of the African continent. These motifs, this narrow spectrum of imagery, did not really gain in breadth until the late 19th century. Then blacks suddenly made a variety of stylized appearances: as tokens of luxury in the salon style of Hans Makart's *Nubian Women* (1876), as instinctual and violent boxer types such as Lovis Corinth's *Othello* (1884), as exotic, impressionistically glittering color complexes such as the *River Pirates* (1914) by Max Slevogt,[48] even as Lesbian contrast figures to the white upper-class women in, for example, the drawings of Franz von Bayros[49] or similar illustrators.[50]

By contrast, the Expressionists generally portray blacks—with an anarchistic-Rousseauian slant—as authentic barbarians, as "genuine" savages. In order to work on these exotic motifs as authentically as possible, some artists such as Ernst Ludwig Kirchner had by 1910 brought "real" black models into their studios,[51] while others—Max Pechstein and Emil Nolde, for example—undertook long journeys to Africa and the South Seas.[52] We are especially well-informed about Nolde's trip in the years 1913–14. After visits to the Berlin Ethnological Museum, he had by 1912 begun planning a book tentatively entitled *Artistic Expressions of Primitive Peoples*. He went abroad, hoping to encounter among the Papuas of New Guinea (parts of which were then a German colony) the "barbaric" and "savage" qualities so sadly missing in Europe.[53] In the pictures and water-colors painted among the Papuas, Nolde sought to portray, not the mythical nor sacredly beautiful that Gauguin had seen, but rather the primitivism, the atavism, the "primeval nature" of these "primeval human beings," something which he feared would be lost "in twenty years" to colonial rapine at the hands of the Europeans.[54] At approximately the same time, Pechstein was staying north of New Guinea on the Palau Islands (likewise a German colony at that time) where he made hundreds of sketches. Between 1915 and 1917, he worked from these sketches to create prehistorically tinged paintings of Polynesian life. Another one who achieved recognition as a painter of blacks in the German colonies of Africa was Irma Stern who, however, quickly sank into purely decorative work and who later settled in South Africa, where today there is still a museum with her art (see plate 3).

Upon closer inspection, much in these pictures does not really strike us as Polynesian or black African. Instead, these images simply reflect the yearnings of white Europeans for the "uncorrupted." Regardless of whether we turn to the South Sea Islanders and blacks in the artistic work of Nolde, Pechstein, and Stern; to the gypsies painted by Otto Mueller; to Alexej Jawlensky's Slavic people with their dangerously glowering cat eyes; or to the "savage" nudes painted by Karl Schmidt-Rottluff and Erich Heckel: in the final analysis, all of these pictures are concerned primarily with the "other," with the strange, powerful, instinctual, elementary, fleshly, i.e., with everything the Expressionists felt to be lacking in themselves or which they wished to possess in heightened measure. Many of their painted figures are therefore mere bogeymen or bogeywomen held up—like the sick, the insane, prostitutes, circus clowns, and similar outsiders—against prevailing bourgeois behavioral norms as idols of an antibourgeois, more intense, and, therefore, richer life. In people like these, the Expressionists could discern like-minded "comrades," among whom Ludwig Rubiner in 1912 included especially "the prostitutes, poets, pimps, bag ladies, petty thieves, good-for-nothings, pairs of lovers in mid-embrace, religious maniacs, winos, chain-smokers, the unemployed, overeaters, hoboes, crooks" and similar "riff-raff."[55]

Expressionist painters were not interested in blacks and other exotic, "primitive" peoples solely as picture content, as themes or motifs. It was not just nakedness and authenticity which fascinated the Expressionists, but also—and just as strongly, perhaps even more so—black and native arts, their masks, statues, totem poles, fetishes, shields, and so on. We have already touched upon the gradual process by which European knowledge and appreciation of these objects as "artworks" grew in the years leading up to the turn of the century.[56] Still, the influence of Ernst Grosse or Leo Frobenius should not be overestimated. Many of their ideas long remained hidden in specialized scholarly journals. It was not until about 1910 that a somewhat broader public became interested in Polynesian and black art, and then

Plate 3. *Three Black Women* by Irma Stern, oil on canvas, 1923. Photo: Courtesy of Bildarchiv Foto Marburg.

chiefly under French influence, via Gauguin and Picasso. In Germany, artists and cultural thinkers of this era finally began to appreciate "primitivism" in the arts of native peoples when the discussion about Expressionistic
form got underway. This was the context for an interpretation of black African sculpture, based on the criteria of "artistic volition" developed by Alois
Riegl, such as was attempted by Paul Germann in a landmark article of 1911
entitled "Sculptural and Figurative Handicrafts in the Cameroon Grass-
lands."[57] In the same year, preparations began for an exhibition of black African sculpture in the Folkwang Museum in Hagen. But the real
breakthrough came in the year 1912, with the publication of the *Blue Rider*
by Franz Marc and Wassily Kandinsky. Throughout this volume, works by
Picasso, Cézanne, Delauney, German Expressionists, and Russian modern-
ists appear directly facing such "primitive" art forms as old votive images,
Bavarian glass paintings, children's drawings, pictures by Henri Rousseau,
as well as works of Eskimo art, Malayan wooden figurines, Polynesian re-
liefs by Gauguin, Japanese masks, Benin sculptures, and black African
masks and statues at large. The book clearly points to the inner affinity between older and newer forms of "primitivism" in art. Marc wrote in the
preface that this was intended to deliver a decisive "no" to the "great centuries," those of classical antiquity, of the Gothic era, of the Renaissance and
Baroque.[58] What "we" value, he continued, is solely the "living," i.e., that
which remains "untouched by the grip of convention" (and in saying, "we,"
he meant especially "the *fauves,* or 'wild animals,' of Germany").[59] The
same point is made by August Macke's contribution entitled "Masks,"
which likewise takes a strong stand against cultural philistines who would
assign "art forms of primitive peoples to the realm of ethnology or handicrafts."[60] And Macke revealed that Germany's modern "savages" would
draw their deepest inspiration precisely from the most foreign and atavistic.

All these ideas were first truly popularized, at least in art circles, by the
book *Negro Sculpture,* which Carl Einstein brought out in 1915. For a number of years, Einstein had been closely following developments both within
ethnology and within French cubism—and, in 1912, he had published Germany's first "cubistic" novel, *Bebuquin.*[61] His new book sees black African
sculpture primarily in terms of formal analysis, despite that art's "religious"
function, which is clearly acknowledged. Einstein interprets it as capable of
creating the impression of a consistent "cubic spatial perception," thanks to
its archaic understanding of the nature of plasticity—an understanding
which Europe had largely lost in the course of the 19th century.[62] And thus
black African sculpture succeeds in an "intensity of expressiveness" sur-
passing that of most modern artists.[63] The impact of Einstein's theses on
contemporary thinking is evident in the numerous, enthusiastically responsive reviews this booklet received. Ernst Bloch emphasized especially the
principle of "plasticity" so clearly pointed out by Einstein.[64] Wilhelm

Hausenstein praised Einstein's analysis of the "absolute" in black African sculpture, the "shaped thing" that exists beyond any "psychologizing" intention.[65] And Hanns Johst also praised Einstein for accentuating the "cubic," near "mathematical," in his interpretation of black sculpture.[66]

Thus Einstein and his reviewers set the tone for any future discussion of primitivism, which became a "central component of the new aesthetics."[67] In programmatic writings of the Expressionists, the modern and the primitive were moved closer and closer together until, finally, they were simply equated with each other. In his book of 1916 entitled *Expressionism,* Hermann Bahr wrote that in art we ought to revert to the "condition of primeval people," i.e., paint like "the savages," in order to escape cooptation and bourgeois society's fatal embrace.[68] In the book *Struggling for New Art* (1919), Theodor Däubler advanced similar views, using the increasingly "abstract" speculations of Alois Riegl and Wilhelm Worringer to equate the primitive, atavistic, and African with the modern, cubist, and Expressionistic. Däubler also wrote that the path of "Negro art" led both to "primitivism" and to the "absolute."[69] Christoph Spengemann waxed even more enthusiastic about the exhibition "Negro Art" mounted by the Kestner Society in 1919. The Europeans had forgotten, he wrote in *Zweemann,* that "being primitive" was a value; that the "infinite" could be seen in the primitive; that the "abstract" as the highest form of art always grows from the primitive; that it is therefore necessary to start "from the very beginning" again, quite "primitively," to create new great art.[70] That *participation mystique* conjured up by Lévy-Bruhl in his accounts of an "original-mystical world" could be regained only by yielding to the "primitive" in black art and by accepting Wilhelm Worringer's concepts of abstraction.[71] Wilhelm Niemeyer made much the same point in 1921, in his essay "On the Essence of African Sculpture." He, too, advocated overcoming egocentrism and psychologism in modern art, in favor of numinousness, cubism, plasticity, mathematicism, and structuralism all schooled on black art; doing so would enable Expressionism to get beyond the merely personal and to achieve a greatness heretofore found only in primitive art.[72] A year later, in his book *Barbarians and Classicists,* Wilhelm Hausenstein emphasized again that modern "artificiality" could be overcome only by yielding completely to instinct, as did exotic and primitive peoples, indeed by developing a "lustiness toward art." The only thing permitted between the "creator and his object" was "sexual ardor."[73] Herbert Kühn was equally timely in his book, *The Art of the Primitives* (1923), combining the primitive and the abstract, the oldest and the newest in the same fantasy image.[74] Even as late as 1926, Herwarth Walden could still write, in his essay "On the Art of Negroes and the South Sea Islanders," that the only great models for today's art are "the savages and children." "The great art of the primeval peoples," he concluded, "is enough to make one wild. One should, one must go wild."[75]

Plate 4. *Self-Portrait with Fetish and Nude Figure* by Max Pechstein, woodcut, 1922.

Such speculations did not remain at the level of mere theory, as is abundantly evident in Expressionist painting and graphics. Not only did blacks appear as figures, or subject matter, but their art was also depicted, imitated, or integrated in the most varied ways in order to achieve the desired impression of simplification, cubification, and, at the same time, of wildness, even barbarism. This is evident at several levels. We might mention first those pictures in which individual African works of art are inserted into an Expressionist framework: still lifes by Nolde or Schmidt-Rottluff, for example, where black sculptures appear next to flowers and jugs, giving the entire work a consciously exotic character. Pechstein even portrayed himself, in a woodcut of 1922, next to just such an African fetish and a black figure he had designed himself; and it is difficult to imagine a more explicit aesthetic statement (see plate 4). Nolde enjoyed bringing exotic masks into his paintings just as much, and he did so in the most demonic and horrifying manner possible, in order to underline the intentionally atavistic. Probably the best known picture of this type is his *Missionary* (1912), in which Nolde—after precise studies in the Berlin Ethnological Museum—gave the title figure the mask of a Korean god, while the woman and her child were derived from a Nigerian wood carving.[76] Indeed, a few Expressionists even attempted to create wooden sculptures in the style of black African statues,[77] beginning with Ernst Ludwig Kirchner's *Blacksmith* (1912) and leading to Rudolf Belling's *Head in Mahogany* (1922), both of which are constantly cited as prime examples of Expressionist sculpture.

But beyond this sort of direct integration or imitation of African artworks, the trend toward primitivism derived from black sculpture also left unmistakable traces in other sectors of Expressionist design. Even when the Expressionists portrayed Europeans, they employed a simplifying, intensified form that evokes the fetishistic in its angular, cubic manner. Some well-known examples are the portraits by such Brücke painters as Heckel, Kirchner, and Schmidt-Rotluff, which vividly recall black African wood carvings with their angular noses, wide lips, and pointed chins. The African influence is even more clearly evident in the woodcuts than in the paintings of this group, since woodcutting is the medium most suited to this urge to simplify. Pointy, bulky, crass, loud, shrill qualities constantly predominate here in order to achieve the greatest possible expressiveness with the greatest simplification (see plate 5). Some of these works almost seem to verge on the botched, since the models that were being followed included not just black African and other exotic artworks but also such books as Siegfried Levinstein's *Children's Drawings to Age Fourteen* (1904) and Hans Prinzhorn's *Pictures by the Mentally Ill* (1922). Indeed, even publications about graffiti and other forms of figuration by the "unschooled" were brought into play, for their primitiveness was regarded as more expressive than the forms of art which had been "schooled" since antiquity.

5

The aesthetic sum of all these trends and urges was—as already noted apropos of Picasso's cubism—constantly marked by the same contradictoriness. The only unifying force apparent in Expressionism lies in the "primitivism" pursued by virtually all artists. But whenever the Expressionists attempted to define this primitiveness or atavism more precisely, then even the appearance of unity once again eluded them. Two chief directions can be

Plate 5. *Seated Woman* by Karl Schmidt-Rottluff, woodcut, 1913.

discerned here. On the one hand, this intentional primitivism meant a lifestyle in accord with all those exotic peoples whose lives still exemplified a
mythic closeness to nature, an unsplintered bond with larger forces, sexual
frankness, even wildness. On the other hand, the arts and crafts of these exotic peoples were admired for their cubic simplification, which provided superb models for all the avant-garde trends toward abstraction,
constructivism, the matter-of-fact, depersonalized, etc. Taken together,

these features actually constituted the broader contradiction of German Expressionism, which in another context I attempted to define as the contradiction, in particularly crass form, between "overt goals" (nature, eroticism, egocentrism) and "covert goals" (object, essence, construction).[78]

Upon reflection, all this turns out to have relatively little to do with blacks and their art. In the years between 1910 and 1925, the invocation of "Africa" was usually a pretense for thoroughly "white" fantasies and aesthetic desires. As invoked in the publications of that era, the "black" feeling for life is largely a substrate for fairly infantile, adolescent, or, at best, liberalistic daydreams of increased acting out on the part of some artists and intellectuals. Older Rousseauian or Romantic forms of neoprimitivism were simply updated and radicalized in a specifically Expressionist manner. The much-touted reestimate of so-called savages, understood to mean heightened esteem for the biological and instinctual, for the atavistic and barbaric, seems constantly to devolve into a tangible devaluation of the humane. At least, very little remains of the humanity or dignity of the blacks whom the Expressionists portrayed—in close association with animals, the insane, or prostitutes—as hormone-powered hulks. This may, in contrast with the earlier denigration of blacks as brainless, soulless creatures, have been intended as an upward evaluation of blacks into the realm of the "vital"—but in many instances the old and the new seem to amount to the same thing.

Something similar was true of the rapid upward evaluation African art underwent during these years, a revaluation that had very little in common with the essence of that art. Its mythical, ritual, cultic character, i.e., everything about it which soars toward the presence of the divine or a transformation into the superhuman—qualities which can scarcely be confined within aesthetic criteria—all this is dealt with inadequately in most of the writings of that era. Like French cubism, Italian futurism, Russian constructivism, and the Dutch Stijl movement, German Expressionism aims not at the ritual, mythical, magical, but instead at the constructed, aesthetically shaped, and matter-of-fact. Religious tendencies are foreign to Expressionism. Its works are not allegories frozen into images which are invested with some kind of transubstantial reality; indeed they have no representative character at all. On the contrary, even Expressionistic pictures of gods and saints are just compounds of color and form, consciously constructed artifacts—only artworks, not cult images. Value is attributed here not to the figure portrayed but to the artistry involved in portraying it. These artworks are therefore products objectified into abstractness, material images or pictorial architecture, whose content is less the organic, natural, humane than a display of the artist's virtuosity.

"Blackness" is, therefore, only a token for highly individual goals within both camps staked out by intentional primitivism, the erotic and the constructivistic. Once again, as in so many spheres, Africa is simply plundered by whites or at least made to serve their ends. On the subjective level, increased interest in blacks was no doubt accompanied by the best of intentions. The objective impact on Expressionist art, however, was another matter entirely. But this contradictoriness is part of the overall nature of Expressionism, for—as already argued—the lack of ideological clarity within this movement usually resulted in a contradiction between forced abstraction and equally forced naturalness. Indeed, Expressionism supported both tendencies equally strongly. The contradiction between instinct and intellect, jungle and metropolis, God and machine resulted in artistically expressed "alienation." But instead of seeking to use dialectical means to place these extremes in a sensible relationship, Expressionism constantly sought to paper over these contradictions with the concept of intentional primitivism, on the emotional-sexual level as well as on the intellectual-technological one. And this contradiction, still unresolved today, is what gives Expressionist art its lasting edge.

It will come as no surprise, then, that Expressionism has always evoked highly charged reactions, whether of acceptance or rejection, on the left and on the right, from Romantics and the avant-garde. In the final analysis, this art, despite its many noble intentions, has highly problematical aspects as well. To return to what I stated at the outset: we have to concede that the Nazi charges about the depravation of human beings in Expressionist art are only partially erroneous. What is completely fallacious, on the other hand, is the Nazi ideology of the hidden string-pullers, making Jewish conspirators responsible for this human depravation because of their supposed interest in racial "mixing." But perhaps the Nazis reacted so vehemently to this art precisely because fascist ideology itself remained largely locked in the same contradiction between myth and technology, religious fanaticism and ice-cold calculation, the Bronze Age and the Atomic Age. And thus they invented a scapegoat. Today, there are no longer any such scapegoats; yet we are still torn between the natural and the technological. The challenge to us is to try to grapple with this contradiction in a nonfascistic, more concrete, and even dialectical manner.[79]

Translated from the German by James Steakley

---

1 On the Nazi position, cf. Jost Hermand, "Bewährte Tümlichkeiten: Der völkisch-nazistische Traum einer ewig-deutschen Kunst," in *Die deutsche Literatur im Dritten Reich,* ed. Horst Denkler and Karl Prümm (Stuttgart, 1976), pp. 103ff.

2 *Führer durch die Ausstellung Entartete Kunst* (Berlin, 1937), pp. 4, 16.

3 Ibid., p. 16.

4 Quoted in *Die bildenden Künste im Dritten Reich,* ed. by Joseph Wulf (Gütersloh, 1963), p. 332.

5 Ibid., p. 327.
6 Ibid., p. 319.
7 See my "Ultima Thule: Völkische und faschistische Zukunftsvisionen," in my *Orte. Irgendwo: Formen utopischen Denkens* (Königstein, 1981), pp. 68ff.
8 Alfred Rosenberg, *Der Mythos des 20. Jahrhunderts,* 3rd ed. (München, 1932), pp. 304, 444.
9 Id., *Der Sumpf* (München, 1930), p. 25. Cf. also Reinhard Wegner, *Der Exotismus-Streit in Deutschland: Zur Auseinandersetzung mit 'primitiven' Formen in der bildenden Kunst* (Frankfurt, 1983), pp. 119ff.
10 Kurt Karl Eberlein, *Was ist deutsch in der deutschen Kunst?* (Leipzig, 1934), p. 33.
11 See my "Das Konzept 'Avantgarde'," in *Faschismus und Avantgarde,* ed. Reinhold Grimm and Jost Hermand (Königstein, 1980), pp. 4ff.
12 Compare Richard Hamann and Jost Hermand, *Expressionismus* (Berlin, 1975), pp. 148ff.
13 See Wegner, *Der Exotismus-Streit,* pp. 22ff.
14 See Jürgen Christoph Winter, "Leo Frobenius' Image of Africa: An Ethnologist's Work and Ethnology's View of It," *Komparatistische Hefte* 2 (1980): 72–91.
15 Ernst Grosse, "Ethnologie und Ästhetik," *Vierteljahresschrift für wissenschaftliche Philosophie* 15 (1891): 392–417.
16 See Wilhelm Hausenstein, "Von ethnologischen Sammlungen," *Die weißen Blätter,* (1913–14), pp. 252–55.
17 See Werner Schmalenbach, "Gauguin's Begegnung mit der Welt der Naturvölker," in *Weltkulturen und moderne Kunst,* exhibition in the Haus der Kunst (München, 1972), pp. 445ff. and Jehanne Teilheit-Fisk, *Paradise Reviewed: An Interpretation of Gauguin's Polynesian Symbolism* (Ann Arbor, 1983), pp. 167ff.
18 Compare Jean Laude, *La Peinture française (1905–1914) et "l'Art nègre"* (Paris, 1968), vol. 1, pp. 123ff.
19 Cf. Laude, vol. 1, pp. 240ff.
20 Ibid., vol. 2, ills. 17, 19, 69.
21 See Josep Palau i Fabre, *Picasso: Kindheit und Jugend eines Genies 1881–1907* (München, 1981), pp. 491, 496.
22 Ibid., pp. 486ff.
23 Laude, vol. 2, pp. 269ff.
24 Quoted by Palau i Fabre, p. 496.
25 See John Berger, *Glanz und Elend des Malers Pablo Picasso* (Reinbek, 1973), pp. 79ff.
26 See the chapter "Natur, Erotik, leuchtendes Ich" in Hamann and Hermand, *Expressionismus,* pp. 111–47.
27 Eckart von Sydow, "Das Weltbewußtsein und die Kunst des primitiven Menschen," *Neue Blätter für Kunst und Dichtung* 2 (1919–20): 70.
28 See my "Expressionism and Music," in *Expressionism Reconsidered,* ed. Gertrud Bauer Pickar and Karl Eugene Webb (München, 1979), pp. 58–73.
29 Carl Einstein, *Werke,* vol. 1 (Berlin, 1980), pp. 397–415, 421–73.
30 See Willfried F. Feuser, "Vom Sklaven zum Proletarier: Erscheinungsformen des Negerbildes in der neueren deutschen Literatur," *Internationales Afrikaforum* 12 (1976): 248ff.
31 *Menschheitsdämmerung,* ed. Kurt Pinthus (Hamburg, 1959), pp. 296ff.
32 Albert Ehrenstein, *Gedichte* (Leipzig, 1920), p. 27.
33 *Lyrik des expressionistischen Jahrzehnts,* ed. Gottfried Benn (Wiesbaden, 1955), p. 50.
34 Gottfried Benn, *Gesammelte Werke,* ed. Dieter Wellershof (Wiesbaden, 1958ff.), vol. 3, p. 9.
35 Quoted by Feuser, p. 259.
36 Richard Huelsenbeck, *Phantastische Gebete* (Zürich, 1960), p. 33.
37 Benn, *Gesammelte Werke,* vol. 3, p. 95.
38 Alfred Brust, "Südseespiel," *Kunstblatt* 1 (1917): 166–221.
39 Reinhard Goering, "Seeschlacht," in his *Prosa Dramen Verse* (München, 1961), pp. 277f.
40 Hans Henny Jahnn, *Medea* (Dresden, 1926), pp. 27, 52.
41 Rolf Lauckner, *Matumbo* (Berlin, 1925), pp. 15, 72.
42 Alfred Knoblauch, *Dada* (Leipzig, 1919), p. 29.
43 Benn, *Gesammelte Werke,* vol. 1, p. 51.
44 Carl Sternheim, *Das Gesamtwerk,* vol. 4 (Neuwied, 1964), p. 433.
45 Ibid., vol. 4, p. 158.

46 Ibid.
47 See the illustrations provided by Alain Locke, *The Negro in Art* (New York, 1968), pp. 141ff.
48 On exoticism as a means of heightened "colorfulness," see Richard Hamann and Jost Hermand, *Impressionismus* (Berlin, 1960), pp. 292ff.
49 See Patrick Waldberg, *Eros in la belle époque* (New York, 1969), p. 158.
50 Compare Hans-Joachim Kunst, *The African in European Art* (Bad Godesberg, 1967), pp. 25ff.
51 See *Tendenzen* 140 (1982): 72.
52 On escaping Europe during these years, compare Helmut Kreuzer, *Die Boheme* (Stuttgart, 1968), pp. 225ff.
53 *Emil Nolde: Reise in die Südsee 1913-1914* (Berlin, 1984), p. 3.
54 Ibid., p. 66.—Nolde had a loaded pistol with him at all times when painting or drawing especially attractive, brightly painted, "savage" natives. When his wife Ada accompanied him, she was likewise usually armed. Papuas that had already been missionized appealed to him less because of their deficient "savagery" (cf. p. 7).
55 Ludwig Rubiner, "Der Dichter greift in die Politik," *Die Aktion* 2 (1912): col.s 645ff.
56 Compare Ferdinand Hermann, *Die afrikanische Negerplastik als Forschungsgegenstand* (Berlin, 1958), pp. 4ff.
57 Reinhard Wegner, p. 43.
58 *Der Blaue Reiter,* 2nd ed. (München, 1914), n.p.
59 Ibid., p. 5f.
60 Ibid., p. 24.
61 Cf. Heidemarie Oehm, *Die Kunsttheorie Carl Einsteins* (München, 1976), pp. 70ff.
62 Carl Einstein, *Gesammelte Werke,* ed. Ernst Nef (Wiesbaden, 1962), pp. 92ff.
63 Ibid., p. 103.
64 *Die Argonauten* 2 (1915): 10ff.
65 *März* 9 (1915): 103f.
66 *Die Aktion* 5 (1915), col.s. 507f.
67 Reinhard Wegner, p. 59.
68 Hermann Bahr, *Expressionismus* (München, 1916), p. 127.
69 Theodor Däubler, *Im Kampf um die moderne Kunst* (Berlin, 1919), p. 43.
70 *Der Zweemann* 1 (1919-20): no. 8, pp. 41f.
71 Sydow, "Das Weltbewußtsein und die Kunst des primitiven Menschen," pp. 71f.; see also his essay, "Grundzüge der Negerplastik," *Gäste* 1 (1921): 82-85.
72 Wilhelm Niemeyer, "Vom Wesen afrikanischer Plastik," *Kündung* 1 (1921): 69-88.
73 Wilhelm Hausenstein, *Barbaren und Klassiker: Ein Buch über die Bildnerei exotischer Völker* (München, 1922), pp. 9f.
74 Herbert Kühn, *Die Kunst der Primitiven* (München, 1923), p. 88.
75 Herwarth Walden, "Zur Kunst der Neger und Südseeinsulaner," *Der Sturm* (1926): no. 2, p. 30.
76 See Kunst, *The African in European Art,* p. 28.
77 See *German Expressionist Sculpture,* ed. Stephanie Barrow (Chicago, 1983); Manfred Schneckenburger, "Bemerkungen zur 'Brücke' und zur 'primitiven' Kunst," in *Weltkulturen und moderne Kunst,* pp. 456ff. and *Primitivism in 20th-Century Art,* ed. William Rubin (New York, 1984), pp. 368-403.
78 See Hamann and Hermand, *Expressionismus,* pp. 96ff.
79 I would like to thank Thomas Wolber, who helped gather source material for this essay.

Them in Our Literature and We in Theirs: Geo-Thematics Reconsidered and Reversed[1]

GEORG M. GUGELBERGER

1

Frida Kahlo, Mexican artist born of a German father and a Mexican mother, and wife of muralist Diego Rivera, during one of her trips to the United States observed that *gringo* faces reminded her of "unbaked rolls."[2] Towards the end of one of the "masterpieces" of the first half of the century, a retracting and bitter Ezra Pound described in typical modernist and bilingual fashion the country from which he had been exiled:

> In meiner Heimat
> where the dead walked
> and the living were made of cardboard.
> (end of Canto 115, 1962)

The latter image might be called an "auto-image" while the first might be called a "hetero-image."[3] Both give us, when taken seriously, pertinent information about a place in time, a people, an ethnic group, and a social class in a way only literature can. At its best, this kind of approach can do what Engels admired in Balzac when he said that he had learned more from this writer than "from all the professed historians, economists, and statisticians of the period together."[4] At its worst, it can lead to descriptions of ironic word games such as Walter Abish's *Alphabetical Africa,* a novel on Africa by a German-American which tells us less than nothing about Africa, its people, or those who oppressed African peoples for so long.

Frequently, readers tend to pass over quickly the criticisms expressed in literary works about other people and places in order to "enjoy" (a most irritating word in literary education) harmless (albeit very harmful) descriptions of depopulated—and if not depopulated, certainly dehumanized—areas of what we now call Third World countries. Such descriptions usually culminate in passages full of "flamboyant red Acacia flowers in the gardens of Mombassa,"[5] giraffes,[6] and elephants, or in an "intriguing" phonetic shift ("she warm like de groun', / she deep like de bush")[7] which can only be understood as downgrading Africans and, in particular, African women as sex objects, even when the speaker is African (albeit in a white man's novel on

Africa such as Joyce Carry's *Mister Johnson*). In the white man's novel on
Africa, blacks take on funny names (Mister Johnson) or remain anonymous
as in Conrad's famous/infamous *Heart of Darkness* of the turn of the century, which an avid André Gide read while being carried through parts of
the Congo. The harm Conrad has done to Africa by pushing it from geography to metaphysics is beyond repair, but for his sake we might at least quote
a few words from this long "short story" which unconsciously reverse what
Martin Steins has called a "Meinungsstereotypie."[8] At one point, there is a
line we normally find whites saying about blacks, but reversed: "white men
being so much alike from a distance."[9] Such unintentional insights, however,
are rare in what has been called "the foreign novel" or "the novel of Africa."[10]

More symptomatic are the depopulated landscapes, an unbearable exoticism, repression of reality even in novels which make claims to being realistic. Typical of this "exploitation" and a sure literary equivalent of what
Walter Rodney has termed *How Europe Underdeveloped Africa*[11] is Karen
Blixen's (alias Isak Dinesen's) account of fellow travelers (obviously hers) on
one of those many typical boat rides in or to Africa where one sits comfort-
ably on the deck of a boat reminiscing about the infamous topos of the *mission civilatrice*. The following citation is from the lady's once adored novel
cum autobiography, *Out of Africa:*

> At the table on the boat to Africa I sat between a Belgian going to the Congo,
> and an Englishman who had been eleven times to Mexico to shoot a particular
> kind of wild mountain sheep, and who was now going out to shoot bongo. In
> making conversation on both sides, I got mixed up in the languages, and when I
> meant to ask the Belgian if he had travelled much in his life, I asked him: *Avez-
> vous beaucoup travaillé dans votre vie?* He took no offense but, drawing out his
> tooth-pick, he answered gravely: *Enormément, Madame.* From this time he
> made it his object to tell me of all the labours of his life. In everything that he
> discussed, a certain expression came back: *Notre mission. Notre grande mission
> dans le Congo.*
>
> One evening, as we were going to play cards, the English traveller told us
> about Mexico and of how a very old Spanish lady, who lived on a lonely farm in
> the mountains, when she heard of the arrival of a stranger, had sent for him and
> ordered him to give her the news of the world.
>
> "Well, men fly now, Madame," he said to her.
>
> "Yes, I have heard of that," said she, "and I have had many arguments with
> my priest about it. Now you can enlighten us, sir. Do men fly with their legs
> drawn up under them, like the sparrows, or stretched out behind them, like the
> storks?"
>
> He also, in the course of our talk, made a remark about the ignorance of the
> Natives of Mexico, and of the schools there. The Belgian, who was dealing,
> paused with the last card in his hand, looked piercingly at the Englishman, and
> said: *Il faut enseigner aux nègres à être honnêtes et à travailler. Rien de plus.*
> Laying down the card with a bang on the table, he repeated with great determi-
> nation: *Rien de plus. Rien. Rien. Rien.*[12]

This is not the place to discuss her novel; its own epitaph should do enough to keep future readers on the alert: "equitare, arcum tendere, veritatem dicere." Needless to say, little *veritas* was revealed. Ngugi wa Thiong'o, the Kenyan novelist, warned his fellow African writers against using such novels as models for their own writings. More recently, he said about Blixen, whom he had been forced to read in school:

> Karen Blixen could describe Kenyans as dogs, hyenas, jackals and the like and be canonized for it: She was once a likely recipient of the Nobel Prize for literature.[13]

So much for the school of "crocodile writers," as Emmanuel Obiechina calls them.[14] There are people who claim that the stereotypes of Africa in the West are still the same and that they shall continue to be the same, that "though the European self-image has changed, the image of Africa has not."[15] Dorothy Hammond and Alto Jablow, two American anthropologists, have recently summarized the descriptions of Africans in Western literature as follows:

> In summary, the descriptions of Africans to be found in the Western literature of the past century conform to a readily definable tradition. It consists of a series of stereotypes and conventions which portray Africans as innately inferior and hence properly subordinate. The intellectual origins of the tradition are in imperialism and Social Darwinism, which gave sanction to the contemporary European society, and particularly to colonial expansion. The social situation and the accompanying intellectual climate have undergone radical change. Such change, however, is not paralleled in the literature. In part, the viability of the tradition can be attributed to the slower rate of change in attitudes as compared to the rapid pace of social change. In effect, the literary image of Africans presented to the readers is not only fantasy, but the obsolete fantasy of an earlier time.[16]

The task, then, of this essay is to analyze what has changed, and why it has changed, in a number of more recent German literary texts which have Africa as fore- or background. While the reflection of reality in literature most certainly is complex, dialectical, and highly mediated, it nonetheless is a reflection of views held by society and its writers.

Thematology and imagology—from the theme of Faust in literature to Donald Duck in comic strips—have had an attraction to formalist describers and cataloguers. This has been so in particular in the discipline of Comparative Literature from its early French days on. Needless to say, most of this preoccupation served little more than exotic interests or the reaffirmation of Eurocentricity. The exotic interest of early utopias and dystopias by now seems to be replaced by science fiction, and a different kind of reality comes to the fore when the former "exotic" places are discussed.

Thematology has been for a long time the domain of the so-called French school which never made an entry into American Comparative Literature because of René Wellek's deplorable attack on the external study of literature; but since the 1960s, Wellek has been corrected frequently. Suffice it to quote Henry Remak's statement:

> Friederich is also right in saying that topics dear to Carré and Guyard but anathemata to Wellek, such as the image of a foreign country reflected in the literature of another country, have, at least, the merit of countering 'ivory tower' tendencies. Fragmentation and overspecialization are greater dangers to our civilization than comparative literature studies bordering on sociology or economics. If comparative literature shut itself off, if it considered those aspects of our discipline contiguous to the fields of history, philosophy, sociology, psychology, etc., as irrelevant, and, by clear implication, inferior, then, by an ironic paradox, the very discipline destined and able more than any other to avert ever narrower specialization will have contributed to the opposite end.[17]

We are all familiar at least with the titles of the French school such as *Les grandes interprétations de l'Italie* (1913), *Images d'Amérique* (1927), *Voyageurs et écrivains français en Egypte* (1932), etc., all to be associated with a founding figure of French *littérature comparée,* Jean Marie Carré, who became instrumental for the institutionalization of the field. His disciple Marius-François Guyard, in his *La littérature comparée* of 1951, presented a revealing chapter entitled "L'étranger tel qu'on le voit" (without defining who this "on" really is). While this approach remained Eurocentric overall and never went beyond the "mirages" of French literature in Germany and England or vice versa, it nonetheless was a beginning for a more sociotelically oriented study of literature, as witness its successful resurgence in Ed Said's *Orientalism.*[18] Although it generally suffered from Eurocentrism, it at least went beyond national parochialism and implicitly opened up directions for an extension into the Third World. In a way, I shall try to continue what is implied in a statement by Carré pointing to some degree of cross-national reception when he asked: "Comment nous voyons-nous entre nous, Anglais et Français, Français et Allemand, etc."[19] I also propose the question of how we more recently in Germany have seen the Third World, in particular Africa, and how they in Africa have seen us and our literature. Without the second part of this statement, I believe such bicameral studies would remain invalid, and their suggested sociotelic nature, a mere allegory of autotelic studies. In other words, we are here mostly concerned with what remained hidden and unexecuted in the abbreviation of Carré's "etc." in the quotation cited above.

Thematology proper (or rather improper) has in the past largely been part of *Stoff- und Motivgeschichte* associated with Paul Merker and Elisabeth Frenzel, theoretically backed up by Raymond Trousson's *Un problème de littérature comparée: Les études de thèmes* of 1965—works which all clearly privilege individual Western heroes in their varied continuity. In Germany, this kind of ill-defined thematology has been replaced by imagology *(Imagologie)* by the Aachen comparatist originally from Belgium, Hugo Dyserinck, who sees in this field a particular extraliterary relevance:

> Vieles deutet darauf hin, daß ihre [imagology's] möglichen Ergebnisse... außerhalb der Literaturwissenschaft tatsächlich auch ernsthaft gebraucht werden.[20]

A statement like this anchors Comparative Literature once again in the necessary nonautotelic domain. Manfred S. Fischer has expanded on the topic when he spoke of "nationale Images" and the "Erforschung genetischer Kontaktbeziehungen," and of "kontaktologische Beziehungsforschung."[21] However, most of this "contact" literature or contactology still remains too literocentric in conception, due to the continued privileging of formalist approaches.

To set my approach apart from such founding statements of thematology, revised thematology, and/or imagology, I propose the term geothematics—the treatment of nations, countries, social groups, and classes by other countries and social groups, in particular the treatment of the Third World people in the literature of Europe and the United States (in our case, Germany) and, reciprocally, the treatment of Europe and the United States by Third World writers (in this case, African writers). A shift from literocentricity to social issues is clearly intended here, and the term "theme" is to be understood in the nonliterary sense given it by Paulo Freire, who in his *Pedagogy of the Oppressed* spoke of "generative theme," "meaningful thematics," and "people's thematic universe."[22] Freire said about this branch of thematology:

> I consider the fundamental theme of our epoch to be that of domination— which implies its opposite, the theme of liberation, as the object to be achieved.[23]

This thematology gains additional relevance if we keep in mind Freire's fundamental and class-conscious distinction between "banking education" and *conscientição*. If we consider the traditional treatment of Africa in German literature, the change of Germany's treatment of Africa in recent literature, and the more recent treatment of Germany by African writers, I think we can draw some conclusions that give the study of literature once again some kind of relevance which goes beyond the privileged study of isolated texts. I would hope that careful studies of such geo-thematic examples could lead to a significant reevaluation of our views of other countries/people/races/classes. They could have the same strong impact a recent book by an African on Greenland had on the falsified and whitewashed anthropology of Greenland. I refer to Tété-Michael Kpomassie, *An African in Greenland.*[24]

2

German scholarly interests in Africa's literature and culture have been extensive, as witness the three most recognized Africanists—Leo Frobenius, Janheinz Jahn, and Ulli Beier. This is not the place to debate the justification of their impact, i.e., Frobenius's on Ezra Pound, or Jahn's on the general and most certainly flawed mythopoeic Western conception of African literature. But a widespread reception of things African has been going on in Germany for a long period of time. In literature itself, however, the "impact" of Africa, i.e., references to Africa in poems, plays, and novels, or entire works dealing with Africa, has been rather negligible as compared to France and England, or even the United States.

This is largely due to a very different development in the history of colonialism, and the absence of a stronger African presence in Germany. In short, works where African topics and people are treated, while not really rare, are seldom of the literary "quality" of such "master"-pieces as *Othello, The Tempest, Heart of Darkness, Mister Johnson,* Gide's *Voyage au Congo,* or Michel Leiris' *L'Afrique fàntome.* But remaining outside of the "canon" can at times be an advantage. Germany has a less falsified attitude towards Africa in her literature.[25] Blacks were positively treated in such early works as *Parzival* (whose brother Feirefîz is half black, half white), in contrast to the general negative treatment of blacks in, for example, Medieval French Literature. Witness the symbolic presentation of Blacks (as categorically negative) in the *Chanson de Roland.* Africans do appear in Grimmelshausen's *Simplizissimus* and even in Lessing's famous *Laokoon,* but they were rarely central. Christian Dietrich Grabbe in his easily overlooked play, *Herzog Theodor von Gothland* of 1822, has Berdoa say:

> Wir Neger haben einen anderen
> Geschmack als ihr: uns ist das Schöne schwarz,
> Die *Teufel* aber sind uns weiß.[26]

It is a known fact that there was considerable interest in Africa during German Expressionism. Perhaps the first significant work on African sculpture is Carl Einstein's *Negerplastik.* But such incidents are rare and, within the context of "World Literature," not comparable to *Heart of Darkness* or *Mister Johnson;* even Einstein's contribution seems minimal when compared with the Yoruba influence on Picasso's early cubist paintings, and with Apollinaire's "collection" of African works of art. Among the exceptions to these relatively *schöngeistig* treatments of Africa in literature, mention has to be made of Heinrich Heine's "Das Sklavenschiff," which has been likened in its attack on organized killing to Paul Celan's "Todesfuge." More interesting, however, are recent treatments of Africa in German literature.

The Nigerian critic Michael J. C. Echeruo, who analyzed the genre of the "foreign novel" or "novel of Africa" (to distinguish it from the African

novel written by Africans) and who focused on Joyce Cary, came to the conclusions that *Mister Johnson* (1939) marks "the finest and the very last example of the 'explorer's novel of Africa'." After Cary, he continues, "it is
almost safe to predict there is not likely again to be another important novel
of Africa by a foreigner."[27] Nothing is safe to predict in literature, however,
and while it is obvious that the "explorer's novel" cannot any longer be written in our times, novels, plays, poems, and essays about Africa will, most
certainly, continue to be written. And, *pace* Echeruo, they can and have
reached a quality which surpasses not only Joyce Cary but Conrad as well.
While this has not necessarily been so in English-speaking countries (witness
one of the last novels of this genre, Saul Bellow's *Henderson the Rain King*)
it has been true to a surprising degree in Germany. That, among other
things, is a criterion of why German literature in our days remains so different from other European literatures, despite the increasing pressure of a canonized Modernism. The reason for the refutation of Echeruo by German
writers can perhaps be found in Germany's peculiar history (corrected) and
in its documentary literature, largely influenced by Bertolt Brecht. The
names of Hans Magnus Enzensberger and Peter Weiss might suffice for our
case. Both writers are strong, albeit by no means concurring, defenders of
the cause of the Third World and literature's turning to this world. We are
perhaps justified to go so far as to propose an Enzensberger-Weiss debate on
Third World Literature which at a point might be recognized as having the
same substantial merit as the Sickingen debate, the Brecht-Lukács debate, or
the Kafka debate (to mention merely the three most important debates in the
archeology of Marxist aesthetics). In this context, we might also emphasize
that Enzensberger is less important for our present topic since he focuses on
Latin America, in particular on Cuba, while Peter Weiss emphasizes Africa
and very easily refutes Echeruo's prognosis.

But before Peter Weiss turned to Africa, many post–World War II German writers have tried using Africa as a theme—not always successfully.
The 1950s in Germany were still obsessed with regaining a lost lyricism or
finding an alternate voice. And while the theme of Africa was rarely treated
in those years, it can be found, usually as a continuation of old clichés, of
the *Meinungsstereotypen*, of exoticism. An example of this deplorable
Entgleisung is an Ingeborg Bachmann poem of the year 1957 entitled
"Liebe: Dunkler Erdteil." The poem continues the stereotypic view of African women, or women falling in love with African men, although it was
written by a women. The black king (he had to be a king) has animal claws;
he hunts and orders the tropical rains:

> Der schwarze König zeigt die Raubtiernägel,
> zehn blasse Monde jagt er in die Bahn,
> und er befiehlt dem großen Tropenregen.
> Die Welt sieht dich vom anderen Ende an![28]

We can still hear Gottfried Benn and his lyricized Africa. This is the language where the rhyme dictates what is to be said. The coasts are loaded with gold and ivory and the caravans move through the desert. For Bachmann, Sahara and tropics seem to be next to each other, most likely as close as Vienna is to Munich. And, of course, love has to be made—wild, animalistic, exotic love:

> Er, fellig, farbig, ist an deiner Seite,
> er greift dich auf, wirft über dich sein Garn.
> Um deine Hüften knüpfen sich Lianen,
> um deinen Hals kraust sich der fette Farn.

This is Tarzan's Africa, full of taboos, snakes, and myths:

> Tabu ist alles: Erden, Früchte, Ströme...
> Die Schlange hängt verchromt an deinem Arm.

Most of these images and expressions of purest kitsch are due to the rhyme structure and a lyrical tradition which still privileges unexamined images to facts. This kind of poetry is never able to go beyond the cheapest tourist expectations or its own visual equivalent—"airport art." Admittedly, it is hard in a short poem (equally hard for Africans themselves, witness the frequent aberrations of most *négritude* poetry) to work realistically. And it is obviously very hard to write a poem about a place one has never seen. But it can be done with a bit of irony, political consciousness, critical distance, and a knowledge of what Brecht has been able to do in his poetry.

Rolf Dieter Brinkmann, in 1971, gave us a pertinent example. He, too, used some of the clichés and, by doing so, makes us question precisely what the beauty of words has tried to achieve in Bachmann's false lyric. Brinkmann's poem, too, deals with the theme of love, with the stereotype of African women seen by white tourists, the theme of commodified love. His verses, entitled "die afrikanische," could be out of the diary of a tourist. But by giving them a most simplistic form, Brinkmann reveals his distancing critical attitude:

> Elefantenfrau
> war am 20. Oktober
> der Gegenstand
>
> unserer Unter-
> haltung. Die Beine
> sind schwarz und
>
> schwer. So geht
> sie herum...[29]

Brinkmann continues with a stereotypic explanation and description which could have come out of a medical book, and he ends with a reference to a photograph of some pygmies in the Berlin Zoo:

> Es gab davon
> Fotos. Als ich vier
> war, sah ich eins.
>   (p. 4)

But Brinkmann is no longer a child and sees things differently. He presents us with a tourist's point of view, the preserved mentality of a four-year-old. The key lines of the poem use compounds which sharply contrast with the lyrical metaphor of the "Elefantenfrau": to wit, *Gegenstand* (there is something here which stands against our traditional views) and the hyphenated *Unter-haltung* (which no longer means only conversation, but also oppression). The traditional views (beautiful words, myth, exoticisms) here are intricately connected with the oppression of those we find so often beautified but unexamined in the former books on Africa.

Another young German poet, F. C. Delius, published two poems dealing with Africa in his collection *Ein Bankier auf der Flucht: Gedichte und Reisebilder* (1975). The first, entitled "Ein Traum von Mozambique," doesn't claim to be the poet's description of Mozambique during Frelimo days, but is a dream. It constitutes the kind of associate images that emerge when mosquitoes are biting one mercilessly. They become little attacking planes:

> Wir rannten in Deckung, statt Bomben flogen aber
> aus den Flugzeugen viele kleine Bombenflugzeuge, schossen
> auf uns zu, die widerlichsten Stechfliegen, und kurz eh
> ich aufwachte, dachte ich, jetzt geht alles wieder
> von vorne los.[30]

The second—and more important—poem is entitled "Reise nach Afrika und zurück in vier Minuten" and forms a counterpiece to prevailing revolutionary tourism. Ironically, Delius starts with the words:

> Nichts ist so weit weg wie Afrika. Also
> fuhr ich gestern abend nach Afrika, obwohl
> mir dauernd Experten im Ohr lagen mit ihren Warnungen:
> Afrika verstehst du nicht. Das weiß ich auch.
>   (p. 65)

The poem is not an attempt at moving from ignorance to knowledge. Delius does not pretend to be an expert writing about Africa. Instead, he describes how others respond to Africa. He sees Archie Moore,

> ...den Boxweltmeister, wie er
> weinend aus dem Getto kam von Soweto...
> es gibt kein schlimmeres Getto, sagte Archie Moore
> den Reportern, meine Brüder werden systematisch
> vernichtet durch Suff...
>   (ibid.)

As in a nightmare, these thoughts torture Delius, and fictitiously he continues his "Reise nach Afrika":

> ...Ich hielt das nicht aus,
> also fuhr ich weiter, fuhr kreuz und quer weiter,
> und freute mich selbst in der algerischen Wüste
> über algerische Fortschritte, so gestärkt
> wieder südwärts. Besuchte in Angola Deutsche,
> die sich breitbeinig auf ihre Plantagen stellen
> und allen Ernstes behaupten, dies Land
> sei ihre Heimat...
> Wenig versteh ich von Kolonisation
> und schickte einige Flüche in Richtung
> England, nach Frankreich, Spanien, Portugal
> und Germany, die hier am Äquator Uneinigkeit
> schürten...

> (ibid.)

The poem continues with an ironic *envoi* against revolutionary tourism:

> Dies Gedicht würd ich gern in Afrika lassen, weil
> die Experten hier es nicht verstehn. Ich widme es also
> den Kämpfern Angolas, von denen einige bekanntlich
> früher mal Dichter waren und die heute überladen sind
> mit der Schwerarbeit Verwaltung und Organisierung
> und der Schwerstarbeit gegen die gutbezahlten CIA-Kämpfer
> und vielleicht mal ein Lächeln übrig haben
> für den bescheidenen Beitrag eines Weißen, der
> nicht mal die Sonne verträgt in Afrika, für Afrika.

> (p. 66)

Another "Reise nach Afrika" in less than "vier Minuten" is Walter Abish's *Alphabetical Africa* (1974). It is a curious and experimental piece of Africana in the form of a fictitious mental journey, considerably less political than Delius's poem. This "novel" is only marginally relevant to our topic, not only because it perpetuates an experimental/exotic tradition, but because it has been written by an American writer. On the other hand, Abish is of German descent and is largely known for his novel on Germany. His African novel, alphabetical in structure (A–Z and back to A) and frequently alliterative, is basically an armchair novel. But Abish's German background is continuously present from the first chapter ("ants are Ameisen")[31] to the chapter based on the letter G, which not only deals with the obvious Ghanians but with "gobbling" Germans as well. An exotic Africa prevails, just compare the letter F where such alliterative excesses as "Fabulous Fulani figures crouch / fabulous fucks..." (p. 12) occur. Here and there, some generally correct and ironic observations are made on colonialism and Germany. Yet a few samples should again suffice to remove this novel from the shelf of relevant items. Here is a brief excerpt from the opening chapter based on the letter A:

> Africa again: Albert arrives, alive and arguing about African art, about African angst and also, alas, attacking Ashanti architecture, as author again attempts an agonizing alphabetical appraisal...asked about affection, Albert answers, Ashanti affection also aesthetically abhorrent, antagonizing all. As alien airforce attacks Angola, Albert asks are anthills anywhere about, agreeing as Alex asserts, all Angolans are absolute asses. (p. 2)

With this, we arrive at what might be considered the low highpoint in terms of our topic, a chapter with a G-string:

> Ghanians are erroneously convinced German gestures can cut floods, can cook beetles, can deafen Africans, but German gestures are all futile, besides being enormously funny...Germany's generals gloomily admit as gifted Gustaf entertains Alva at Gabon's best diner. Good Gabon food. But everyone at diner genuinely alarmed by German's great girth, by German's great appetite. Gobbling gestopfte Gans, gobbling Gabelfrühstück, gobbling goulash, gobbling geschwind, Gesundheit, goppling Gurken, Guggelhupf, Gash Gash, Gish Gish, groaning, grunting also complaining, chewing Grüne Bohnen, Geschmacksache, as Germany grows greater. Alarmed, Gabon grows additional food for Gustaf, and Gustaf's children, Gerda, Grete and Gerhard. Gifted Größeres Germany consumes energy and guarantees greatness, get going, grow another Goethe, great guy, claims Gustaf, as all Grundig gramophones in Gabon, gently groon: Goethe, Goethe, Goethe...are Germans convincing in Africa? A glowing G-man arrives, gripping black gloves, bearing a granite chin cheerfully granting Germany a concession...Also Gabon ganz gemütlich: broad avenues built along French design, also few bars and boutiques, fortunately Gabon bush "ganz echt Afrika." (pp. 14–15)

This *tour de force* of an alliterative stream of consciousness (a fine example of literary logorrhea) leads to a convincing self-indictment as early as the chapter which exploits the letter E: "Enough" (p. 10).

Let us turn to more relevant and accurate treatments of Africa as they appear in recent German literature. Perhaps the best known and most enthusiastically received play (particularly in Third World countries) by a German playwright focusing on things African has been Peter Weiss's *Gesang vom Lusitanischen Popanz* (produced during the heydays of the 1960s in 1966/67, and published in 1974). With this play, Willfried F. Feuser concluded his "Das Bild des Afrikaners in der deutschen Literatur," an important fact-finding essay in geo-thematics. Unfortunately, at the time when his essay was written, the play was not yet widely known. Feuser correctly perceived the new "Tendenz in der deutschen Afrikaliteratur...die auch in ihren anderen Werken zunehmend zutage tritt und der Schablone vom 'master image of Africa' in der westlichen Literatur ('the tradition is transigent') widerspricht."[32] His survey ended with the concluding prophetic song of the chorus from Weiss's play:

> Und mehr werden kommen
> ihr werdet sie sehen
> schon viele sind in den Städten
> und in den Wäldern und Bergen
> lagernd ihre Waffen und sorgfältig planend
> die Befreiung
> die nah ist.[33]

This Brechtian/Fanonian play, with its call for permanent class struggle, is not a *laudatio* for a liberation war which has already taken place. It focuses, rather, on a time period prior to such a rupture and, by doing so, is considerably more accurate and relevant (after all, this liberation has since taken place). Although the play clearly deals with events in the former colonies of Portugal, the relevance of the play goes far beyond—it is international in character, while at the same time implicitly criticizing Germany. Weiss's turn to the documentary theater, in literary terms, completes his necessary liberation from Modernism (in its canonized version), from experimental literature and art. Documentary theater as he sees it is conceived as a counter medium to the consciousness industry. Its task is to criticize the fraudulent practice of mainstream media. Even the play's title, *Gesang vom Lusitanischen Popanz,* is less baroque than that of Weiss's *Marat/Sade* play. According to Weiss, his *Gesang* is located ("liegt genau dazwischen") between his *Marat/Sade,* an orgiastic Artaudian play, and his *Vietnam Diskurs,* an ascetic Brechtian play. It attempts to correct the image of liberation presented by the media. It is factual "scientific theater" *(wissenschaftliches Theater)* without fully giving up aesthetic dimensions. The adjective *lusitanisch* obviously alludes to Portugal, hence we correctly assume a play on Mozambique, Angola, and/or Guinea-Bissau. But Weiss goes beyond such stereotyping. By not mentioning Portugal, but rather Lusitania, he calls attention to the fact that a colonizing power had once been a (Roman) colony itself. During the events presented, the colonizer itself is colonized (and used) by NATO.

This gives Weiss's "African" play a more than topographical relevance. Places are not directly mentioned (although some productions indicated Africa by using a large map in the background). The same holds true for the characters: originally, some were named (e.g., Richard Jäger, former West German Minister of Justice who defended Portuguese colonial terror), but then Weiss reduced almost all persons to numbers (numerically/symbolically from 1–7)—a brilliant strategy which avoids individualization, identifiable characterization, and hero-worship while allowing the actors tremendous flexibility. Thus Weiss fulfilled one of the main assertions of his essay "Notizen zum dokumentarischen Theater," in which he stated: "Nicht individuelle Konflikte werden dargestellt, sondern sozial-ökonomisch bedingte Verhaltensweisen."[34] With similar consistency, the actors do not have to be black (only the 1968 New York performance used black actors) and no cosmetic tricks have to be used since the play is about class, not race. There are seven actors, four female and three male, who simultaneously represent whites and blacks, oppressors and oppressed (with the implicit possibility that the oppressed, if they are not class-conscious, can turn again into the oppressors).

The main character (until 1966 Weiss used—according to Manfred Haiduk—the name Salazar)[35] is a construct entitled *Popanz* which is a kind of technological skeleton ("ein klappriges Gerippe"); in the GDR production, a TV screen was used for its head to point out the connection between TV and capitalism—a gigantic allegory of steel, cross, and whip which clearly stands for militarism, colonialism, and imperialism. The figure appears as dangerous as it is ridiculous and is characterized by continuous yawning. Ernst Schumacher has called this *Popanz* "ein künstliches Monstrum mit einer 'Sprachröhre,' aus der die 'abendländische' Gebetsmühle leiert."[36] Rüdiger Sareika provides us, via the *Brockhaus Enzyklopädie,* with the etymology of the word:

> *Popanz*/wahrscheinlich tschechisch-polnisch/*der,* ein seit dem 16. Jahrhundert zuerst in Ostmittel-Deutschland verbreitetes, dort mit dem gleichbedeutenden "Popelmann" sowie "Popelhans" vermengtes Fremdwort für Trugbild (für Kinder erdachtes Gespenst), Vogelscheuche, auch spaßige, leicht tragisch wirkende Figur.[37]

The image of imperialism and colonialism as a bogey is brilliant not only in its Portuguese-African context, but in its international ramifications as well.

The play consists of two acts with eleven scenes. It first shows us the nature of *Popanz,* its connection with Christianity and lust for power:

> Ich erhalte mein Befehle
> von Gott dem Herrn
> Es ist Lusitaniens Aufgabe
> die göttliche Botschaft zu verbreiten.[38]

In this realistic/ficticious setting, the exploitation of (Ju)Ana is shown in exemplary form. Scene 2 gives us briefly the history of the Portuguese colonies in Africa. Scene 3 pictures colonial exploitation at large: Portugal's (in)famous "exception to racism," the *asimilado* (the exception of 1 percent), and the rule (exploitation of the remaining 99 percent of the indigenous population). Scene 4 displays typical examples of colonial terror and the destruction of the native family structure: Poverty is a crime. Scene 5 demonstrates the different treatment of white and black proletarians, capitalism's famous invention of "divide and rule." This scene culminates in a more individual treatment: a story narrated by Ana.

Act II, scene 6 shows the black as pariah. The creation of intellectual inferiority of the indigenous population is being contrasted with the intellectual potential of the native population. Torture reigns supreme in Angola. Scene 7 presents Angola as the center of Portuguese capitalism. Scene 8 demonstrates how its colonies made Europe rich and also presents the beginning of the liberation struggle. Scene 9 denounces the propaganda of a European Minister of Justice. Scene 10 reveals a foreign bank director as partner; Portugal offers Germany military bases and places for its war industry. In scene 11, capitalism and tourism are contrasted with poverty and oppression. Resistance is on the increase in the colonies as well as in Portugal, despite Western support for the Salazar regime. Scene 11 culminates in the destruction of the *Popanz*—a symbol of liberation from foreign colonialism.

This short summary, however, shows little of the play's aesthetic dimension, its combination of folkloristic African elements with Brechtian straightforwardness, its songs combined with statistics and facts. *Gesang* is a veritable example of what a socially conscious art can do, which is particularly due to the enormous variability of the performance, the script by itself being no longer the sole "text." It is indeed an example of an "Aesthetics of Resistance" *(Ästhetik des Widerstands)* which for the first time clearly demonstrates how close Africa, the Third World, and all oppressed people in the First and Second worlds really are, once one has learned to approach things from the point of view of class. In a way, this play comes closest to Peter Nazareth's definition of Third World literature (a nongeographical definition) which reads:

> To belong to the Third World is...to accept an identity, an identity with the wretched of the earth spoken for by Frantz Fanon, to determine to end all exploitation and oppression.[39]

By using the "theme of Africa" in a nonexotic, class-based manner, Weiss has shown that a factual treatment of the Third World can be of uttermost educational importance for non-Third World as well as for Third World audiences. Through his play, he himself became one of the foremost Third World writers. This is amply demonstrated by its wide use in Third World countries (witness the version of the Teatro Estudio of the Universidad de los Andes).

For those who thought German colonialism any better than other European or American brands, Peter Weiss has amply demonstrated the affinity between Germany and Portugal (both are/have been colonizers who are/were at the same time colonized). Weiss's critique of German colonialism is implicit in the bogey's words to some officers:

> Ich habe Sie
> Meine Herren Offiziere
> zu einer Expedition zusammengerufen
> bei der Sie das Wort Mitleid
> aus Ihrem Gedächtnis
> streichen müssen.
> Wir kämpfen nicht gegen Menschen
> wir kämpfen
> gegen wilde Tiere.[40]

Sareika, in his discussion of Weiss's play, has pointed out reminiscences of this speech to Kaiser Wilhelm II's "Hunnenrede" (1900): "Pardon wird nicht gegeben, Gefangene werden nicht gemacht..."[41] How German colonialism really worked in Africa can be learned from the two works following: Uwe Timm's *Morenga* and—once we have turned to the topic of how Africans see Germany and Germans—Ebrahim Hussein's play on the abortive Maji-Maji rebellion in former German Tanganyika.

In the history of pre-concentration camp Germany, two atrocious genocidal moments occurred: the excessive killing of blacks during the Maji-Maji rebellion (Wahehe uprising) in East Africa and the almost complete annihilation of the Herero in Southwest Africa ("Von ehemals 80,000 Hereros überlebten 15,130").[42] Both events have been largely repressed in Germany to preserve the myth of German colonialism as a "better" form of colonialism. History, however, teaches us the opposite. With the intention of correcting that German myth, Uwe Timm wrote his novel *Morenga* (1978; in its second [1981] edition properly subtitled "Aufstand in Deutsch-Südwestafrika: Ein Roman um ein verdrängtes Kapitel deutscher Geschichte"). It is easily the most important and impressive publication to date in the revision of the literary image of Africa in Germany.

In the history of anti-imperialist struggle prior to SWAPO and its leader Sam Nujoma, two guerrilla figures stand out: the Nama chieftain Hendrik Witbooi, who fought the Germans while keeping a detailed diary from 1884–94,[43] until he succumbed to German pressure and went over to the enemy, and the Nama/Herero Morenga, a considerably more political figure, with whom Witbooi later sided when he realized that the Germans could not be trusted.

Timm, largely known for his novel *Heißer Sommer* of 1974, in which he examined the connection between Third World uprisings and the German student movement during the late 1960s, has for a long time demonstrated interest in Africa. In 1971, he published a collection of poems entitled *Widersprüche*. One of them, entitled "Lob der Idylle," readjusts the topos of exotic Africa; it ends:

am schönsten
in der Nacht auf einer Safari in Südafrika
das gleichmäßige Äsen
eines weißen Nashorns zu beobachten
wissend
daß der Boy den afrikanischen Hummer im Wasser siedet
während die südafrikanischen Streitkräfte mit dem CIA
für Ruhe und Ordnung im Lande sorgen

Beunruhigend aber der Gedanke
daß es Leute gibt
die keinen Sinn für Schönheit haben.[44]

This Brechtian anti-aesthetic attitude (compare Brecht's poem "Literature Shall Be Scrutinized," which culminates in the insight central for an unexotic and politicized aesthetics, namely that "The delicious music of words will only relate / That for many there was no food")[45] is also the driving force behind Timm's latest Africa novel. It contrasts not only oppressors (Germans) and oppressed (Nama and Herero) but also Germans who believe in the aesthetics of exoticism (thrilled by such words as "Gewürzinseln" and by sunsets over the Namib desert, without ever feeling anything for the starving native population) and those who, like Brecht, side with the native population, learn from them, and see their problems as being related to their own class problems. In between, there are others for whom there is hope that they might learn to adjust their nonvisions: for instance, the main protagonist of the novel—a veterinarian from Hamburg named Gottschalk—and, of course, the reader of the novel. About the latter, Timm had the following to say when asked in an East German interview: "Welche Wirkung wünschst du dir von dem Roman? Daß sich der unpolitische Leser politisiert und der unorganisierte organisiert."[46]

The story of the novel is simple. What makes it interesting is Timm's combination of fiction and fact in the tradition of Weiss's emphasis on documentary literature (all the main secondary sources from archives down to the books on Southwest Africa by Bley and Drechsler have been incorporated). The work is a masterpiece of Brechtian "learn and have fun." Timm does not focus on the entire period of Germany's exploitation of Southwest Africa, but instead emphasizes the crucial years from 1904 to 1907. However, he also brings in the fifty years prior to that time, as well as its connection with the present. Though entitling his novel *Morenga,* he does not commit the error of glorifying a black guerilla leader from a guilty white man's perspective, but rather leaves Morenga relatively absent. Yet this absence is a very powerful *présence d'absence.*

The main figure among the many bellicose Germans who are largely "gutmütig" and naïve is Gottschalk. During his early days in Africa, Gottschalk meets another German from Berlin, who is also a veterinarian and who appears to be rather skeptical about Germany's engagement in Southwest. Wenstrup (a fictitious character) is the political center of the novel and merges with political figures of recent years. Likewise, he often takes on aspects of Morenga himself. He later disappears—some claim to have seen him in Latin America—and his photograph is described as reminiscent of "jene Bilder, die es von Che Guevara aus dem bolivianischen Urwald gibt" (p. 173). Wenstrup refuses to fight with the Germans and sides with Nama and Herero. For this, he is court-martialed but manages to escape. He leaves a book with the less "gutsy" Gottschalk which contains many marginalia that allow the latter to figure out not only his former friend but also what was really going on in Southwest Africa. Gottschalk's interest in Wenstrup would not have been possible had he not been somewhat skeptical himself. From the beginning, he knew: "Da wurde ein Krieg geführt, der ihn, genaugenommen, doch gar nichts anging" (p. 11). Both men stand out among their many compatriots that make every reader laugh with guilt and recognition (the "typical" German who calls the Hottentot women "Hottentitten," buys the love of native girls with a spoonful of sugar, calls the natives "Pavians," or has ashtrays made out of Hottentot skulls). One German has a large barrel on wheels constructed and moves it across the terrain to sell "Branntwein" to the natives. An *Unteroffizier* Rattenhuber, keen on starting ice-skating in Southwest, is described as follows:

> Er wollte für Südwest einmal das werden, was Klopstock für Deutschland geworden war, nachdem der dort das Schlittschuhlaufen bekannt gemacht hatte ...daß es bis heute nicht möglich ist, in diesem Lande Schlittschuh zu laufen, liegt möglicherweise daran, daß der Unteroffizier Rattenhuber zwei Monate später in einem Gefecht mit Leuten von Morris gefallen ist. (p. 53)

Among these typical German "clowns," Gottschalk and Wenstrup distinguish themselves by the mere fact that they are informed, that they read and—in the case of Gottschalk—keep a diary (as did Witbooi and Morenga). That which they read, however, is what makes the difference: Gottschalk brought along Fontane's *Stechlin* and some Hölderlin, whom he only understands after having come across Wenstrup; Wenstrup is reading and annotating nothing less than the Russian anarchist Kropotkin's *Mutual Aid: A Factor of Evolution,* or rather its German version, *Gegenseitige Hilfe in der Entwicklung,* in which the Herero are praised for having not the slightest interest in competition. The combination of Fontane, Hölderlin—Gottschalk is particularly fond of the line, "so komm! daß wir das Offene schauen" (p. 273)—and the anarchist Kropotkin is not only characteristic of Timm's interest in anarchism, but it also reflects the politicization of mainstream German literature (witness Weiss's interest in Hölderlin due to Pierre Bertaux's biography). The Kropotkin book Wenstrup gives to Gottschalk bears the inscription: "nicht weil es Weihnachten, sondern weil es Zeit ist" (p. 54).

In this novel where almost every German seems to have fun, Wenstrup remains serious and observant: "Alle lachten, nur Wenstrup nicht" (p. 15).

When they arrive by boat and are carried to the shore by blacks, Wenstrup "lehnte es ab, sich von einem Neger an Land tragen zu lassen" (p. 16). He constantly tells Gottschalk that "wir stehen auf der falschen Seite" (p. 42). Wenstrup even learns Nama—the only figure in the novel to do so. In every respect, he is "ein wirklich ungewöhnlicher Zufall," probably "der einzige anarchistische Veterinär des deutschen Heeres" (p. 49). And a few pages later, Wenstrup merges with those he was sent to fight: "Er begann langsam denen zu ähneln, die zu bekämpfen er hergeschickt worden war" (p. 52). About the various uprisings quelled by the Germans, he notes: "Wahehe-Aufstand, Boxer-Aufstand, Herero- und Hottentottenaufstand. Wer da schläft, den muß man wecken, notfalls mit Krach" (p. 116).

A new, positive, and progressive image of Africa is presented via these two veterinarians. For instance, the Nama learn fast while the Germans (with the exception of Wenstrup) learn very little. Also, another friend of Gottschalk comes to the proper conclusion: "Er dachte, man verteidige das Vaterland, aber genaugenommen seien es die Hottentotten, die ihr Vaterland verteidigten" (p. 193). The critique of Germany makes room for a defense and praise of the native population and their cause. Through a Kropotkin citation, we learn: "Im Stammesverband der Hottentotten aber ist die Konkurrenz durch das Prinzip der gegenseitigen Hilfe außer Kraft gesetzt" (p. 252). What do we really know about Africa, we colonizers and heirs of colonizers, brainwashed by exotic literary writings? Timm asks himself this question and reaches the interim conclusion: "Einstweilen müssen wir also offen bekennen, daß der Hottentotte uns besser kennt als wir ihn" (p. 255).

In the end, Wenstrup disappears, Gottschalk returns to Germany, and Morenga is killed. But the latter's message remains as strong today as it was in an interview of May 29, 1906, which was printed in the *Cape Times:*

> Auf die Frage des Reporters, ob er wisse, daß Deutschland einer der mächtigsten Staaten der Welt sei, antwortete Morenga: 'Ja, darüber bin ich mir vollkommen im klaren, aber die Deutschen können in unserem Land nicht kämpfen. Sie wissen nicht, woher sie das Wasser nehmen sollen, und sie verstehen nichts von der Guerillakriegsführung.' (p. 32)

The image of water, which has many connotations, here symbolizes unity in anti-imperialist struggle worldwide. I shall come back to this image when I examine the literary treatment of the Maji-Maji rebellion by Ebrahim Hussein of Tanzania.

3

At one point in the novel, the veterinarian Gottschalk, recently involved in making the camel the main animal for the German troops, hires a steward "Bambuse," a Nama by name of Simon. Simon speaks German and has been in Germany with his missionary. Gottschalk asks him how he feels about Germany and what impressed him most. Simon answers, the mortuaries ("die Beerdigungsinstitute," p. 244). While this is merely a minor episode in that highly episodic novel, *Morenga,* it does anticipate what we can see in many an African text: namely, the Africans' ability to be much more critical when they visit "our countries" than we are when we visit theirs. Contrary to English and French works stemming from Africa—where the so-called been-to topos has been central, at least in the first twenty years after independence—references to Germany in African literature are relatively hard to come by. But they do exist. The Nigerian poet Wole Soyinka refers to Tegel in his poem "Idandre," but the word "Tegel" hardly functions much differently from the word *baluba* in Pound's *Cantos.* John Pepper Clark's *America, Their America* (1964) is perhaps the strongest indictment of a Western nation by an African writer to date, but it is, naturally, not about Germany. In Africa in recent years, we can generally observe an increase in what J. E. Lip has called *The Savage Hits Back* as early as 1937, and which he described, not so much in literature but in the visual arts, by analyzing sculptures from Africa that ridicule the *colon.* According to Jens Jahn, it is "Lip's Sicht des außereuropäischen Künstlers, der uns in seinen Bildwerken einen Spiegel vorhält, als ob er sagen wollte: 'Schaut! Das ist, was ihr Weißen seid'."[47] This *Position der Umkehrung* (for which there are so many visual examples, indeed an entire genre called *colon*) can be found in a play by the Tanzanian Ebrahim Hussein which extensively examines Germans and German colonialism in the late 19th century.

Kinjeketile is a relatively unknown work (unknown even to literary Africanists) based on the records of the Maji-Maji rebellion (1905-7). An 18-year-old schoolgirl in the 1890s wrote about that time of German atrocities in Tanganyika: "Our news is this, that the Germans treat us badly and oppress us much, because it is their will."[48] The Germans, along with Arab accomplices who dealt in the slave trade, instituted the production of cash crops for export, chiefly cotton, at the expense of native food production. Forced labor with whippings and beatings was employed. The Germans also tried to tax the population, even after stopping payment for labor in 1903. As a contemporary of the period said: "The good thing about the Germans was that all people were the same before the whip."[49]

The play by Ebrahim Hussein was originally written in Swahili and then translated by the author. It starts out with two women conversing about economic exploitation and oppression by the Germans. The men of a village dream of an uprising but they are disunited. Kitunda, a leader, has to face his daughter being raped. The brutality of the Germans and their henchmen, the Askaris, is presented.

Against this background emerges Kinjeketile, a poor man immersed in solitude and mysticism. He sees visions and acts strangely, bewildering his neighbors. In a state of trance, he falls into the Maji River and fails to surface for an entire day. Kitunda, his closest aide, pronounces him dead. But Kinjeketile does emerge. People believe that this is the work of Hongo, a spirit of the Maji River. Kinjeketile proclaims a new dawn to the people, a dawn of unity, resistance, and victory. He gives orders that they must start a "whispering campaign" and spread the words of rebellion. Kitunda is appointed general of the people's army and given instructions that he must patiently train them to form such an army. He is to wait until arms have been procured. Kinjeketile consecrates the new spirit of the assembled people with the waters of the Maji. He pronounces the fighting men protected by the waters of the river, and invulnerable to the bullets of the Germans. The people unite.

But an uncontrollable and dangerous fervor possesses the people. Because of the promise of the protection of the water, they know no bounds and finally revolt in spite of Kinjeketile and Kitunda. In a final confrontation with the Germans, the people are crushed. Many are killed by the German use of the machine gun. The rebellion collapses and the people sink back into the depths of despair and defeatism and denounce Kinjeketile. The final scene takes place in a German prison where an attempt to lynch Kinjeketile is barely averted. For the lives of the captured warriors, the Germans demand a recantation from Kinjeketile, his repudiation of the Maji myth so that the spirit of rebellion will die. Kinjeketile refuses, maintaining that, ultimately, the myth is not a lie because it has produced a historical truth: namely, the absolute necessity for the Africans to fight and defeat the German colonizers.

In Tanzania, this movement of Kinjeketile and his *maji* went around as TANU. Although the play is based on historical fact, Hussein deliberately alters and politicizes his protagonist. Hussein himself states his intentions in his introduction:

> In my play, I have tried to demonstrate three things. First, I have tried to show how the Wamatumbi felt about the cruel invasion by the Germans, especially to show the master-servant relationship then pertaining. Secondly, I have tried to show briefly the political climate of that period (1890–1904). Thirdly, I have touched on the theme of economic exploitation of the African by the Germans.[50]

The function of myth in this play is considerably different from literature in the mythopoeic tradition. As Biodun Jeyifo has stressed in his essay "Tragedy, History and Ideology," in which he compares and contrasts a bourgeois play by Wole Soyinka *(Death and the King's Horseman)* with Hussein's play:

> Kinjeketile used the Maji myth to unite the divided peoples and to instill a spirit of resistance in them. But having done that he then secularizes the myth by founding it on the bedrock of practical and military realities. It then remains for Kinjeketile to articulate, albeit in tragic recognition, the inevitable transcendence of the myth as an irreversible process of struggle and history.[51]

The use of myth and symbol to fight an invader is clearly seen as what it is: a myth. But precisely through the failure of the myth to fight German colonialism, reality breaks in with its demand to unify and to organize. A word is merely a word. For some time, it can function to wake people up. But then the necessity of the fight will become clear. Kinjeketile during his trial formulated this essence when he said:

> A word has been born. Our children will tell their children about this word. Our great-grandchildren will hear of it. One day the word will cease to be a dream, it will be a reality! (p. 53)

Slightly to the North of Tanzania, another East African writer has tried to come to terms with Germany. This time, the genre is not a "realist or socialist African historical tragedy" (Biodun Jeyifo on *Kinjeketile*) but a novel. And its events do not take place in the past, but in the present. *Sunset on the Manyatta* (1974) by the Kenyan Masai writer Kenneth Watene is the story of Harry Nylo ole Kantai ole Syambu. Harry grows from a tribal Masai *maran* (youth/warrior), and passes through schools in the plains, unrespected work in Nairobi, and, finally, training in Germany as an automobile factory engineer, into an adult ready to take on the problems of Kenya's new independence. It is the familiar African "been-to" story, with the difference that the place the protagonist has been to is Germany. We are mostly concerned with what will function as the turning point and politicization in the life of this young Masai: namely, his stay in Germany, where he first fancies himself "an unofficial ambassador from the new-born sovereignty."[52]

Harry lives in a small German village with some other Africans. He quickly becomes alienated by people's reaction to blacks; "their unconcealed curiosity makes him uncomfortable" (p. 133). Children run in fear to their parents at his appearance. Racial insults then lead him to Pan-African awareness. "And Harry, for the first time, saw Africa against the world" (p. 136). He is slowly becoming politicized, but only in an isolated, individual sense. The few Africans around him are united in bitterness, "aggravated by the continuous rain and snow" (p. 138). Harry moves on to work in a factory in the north in an even smaller, even colder village. The old couple he lives with is naïve but kind. They wonder if Africans defecate like Germans, and if their blood is red. Encountering more real as well as imagined prejudice, Harry writes to a former girlfriend in Africa about the Germans he has so far encountered:

> It is curious, but they seem to belong to no one except themselves and their country. Anything that does not surpass their expectations is something to mock at, to jeer at, to abuse and even, at times, to violate. Ever since I came here, I have not met a humble heart. There seems to be a mocking turn of the lip in every one of them. (p. 143)

One day Harry is invited to see a film about Africa. He is "almost delighted" (p. 158) until he hears the familiar clichés in the commentary:

> This is Africa...where the sun rises every morning beneath gentle mountains, where the virgin forests stretch and animals roam the plains in freedom, etc., etc. (p. 156)

Harry shuts his ears. "He rose to his feet. 'Rubbish!' he shouted, 'Rubbish' " (p. 160).

To another friend he writes, "I am living malice" (p. 156), after he has struck a child in a group of boys that taunted him. The only unifying experience he has is with a fat and lonely German girl. While making love, they become people without color. But Harry's sense of isolation does not permit him to open up to anyone and his attempt at sexual union with a whore who says, "Europe is cold, hard, and cruel. I want to go with you to sunny Africa and live there with my darling sonny boy" (p. 166), leads him to withdraw totally from the company of others. As the end of his stay in Germany approaches, Harry looks forward to Africa. He realizes, slowly and painfully, that he has had the opportunity to see his country and culture from the outside. Before leaving, he writes in his diary: "When I look at them from my own world, they seem to be some big, naughty children that will stop at nothing to satisfy their curiosity" (p. 244). At home again, his initial happiness turns to bitterness because he has no identity in Africa, either. He adorns his house with the symbols of his old self, the Masai spear and the Masai shield, along with books ranging from philosophy to engineering. His future wife is a nurse devoted to social work; Harry himself turns to writing. Reflecting upon his past experience, he states:

> Poverty...shapes the dreams of a million lives. The rich continue to get richer. Bitterness and jealousy increase every day of the year, and violence threatens the delicate structure of our society. (p. 263)

He now acts out his realization that "it is not a matter of returning into the past, but looking forward into the future with the eyes of the past, strengthened by the wisdom gained through time and inherited from the blood of our forefathers" (p. 260-61). As the novel ends, Harry abandons his Christian name and plans to purchase the largest Swahili dictionary available.

The experience of Germany here functions as a catalyst for awareness: that is, almost as the experience of the Third World has functioned for some First and Second World writers to raise their consciousness. In this overall process of solidarity and consciousness-raising which goes far beyond imagology and geo-thematics, and most certainly beyond what comparatists have called influence studies, two other African writers have to be mentioned who do not merely reflect their experience as been-to's—Alioum Fantouré of Guinea and Ngugi wa Thiong'o from Kenya. Their interest in a German writer, Bertolt Brecht, is not an attempt to emulate Brecht, to borrow from a European writer, but a clear case of political solidarity.

Brecht has had a significant reception in recent years in an African literary context. It is interesting to observe that his plays became influential largely in a bourgeois context (e.g., Soyinka's *Opera Wonyosi*), while his poetry became relevant for, and is frequently cited by, progressive writers such as Fantouré and Ngugi. Brecht's political aesthetics, however, can be seen as the most important background for a nascent African literary criticism.[53] This increasing dialogue with Brecht should not be misconstrued as an example of literary influence or a return to Eurocentric models. It is rather a dialogue in solidarity, an expression of the awareness that class-consciousness is replacing ethnicity.

Fantouré uses a Brecht poem[54] in a very striking way in his novel *Le Cercle des Tropiques*. In a fictitious, but all too real, postindependence country, Les Marigots du Sud, people get more and more intimidated in an Idi Amin–like situation of horror and neocolonialism. In the middle of excessive repression, a young boy distributes leaflets of a poem entitled "Ballad of the Trouble-Maker in a Zinc Coffin" (from the 1934 collection *Lieder Gedichte Chöre* by Brecht). Nothing, apparently, can shock a tyrant more than being mocked in literature. Culture—real culture, not media culture— is anathema to fascism. Fantouré tells us that the Messíah-Koí, the ruler of the fictitious African country in a state of siege, "was said to have had a blackout after reading the poem."[55] He demands the head of the poet, oblivious to the fact that no Bertolt Brecht is living in Les Marigots du Sud. Three days later, a boy of sixteen is arrested as the culprit and shot publicly. The violence escalates, but eventually the tyrant falls. Brecht—or rather, a Brechtian poem (in other words, literature, German literature)—functions as a catalyst to unify, indeed radicalize, the people. Seldom, particularly in an African context, has so much power been allotted a poem by a foreigner.

Ngugi wa Thiong'o, while not directly using either Germany or Brecht in his literary work, is constantly making references to Brecht in his critical writings. In his latest collection of essays, *Barrel of a Pen,* he quotes a Brecht poem to describe the fear tyrants have of writers, and implicitly postulates the latter's task:

> Driven by anxiety
> They break into homes and search the lavatories
> And it is anxiety
> That makes them burn whole libraries. Thus
> Fear rules not only those who are ruled, but
> The rulers, too.[56]

In this collection, Ngugi also spells out the European writer's task as follows:

> He must expose to his European audience the naked reality of the relationship between Europe and the Third World. He has to show to his European reader that, to paraphrase Brecht, the water he drinks is often taken from the mouths

of the thirsty in the Third World, and the food he eats is snatched from the mouths of the hungry in Asia, Africa and South America.[57]

The increasing interest in Brecht, as well as the use of Brecht to affirm one's class position, must certainly be seen as part of that recent treatment of Germany in Africa which parallels the reversal of the image of Africa in German literature.

The ten authors here discussed show us four major developments. 1) A significant change has taken place in the treatment of Africa in German literature since the late 1960s. Formerly exotic treatments give way to the new theme: oppressor vs. oppressed. 2) For the first time, Germany has been treated by African writers since the 1970s. 3) The enormous interest in Brecht as an expression of solidarity coincides with the change and reversal of the Africa theme in Germany. 4) Historical plays and documentary novels (more so than poetry) are the appropriate genres, both in Africa and in Germany, for a literature which liberates itself from colonialism and its by-products, literariness and exoticism. In Africa as well as in Germany, literature tries to become "useful" and politically relevant.

Geo-thematics thus conceived provides a momentous expansion of the "discipline" of Comparative Literature, going beyond both the former French school and even the imagology of the Aachen school. Most important, however, it strongly and firmly militates against the parochialism and literary reductionism of the American school. Furthermore, geo-thematics goes beyond the narrow notion of "masterpieces" (since reflections are seldom found in "mainstream" texts) and also beyond a formalistic concept of modernism. It opens up to the task we all should confront: namely, an understanding through literature of the problems of the Third World and, through such an understanding, an awareness that the problems of the Third World are ours as well. It provokes not only solidarity with the "wretched of the earth" (Fanon) but leads to "conscienticisation" (Freire) and to skepticism against the beauty normally associated with literature. Former imagology and treatments of Africa were most frequently misplaced beautifications. Literary studies which deal with place, otherness, themes, and images can learn a lot from these words by a Bolivian campesino:

> Ecuador es grande y lindo, dicen: Yo de verdad no creo que sea así. Creo que hay sufrimientos para campesinos, que sufrimos de hambre. Yo no veo nada en favor del pobre.[58]

---

1 My main title alludes to Paul O'Flinn's Marxist popularization *Them and Us in Literature* (London, 1975).
2 Quoted in Hayden Herrera, *Frida: A Biography of Frida Kahlo* (New York, 1983), p. 119: "I

don't particularly like the gringo people. They are boring and they all have faces like unbaked rolls (especially the old women)."

3 Hugo Dyserinck, *Komparatistik: Eine Einführung* (Bonn, 1977), p. 132.

4 Lee Baxandall and Stefan Morawski, eds., *Marx and Engels on Literature and Art* (St. Louis/Milwaukee, 1973), p. 115.

5 Isak Dinesen, *Out of Africa* (New York, 1952), p. 298.

6 Alfred Andersch titled one of his short stories which dealt with Algeria, "Giraffe," by which he meant General de Gaulle; see his *Geister und Leute* (Olten und Freiburg, 1958). This collection of short stories also includes "Weltreise" with its—for German literature—relatively rare Namibia references.

7 Joyce Cary, *Mister Johnson;* quoted in Michael J. C. Echeruo, *Joyce Cary and the Novel of Africa* (London, 1973), p. 125.

8 Martin Steins, *Das Bild des Schwarzen in der europäischen Kolonialliteratur 1870–1918: Ein Beitrag zur literarischen Imagologie* (Frankfurt, 1972), p. 16.

9 Joseph Conrad, *Heart of Darkness* (New York, 1971), p. 16.

10 Echeruo, *Joyce Cary,* p. 1.

11 Walter Rodney, *How Europe Underdeveloped Africa* (London and Dar es Salaam, 1972).

12 Dinesen, *Out of Africa,* pp. 304–5.

13 Ngugi wa Thiong'o, *Barrel of a Pen: Resistance to Repression in Neo-Colonial Kenya* (Trenton, N.J., 1983), p. 63.

14 Emmanuel Obiechina, " 'Through the Jungle Dimly': European Novelists on West Africa," *Literary Studies* 1 (Fall 1970): 115.

15 Dorothy Hammond, Alta Jablow, " 'The Africa' in Western Literature," *Africa Today* 8 (1981): 13.

16 Ibid.

17 Henry Remak as quoted in Steins, *Das Bild des Schwarzen,* p. 9.

18 Ed Said, *Orientalism* (New York, 1978). Said states: "But there is no avoiding the fact that even if we disregard the Orientalist distinction between 'them' and 'us,' a powerful series of political and ultimately ideological realities inform scholarship today. No one can escape dealing with, if not the East/West division, then the North/South one, the have/have-not one, the imperialist/anti-imperialist one, the white/colored one. We cannot get around them all by pretending they do not exist" (p. 327).

19 J. M. Carré as cited in Manfred S. Fischer, *Nationale Images als Gegenstand Vergleichender Literaturgeschichte: Untersuchungen zur Entstehung der komparatistischen Imagologie* (Bonn, 1981). An important American summary contribution to the Aachen school of "Imagologie" is Peter Boerner, "National Images and Their Place in Literary Research: Germany as seen by Eighteenth-Century French and English Reading Audiences," *Monatshefte* 67 (1975): 358–70.

20 Dyserinck, *Komparatistik,* p. 133.

21 Fischer, *Nationale Images,* p. 163.

22 Paulo Freire, *Pedagogy of the Oppressed* (New York, 1968), p. 86.

23 Ibid., p. 93.

24 Tété-Michael Kpomassie, *An African in Greenland* (New York, 1983).

25 Willfried F. Feuser states: "...doch scheint mir insbesondere im Hinblick auf die deutsche Literatur...ein konstantes Afrikabild mit rein negativen Zügen...im Ablauf der Jahrhunderte nicht gegeben"; see his "Das Bild des Afrikaners in der deutschen Literatur," in *Akten des V. Internationalen Germanisten-Kongresses, Cambridge 1975* (Bern, 1976), p. 306.

26 Ibid., p. 308.

27 Echeruo, *Joyce Cary,* p. 1.

28 For this and the following two quotations, see Ingeborg Bachmann, "Liebe: Dunkler Erdteil," *Akzente* 6 (1957): 494.

29 Rolf Dieter Brinkmann, "die afrikanische," *Akzente* 1 (1971): 3–4 (pagination for further citations in the text).

30 Friedrich Christian Delius, *Ein Bankier auf der Flucht: Gedichte und Reisebilder* (Berlin, 1975), p. 64 (pagination for further citations in the text).

31 Walter Abish, *Alphabetical Africa* (New York, n.d.), p. 1 (pagination for further citations in the text).

32 Feuser, p. 314.

33 Peter Weiss, *Gesang vom Lusitanischen Popanz.* Mit Materialien (Frankfurt, 1974), p. 74.

34 Peter Weiss, *Rapporte 2* (Frankfurt, 1971), pp. 98–99.

35 Manfred Haiduk, *Der Dramatiker Peter Weiss* (Berlin, 1977).

36 Weiss, *Gesang,* p. 74.

37 Rüdiger Sareika, *Die Dritte Welt in der westdeutschen Literatur der sechziger Jahre* (Frankfurt, 1980), p. 200.

38 Weiss, *Gesang,* p. 12.

39 Peter Nazareth, *The Third World Writer: His Social Responsibility* (Nairobi, 1978), p. xxi. For a further definitional study on Third World Literature, see my "Blake, Neruda, Ngugi wa Thiong'o: Issues in Third World Literature," *Comparative Literature Studies* (forthcoming).

40 Weiss, *Gesang,* p. 12.

41 Sareika, *Die Dritte Welt,* p. 215.

42 Uwe Timm, *Morenga* (Reinbek, 1983), p. 27 (pagination for further citations in the text).

43 See Georg M. Gugelberger, ed., *Hendrik Witbooi: Freedom for Namibia* (Lagos, 1982), and *Nama/Namibia: Diary and Letters of Nama Chief Hendrik Witbooi, 1884-1894* (Boston, 1984).

44 Sareika, *Die Dritte Welt,* p. 284.

45 Bertolt Brecht, *Poems 1913-1956* (New York and London, 1976), p. 344.

46 Ursula Reinhold, "Interview mit Uwe Timm," *Weimarer Beiträge* 7 (1976): 64.

47 Jens Jahn, ed., *Colon: Das schwarze Bild vom weißen Mann* (München, 1983), p. 16.

48 G. C. K. Gwassa, John Iliffe (eds.), *Records of the Maji-Maji Rising* (Dar es Salaam, 1968), p. 3.

49 Ibid., p. 4.

50 Ebrahim N. Hussein, *Kinjeketile* (London and Dar es Salaam, 1970), p. vii (pagination for further citations in the text).

51 Biodun Jeyifo, "Tragedy, History and Ideology," in Georg M. Gugelberger, ed., *Marxism and African Literature* (London, 1985), p. 105.

52 Kenneth Watene, *Sunset on the Manyatta* (Nairobi, 1974), p. 126 (pagination for further citations in the text).

53 See my "Beyond Neo-Tarzanism and Ogunism: Marxist Aesthetics (Lukács vs. Brecht) and Their Relevance to African Literary Criticism," in *Proceedings of the 23rd Meeting of the African Studies Association* (Waltham, Mass., 1981); also, see Edith Ihekweazu, "Brecht-Rezeption in Afrika: Die Adoption von Lehrstück und Parabelstück im zeitgenössischen afrikanischen Theater," *Monatshefte* 57 (Spring 1983): 25–45.

54 Alioum Fantouré, *Le Cercle des Tropiques* (Paris, 1972); English edition: *Tropical Circle,* trans. by Dorothy S. Blair (London, 1981). For an extensive treatment of Brecht and Fantouré, see my "Solidarity, Not Influence: An African Novelistic Incorporation of Brecht's 'Ballad of the Trouble-Maker in the Zinc Coffin'," *Monatshefte* (forthcoming).

55 Fantouré, *Tropical Circle,* p. 183.

56 Ngugi wa Thiong'o, *Barrel of a Pen,* p. 69. This collection of essays is full of references to Brecht, even more so than Ngugi's previous *Writers in Politics* (London, 1981).

57 Ibid., p. 74.

58 Juan Chimbo's introduction to Jorge Sanjinés y grupo ukaman, *Teoría y práctica de un cine junto al pueblo* (Mexico, 1980), p. 10.

Blacks in Germany and German Blacks:
A Little-Known Aspect of Black History

ROSEMARIE K. LESTER

It's not the color of the skin that counts, but the person within. A statement like that comes easy to the enlightened citizen of the Federal Republic of Germany—until the girl next door shows up with a black husband!

Thus, in 1972, West Germany's best known illustrated weekly, *Stern,* introduced a serial feature about German women who had married African or American blacks.[1] 1972 was the year of the Olympic games in Munich and the series was well timed to remind people of latent as well as open racism in their own society—at a time when the beautiful myth of international peace and understanding through sports was very much in the public consciousness. The interviews in this series, which was entitled "My Son-in-law the Negro," were accentuated by one leitmotif: "I have nothing against Negroes—but what are the neighbors going to say?"

He'd pay a fortune if he could find a "whitener" for his black son-in-law, declared a wealthy businessman. He, too, has nothing against blacks, but miscegenation was simply against his principles. Said he: "After all, the animals don't mate outside of their race, either!" Nurse Elke B. had no problems with her family when she decided to marry an African. But things were not so good at her place of work. "We can't have whores around here who spend their time in niggerbars," she was told by the pastor of her nurses' association; and the mother superior at the hospital where she worked hissed, with a sidelong glance at Elke's obvious pregnancy: "Such children shouldn't even be born."[2]

Alas—by December of 1951, roughly three thousand of "such children" had been born by German women.[3] Their fathers were black members of the American occupation forces; and when the first several hundred of them entered grade school in 1952, a tiny but very visible new minority—an indigenous colored minority—stepped into the public eye of this formerly all-white society, to be met almost immediately by a new variety of racist sentiment.

But perhaps not so new, after all. There had been black occupation troops in Germany once before, though not American. From 1919 to 1923, in the course of enforcing conditions of the Versailles Treaty after the First

World War, sizable contingents of French colonial troops from North Africa, Madagascar, and the Senegal were stationed in the left Rhenish areas and briefly in Mainz and Frankfurt: a fact that so incensed racial feelings of Europeans as well as white Americans that it soon ballooned into an international scandal under the catchword *Die schwarze Schmach* ("The Black Disgrace"). In his study "The 'Black Horror on the Rhine': Race as a Factor in Post–World War I Diplomacy," historian Keith L. Nelson writes:

> Originally, the French had begun the process by assigning Africans to the occupation at least in part in order to demonstrate to the enemy the extent of his defeat. Before long, the Germans had retaliated with a concerted propaganda effort, attempting to utilize the "black horror on the Rhine" to discredit France and the occupation in the eyes of the "civilized" world.[4]

It was not hard to predict that the Germans would receive support in this matter, as an American liaison officer pointed out to a French colleague:

> One or two cases of rape committed by your Blacks on the German women well advertised in the Southern states of America where there are very definite views with regard to the Blackmen would likely greatly reduce the esteem in which the French are held.

He was right, of course. There were rapes; there were great economic hardships caused by the demands of the occupation; and there was a good deal of voluntary fraternization. But German pamphlets of protest (a few of them bordering on the pornographic) focused almost entirely on the theme of sexual abuse. The most popular ones were translated into six major languages—and Esperanto. Encouragement for the Germans came from France, Italy, England, Sweden, and the United States, where at one point, during Harding's election campaign, word went out that one ought to vote for him because "he'd do his best to get those niggers out of Germany." Not without interest in this context, however, was a letter written by Germany's Foreign Minister Dr. Adolf Koester to the French military government in which he pleads, "we would gladly accept the inferior discipline of your white soldiers if you would only rid us of this black plague."[5] And Germany's famous satirical weekly *Simplicissimus* commented on the situation in its own way (plates 1 and 2).

While German nationalists played the theme of racial and cultural pollution to the hilt, a few moderate and liberal elements in the *Reichstag* tried in vain to put things into proportion. In May of 1920, one scrappy delegate of the USPD *(Unabhängige Sozialdemokratische Partei Deutschlands),* Luise Zietz, dared to point out the hypocrisy of those who (quite rightly) condemned rapes and brutalities of the colonial soldiers but did not find a word of protest for the same kind of outrage committed by German *Freikorps* members against German women, nor, for that matter, by German troops in the colonies. And after a spirited attack on militarism as being the first

Plate 1. Down with International Peace, cover from *Simplicissimus* 52 (24 March 1920). Spring is not allowed to enter Germany until peace conditions are fulfilled to the letter.

cause for the brutalization of human beings, she closed by calling German colonial politics a "history of atrocities and oppression of colored peoples by the Germans."[6] Needless to say, her contribution was not appreciated; and *Simplicissimus* promptly dedicated a poem to her—right beneath one of the nastier depictions of blacks in Germany at the time (plate 3).

Meanwhile, the French were busy refuting all accusations of ceaseless rape, murder, and mayhem, collecting favorable testimonials on behalf of the African troops from German clergy, mayors, innkeepers, and publishing favorable letters written by ordinary citizens—as well as love letters to black soldiers written by German women. The caricature from *Le Rire* points to the direction their arguments tended to take (plate 4).

Plate 2. Justice in the Ruhr Region, cover from *Simplicissimus* 9 (28 May 1923). Oh, Judgement, thou hast fled to the stupid beast!

Ultimately, President Woodrow Wilson was compelled by angry citizens' letters to order a formal inquiry into the matter, and both the American commissioner in Berlin, Dressel, and the American commander in Coblenz, General Henry T. Allen, submitted detailed reports that included figures and data showing that much of the German claims was wildly exaggerated and, in part, pure fiction.[7] Interestingly, though the report was written in 1920, it was not made public until 1923.

To be sure, there were incidents of sexual abuse as well as a number of murders. And any attempt at objectivity must not be construed as even the slightest apology for, or justification of, rape or murder. However, at the

Die fchwarze Befaßung

Eine Schmach für die weiße Raſſe — aber es geſchieht in Deutſchland.

Plate 3. Black Occupation, cover from *Simplicissimus* 11 (21 May 1920). A disgrace for the white race—but it is happening in Germany.

core of the controversy was something else. The anonymous writer of an essay in a widely distributed pamphlet by the Rhenish Women's League, *Colored French Troops on the Rhine,* states it quite clearly:

> It is not the behavior of the colonial soldiers that causes the greatest and most
> righteous indignation. It is rather the circumstance of...one civilized Euro-
> pean nation, actuated by the fiendish desire to humiliate...letting loose on an-
> other civilized European nation a mercenary host recruited from a semi-savage
> and far inferior race with which to attain its horrible ends.[8]

All in all, it can safely be said that the African blacks in Germany at that

Infamie

Plate 4. Infamy, from *Le Rire* (10 July 1920). We wanted to guard an
eagle; instead, we have to fend off a pig.

time were misused by both sides, the German as well as the French, for political propaganda purposes (plate 5).

The number of racially mixed children from that occupation is estimated to have been no more than five hundred or so; nothing was known
about them until 1979 when historian Reiner Pommerin brought out his
book *Sterilization of the Rhineland Bastards: The Fate of a Colored German
Minority, 1918–1937.*[9] Pommerin had come upon secret documents in the ar-

An das Weltgewissen

(Karl Arnold)

Über das Märchen von den abgehackten Kinderhänden hat sich die ganze Welt entrüstet. Aber die Wahr-
findet taube Ohren.

Plate 5. To the World's Conscience, cover from *Simplicissimus* 45 (5 February 1923). The world was outraged over fairy tales about hacked-off children's hands. But the truth fell on deaf ears.

chives of the German Department of State from the time of the Nazi regime, documents which revealed that in 1937, secretly, and after considerable pressure had been put on the mothers by the Gestapo, sterilizations had been performed on 385 of these officially so registered "Rhineland Bastards." The papers also revealed that similar actions had already been considered in the 1920s. The proposals were ultimately rejected by the commissioner in charge of the occupied zone, who decided—"bastard or no bastard"—the children were, after all, legally German. Yet the tirade of one Dr. F. Rosenberger in the *Ärztliche Rundschau*—only one of many similar opinions expressed by German physicians—demonstrates that the concept of "racial hygiene" that was to become so important for the Nazis was already in full bloom at the time, ready for the picking:

> Shall we tolerate...that in future, instead of enjoying the cheery songs of White, handsome, well-built, mentally superior, lively and healthy Germans along the Rhine, we shall hear the croaking sounds of gray-mottled, low-browed, wide-snouted, half animalistic, syphilitic mulattoes?[10]

The situation after 1945 is hardly comparable to that of the Rhineland occupation. As a matter of fact, immediately after the end of World War II, relations between black American troops and civilian population were quite good. Open expressions of racial hatred were taboo, anyway, in view of Germany's recent history; and the special generosity of the black Americans with the treasures of PX and commissary, the shopping centers for the military, went a long way in advancing good human relationships. There is no doubt at all that black Americans, an oppressed minority in their own country, showed an especially high degree of friendly helpfulness to those who were now the underdogs, as it were (an observation, incidentally, that one hears almost unanimously from former prisoners of war who were interned in American camps). For quite a number of blacks, this was a first chance for free and easy, unrestricted interaction with whites—and I do not mean sexual encounters only—and contact with Germans was, indeed, looked for and appreciated. All of which becomes even more significant when we recall that segregated army units were not officially dissolved until 1951.

However, as the situation began to stabilize, as the material dependence on the occupation forces lessened, and, particularly, as more of the so-called brown babies were born (in German, they were called "colored occupation children," conferring a double stigma), latent or repressed prejudice began to surface: the mothers were looked down upon, if not ostracized, by Germans and white Americans alike.

To be sure, sympathetic and sentimental stories were printed about the children in the illustrated press as early as 1949. But the fact that these children were labeled "problems" from the start, that dire difficulties were predicted for their future lives, sympathetically yet as a matter of fact, shows clearly that widespread racial discrimination was taken completely for granted. And the following quote from a feature story in *Constanze,* at the time the best known women's magazine, reveals involuntarily how dearly one would have liked to be rid of the problem:

> Many American Negro families are trying to get permission to adopt one of these children. The requests were always denied up to this point. The children are considered to be German citizens and...are not permitted entry into the USA. Yet they would hardly be conspicuous among the Negro population and would have better chances for the future than here, although the coloreds in the USA are still disadvantaged.[11]

Nor did the famous Albert Schweitzer have any better ideas, who advised a small confessional school for racially mixed children to begin immediately with teaching foreign languages, for most of the children would have to emigrate if they could not "find a home" here, as *Revue* reported in 1955.

In December of 1951, a committee met in the West German parliament to try to disentangle the legal status of all the illegitimate occupation babies—the children had virtually no rights at the time, since the allies were extremely uncooperative in the matter of child support until the late 1950s. During this session, one of the women delegates—a Dr. Rehling (CDU)— remarked: "The officials have long been searching for ways to do right by these racially mixed children *for whom not even the climate in this country is suitable*" (my emphasis). Public attention, she continued, must be directed toward this problem, but not as was done during a recent carnival parade in a large Rhenish city. One of the floats there carried large signs with the legend "made in Germany." On the float, there stood German children made up in black-face. The delegate closed her presentation with the remark that here would be a chance for Germans to atone at least in part for the guilt which the Nazi regime had heaped upon Germany with its racism.[12]

Rehling's report contains in a nutshell the three major elements that make up the attitude of many, if not all, West Germans toward blacks yet today: a truly abysmal ignorance (the climate); a deep-seated, mostly unreflected racism (the float is only one of its manifestations under the popular guise of "just fun"); and a fair amount of good will, sometimes stemming from a guilty conscience (the reference to the Nazi regime).

In the 1950s and early 1960s, a number of research reports and pamphlets directed at teachers, social workers, and concerned parents were published whose intent it was to make people aware of the very special problems of the dark-skinned Germans in their midst, how they lived, and how hard their mothers often had to struggle. The most voluminous one, *Farbige Kinder in Deutschland* ("Colored Children in Germany") came out in 1961, at a time when the youngsters were about to reach puberty and would be in need of job training, higher education, etc.[13] It was a thoughtful and thorough analysis conducted by the Department of Psychology of the University of Hamburg under the direction of Klaus Eyferth. One of its special merits was that it did away with many popular misconceptions. It showed, for example, that only a tiny minority of the women was willing to give up their racially mixed child (9 percent of the Eyferth study); instead, there was rather a tendency to be overly protective. It also showed that the mothers came from all walks of life (though lower-class women predominated) and not, as was commonly assumed, only from the "dregs of society"; and that young women with an upper-middle-class background often were rejected most harshly by family and neighborhood. The sacrifices many of these mothers had to make were tremendous; not a few of them gave up marriage prospects if a white man would only marry under the condition she give up her colored child. All of the studies stressed, again contrary to popular notions, that there was no difference in learning capacity or intelligence between the white and non-white children. But for all of the racially mixed children, the discovery of being irrevocably "different" had been the first serious trauma, and desperate efforts to scrub the skin white were quite common. One medical study showed a high incidence of skin disease among children in homes where personnel were unwilling or untrained to fulfill the special emotional needs of the "brown babies."[14]

But studies like these never reach as large an audience as do the popular media and, in particular, the so-called topical illustrated weeklies—such as *Stern, Bunte, Quick, Neue Revue*—that reach well over 50 percent of the West German reading public. These magazines are, in fact, important *Meinungsträger* and *Meinungsmacher* (i.e., carriers as well as makers of opinion) and, for large segments of the public, represent major sources of topical information (as well as entertainment, of course).

It is true, these publications also carried human interest stories designed to arouse concern for the racially mixed children; *Revue* at one point launched a project that brought about a number of adoptions—to the United States, incidentally, which then led to another sentimental story. But the very tone of these features, the persistent talk of "sweet little chocolate babies" or worse, "cute little pickaninnies" *(niedliche kleine Negerlein),* at once trivialized the very real social problems and evoked, perhaps unconsciously, old racist clichés. And that was not all. Sometimes in the same issue with such stories, and also as early as 1949, these selfsame magazines were disseminating an image of blacks—African blacks, that is—which was nothing short of a revival of the worst colonialist traditions and, at times, of shades of the *Schwarze Schmach.* During the first decade of decolonization in Africa, the illustrated weeklies provided a running commentary to the events taking place there, under headlines such as "White Man, You Must Die!" (*Münchner Illustrierte,* 1953) or "The Naked and the Red" (*Stern,* 1961), and with interpretations of African complexities that were ever accentuated by the leitmotif "In South Africa, Communist Incited Negroes Bash Their Opponents' Heads In!" (*Quick,* 1951). The arrogant tone of the texts left no doubt as to what one was to think of African aspirations to independence; for instance, the pictorial commentary to the first elections in French Equatorial Africa began:

> On the way to the jungle elections: Naked and piggy-back, like this black beauty from Ubangi—that has got to be the *dernier cri* to motivate reluctant voters. (*Münchner Illustrierte,* 1953)

And those evergreens of German "humor," cannibal cartoons and grotesque Negro caricatures, enjoyed a remarkable increase in popularity in the 1950s and 1960s (plates 6–8). Feature stories focused on the sensationally exotic, the most unusual, and, if possible, bloody ethnic rituals, or ridiculed African dress and hair styles. And at a time when Britain was about to have to let go of her colonies—the so-called Mau Mau uprising began in 1951—lengthy illustrated reports revived the "good old days" of German colonialism, and General von Lettow-Vorbeck and his faithful Askaris relived their heroic deeds for months on end.[15] Noticeable from the start was, in all of these features, an open and strong show of sympathy with the old friend and business partner South Africa. And, in addition, six novels published in serial form between 1953 and 1961 took up the African theme, reviving the worst of colonialist clichés, now enriched, during the height of the cold war (and the influence of the Hallstein doctrine) by the specter of the "red blacks."[16]

This digression illustrates that the negative Africa imagery, the cheaply ironic language used to describe everything African (and that meant, black), the viciously racist cartoons—all that pervaded the popular printed media (all the more important in the 1950s since TV was still in its infancy)—was still present in school books as well as in children's and young people's literature (research in those areas did not begin in earnest until the early 1970s): and, consequently, was very much part of public consciousness during the time in which the black Germans were taking their first steps into society.

The year 1952 was virtually the year of the black Germans. As the first (approximately) five hundred of them entered public school, the popular press was never far behind. Cartoonist Brinkmann gave his comic strip hero Herbert, a kind of German Dennis the Menace at that time, an adopted black sister for about a year (plate 9). The Number One on the hit parade of the NDR (North German Radio) was a schmaltzy tune entitled "Mach nicht so traurige Augen, weil du ein Negerlein bist" ("Don't make such sad eyes because you are a little pickaninny"), sung by a black teenager, Leila Negra. And public sympathy reached an all-time high with the release of the movie *Toxi,* the story of a "chocolate brown" youngster, placed at the doorstep of a wealthy German family. Toxi was played by Elfie Fiegert, daughter of a black GI and a German woman, a talented and charming five-year-old who at another time and in another place might have become a brown Shirley Temple. The story was pure soap opera—and tremendously successful pre-

Plate 6. Cartoon from *Neue Illustrierte* 19 (7 May 1955), p. 28. "How long do you have to wear black?"

Plate 7. Advertisement for suntan lotion from *Stern* 30 (23 July 1960), p. 66. Not he...but we need Tschamba-fii...

cisely because it sugar-coated and simplified the issues completely. After Toxi melts the heart of even the most hard-nosed racist in her involuntary German foster family, along comes rich and handsome daddy Al Hoosman (a well-known black actor at the time) clear across the ocean to sweep up his little daughter who immediately and happily takes off for the United States with him. And thus relieves the German family of any responsibility.

"Oh mommy, why can't I be a little brown girl like that," a German youngster was overheard to say coming out of the movie theater. And that, commented one critic, said more about the movie than he could have writ-

Plate 8. Cartoon from *Deutsche Illustrierte* 50 (13 December 1952), p. 1566. "Thanks for letting me go, Chief—and enjoy your dinner."

Plate 9. Comic strip from *Revue* 15 (12 April 1952), p. 48. Herbert—now with his adopted little sister.

ten in two newspaper columns. The film's total lack of sensitivity to the many forms of "everyday racism" pervading West German society reveals itself most strikingly in one key episode. A young man obviously intended to be a positive identification figure (he is about to get married and wants to adopt Toxi) finds fame and success as a commercial artist by creating a huge poster of Toxi—advertising chocolate.

Still, a critique of popular culture must never forget the recipient. Some time ago, I participated as a speaker in the annual workshop for Parents of Black Children held by the Frankfurt Ecumenical Center. Several black Germans present vividly remembered the movie, which they had seen as seven- or eight-year-olds. They all agree as to how deeply the film had moved them, how they had cried over Toxi—but with a feeling of relief at being able to cry about themselves, in public. Of course, all of them also remembered how much they all wanted a cute little white fur coat, just like Toxi's. In any case, *Toxi* became synonymous with "colored occupation child" for the next two decades.

In the early 1960s, the oldest of the "sweet little chocolate babies"— whose curly heads were often patted by complete strangers on the street "like little poodles," as one embittered mother reports—then reached the age when it was time to make decisions about the future, and job training, higher education, and, of course, love and partnerships became major concerns. A job or vocation might perhaps be the only thing to help these young people overcome personal disappointments, speculated a vocational counselor, because "there will be massive protests if the son of the local paint shop owner or postmaster suddenly wants to marry a curly-headed, dark-skinned girl," as he predicted.[17]

But schooling and job training presented more problems. As was pointed out in one television documentary some years later, "society gets rid of its unwanted quite easily by sending all too many of the racially mixed children into the ghetto of the *Sonderschulen*"—a not very well reputed special education program— "even in cases where an above average IQ had been determined."[18] The reason: behavioral difficulties—generally caused by society itself. Thus an unreasonably high percentage of the black Germans tended to remain in the lower social strata. Though matters have improved somewhat in the past decade or so, certain positions requiring public contact are still not open to dark-skinned people; there is, after all, no Affirmative Action or EOC in the Federal Republic. On the other hand, as "attractive for our guests," the foster son of a Frankfurt woman was quite welcome to work in a spa in the Black Forest, and a jewelry shop at a seashore resort was willing to hire one of her black foster daughters for the same reason.[19] One thing soon became clear: The well-known American saying, "I have nothing against Negroes, but would you like your daughter to marry one?" applied to West Germany as well. "Everybody wants to sleep with me—but no one wants to marry me," was the sad refrain of many interviews with those young women—and certain magazines just loved to expound upon that subject.[20]

At this point, black Germans—at least those of the female sex— became interesting to popular literature. Two novels—*Meine schwarze Schwester* ("My Black Sister," 1961) and *Mach mich weiß, Mutti* ("Make Me White, Mommie," 1963)—were published in serial form before the books came out.[21] There are similarities between them. Both protagonists, twelve-year-old Gisela and eighteen-year-old Harriett-Rose, are the result of a rape. Both fathers come to Germany when they learn about their daughters, hoping to take them to the United States with them. But, unlike Toxi, both girls remain in Germany; after an inane double suicide attempt, Harriett-Rose's plight dissolves in a weepy happy end, and Gisela's German stepfather learns to cope with societal discrimination and his own unreflected racist feelings more honestly, though not until Gisela runs away from home and also attempts suicide.

Make Me White could be dismissed as altogether too inconsequential for discussion, were it not for the depiction of the rapist father. A flashback to the Germany of 1945 shows him to be a friendly simple soul (the popular stereotype of the utterly naïve black giant) who one night rapes a young woman who had been coming to the American mess hall, hungry and fascinated—he rapes her, overwhelmed by whiskey and the heady feeling of no longer living in a country where he might risk his neck for merely whistling at a white woman. The reference was not accidental: This was 1963 and, some years back, the Emmett Till case had made German headlines, too. By now, the West German press had begun to focus increasingly on the Civil Rights issues in the United States, at first following the nonviolent phase of Martin Luther King's movement with a fair amount of sympathy (if slipshod research). The honeymoon was over, however, as soon as blacks began to assert themselves, and, particularly, when Black Power came into being. At any rate, the author draws a vivid picture of racial oppression in the man's hometown in Alabama, obviously drawing on material presented in news features and reports. The ex-soldier and his mother ultimately get killed by a white mob—a somewhat underhanded Old Testament punishment for the rapist, one might suspect. But lest German readers forget, the author makes pointed reference to Germany's own recent racist past (which was deleted for the serialized version of the novel, however).

In *Black Sister,* the girl's mother is raped the night armistice is announced and the soldiers break out in wild celebration. The young black GI returns to the woman's house the next day in abject remorse to plead forgiveness—and receives a bloody beating by military police for trying to "fraternize." Much later, when his past catches up with him, he is portrayed as a responsible loving family man who has long suffered pangs of guilt and is eager to atone for his wrong.

All in all, *Black Sister* presents a surprising number of believable characters and conflicts—all of which one could easily find documented in the Eyferth report and similar studies. What the author does with this material, however, ultimately conforms to the requirements of popular magazine fiction: she takes the edge off. One example may stand for many here. When a classmate who "hates" Gisela's skin pulls a particularly nasty trick on her, she does so, it turns out later, because she has lived in the Congo where "men with black skin" had brutalized her family. And in 1961, the papers were overflowing with gore from one Congo crisis after another.

Still, readers' reactions in the form of spirited letters to the editor in reference to *Black Sister,* at least revealed that the novel was taken quite seriously. About half of the letters hurled contempt at "such women" who threw themselves at "black or white occupation soldiers" and later claimed to have been raped—comments which serve to illustrate once again the close relationship between racism and sexism. Conversely, three of the black Germans from the workshop mentioned earlier had read the novel and felt that it represented their problems quite well. At any rate, *My Black Sister* is still a steady seller, now in its third paperback printing.

The question remains: why did the black fathers have to be rapists when, contrary to the time of the *Schwarze Schmach,* rape had never been an issue after the Second World War (save for one spectacular gang rape for which several black soldiers were court-martialed and given life sentences)?[22] The answer lies within the medium itself, I believe. The *Illustriertenroman* ("serial novel"), an important selling point for a magazine, is a veritable seismograph of contemporary moods and mores, and never ahead of accepted social norms. In the early 1960s, black/white sexual unions (though existing) were not yet a part of the officially (if grudgingly) accepted moral code. Much as in the United States, incidentally, where it took until 1967 for a black to marry a white woman on the screen—Sidney Poitier in *Guess Who's Coming to Dinner*—to gain full sympathy for the black Germans *and* their mothers, there had to be an extraordinary excuse for the children's existence. And tears and sympathy the media and their readers had been willing to give to the new minority all along. Moreover, tearful sympathy is always a guarantee for popular success—but not the only one, as we shall see presently.

About ten years later, *Praline,* at that time West Germany's favorite soft-porn bourgeois breviary, featured the novel *Mischlingsmädchen Billie* ("Billie the Mulatto Girl"), the story of a sixteen-year-old "colored occupation child."[23] The tale is held together by a loose frame in which a wealthy young man who fancies himself a maverick writer adopts Billie as his little black sister, listens sympathetically to her tales of woe, and recycles them into a novel. A critical one, of course, meant to expose the hypocrisy and immorality of society. Let's take a look:

> There was a magic about this Wilhelmine Schwarze...called Billie for short. Every man who had met her just once could think of nothing else anymore but to possess her. Yet there was not one among them who ever thought of properly courting the pretty young girl with the dark skin, to really win her hand. (No. 18)

With such silver-tongued sympathy the author introduces his hapless heroine. But it is hardly compassion his novel seeks to give rise to. In no less than

48 installments—that's 48 weeks—the barely sixteen-year-old with the symbolic name is literally and figuratively used by more than a like number of German males. A chain reaction is set in motion when some curious chap watches unnoticed—Peeping Tom as identification figure for the reader—who is then mightily moved to be next. Only once is it the black chauffeur of a white gangster who spears the desperately struggling Billie upon his (naturally supersized) penis in a private underwater show, whereupon Billie pulls off her oxygen tank and attempts—what else?—suicide. But in general, says the narrator,

> Billie did not consider these things all too important. She did not enjoy them, to be sure, but they did not bother her very much, either.... Whatever happened to Billie, ultimately it bounced off her happy innocence and did not touch her soul.... Yes, the young colored girl was innocent, and in a way that cannot be measured by traditional standards, because it goes deeper than the merely physical. (No. 19)

What the author is, obviously and hypocritically, alluding to here is the 18th-century idealistic concept of the untouchable moral innocence of nature's child. What he is in fact selling, however, is the colonialist flip side of that image, the justification stereotype of the sexually inexhaustible black woman who, fortunately for the white male, lacks the emotional *Tiefe*, the depth and sensitivity of "civilized" white humanity. It has been well documented in recent years how viciously German colonials, notorious among them Carl Peters, acted upon that premise. But that is the subject of another analysis.[24]

Billie represents a high point in sheer hypocrisy and exploitation of the very real social problems of black Germans. That it was so successful—48 installments are unheard-of for a serial novel—does tell us a great deal about the level of consciousness of its more than a million readers. However, the novel did not exist in a vacuum, as it were. *Praline,* until 1969 a pleasantly entertaining travel and fashion magazine, changed its image almost overnight in 1970 to become the strongest *porno-polit* sheet of the Heinrich Bauer Publishing Company, a house that is second only to Springer in the magazine market, and whose success formula consists of a clever mixture of reactionary politics and medium-soft porn. Throughout the 1950s and 1960s, the Bauer products have held the record for publication of cannibal cartoons; they are still around in the 1980s, from time to time (plates 10 and 11). In the 1970s, features and novels about postcolonial Africa were planted in Bauer's publications at certain critical times, with the obvious function of image making, if not ideological support, in favor of the old and current business partner South Africa. It goes without saying that SWAPO and ANC were always roundly condemned as Moscow-inspired terrorists. An opinion, incidentally, that is held by Franz Josef Strauß and his political followers as well.[25]

In the early 1970s, then, *Praline* became something of a trade journal

Plate 10. Cartoon from *Neue Revue* 27 (27 June 1981), p. 43. "Don't you dare, Karl-Heinz!"

Plate 11. Cartoon from *Praline* 4 (15 January 1981), p. 14. "Bimbo, now take your finger out of the soup!"

for black sex, and Billie appeared as an integral part of a massive onslaught of exotic erotica that did not subside until about 1975. "Human interest" stories in the style of *Billie* were published regularly, richly illustrated with scantily (if at all) clad colored young women. But the most successful feature was the weekly ethno-porno in color, a two-page product entitled "Sexual Customs of Primitive Peoples." These "ethnological reports," mostly set in Africa, were pure invention; but readers apparently loved their black skin-flicks and the series remained a regular feature with *Praline* for seven years.

A last note should be added to this unsavory chapter. In 1978, *Praline* had to change its image once again. The *Bundesprüfstelle für jugendgefähr-dende Schriften* (a commission for the control of publications endangering young people) put the magazine on its index because of too much sexual violence and brutality. Typically, no protest was ever heard against the pervasive racist elements in that publication.

Billie has brought us back to 1972, the chronological starting point of our discussion. Was it an average year for blacks in German culture? There was *Billie,* of course, demonstrating *ex negativo* that racism and sexism make very common bedfellows indeed, while *Stern,* with its fairly honest series about the black sons-in-law, provided facts about racial discrimination in the Federal Republic. Concurrent with both, *Bunte,* one of the four major illustrated weeklies, published the first and only novel whose romantic hero was a male black German. However, this handsome university student Robert Black has been brought up by his father in the United States and comes to Munich to win a gold medal at the 1972 Olympic games *in fiction*—while those games are taking place there *in fact.* A secondary story line tracing back the unhappy love story of Robert's father, the black GI in the Germany of 1946, is intended to serve as a contrast model, as proof that race relations have vastly improved over the years: there is a happy ending for Robert and his German sweetheart.[26]

But not to confuse fact with fiction: *Pardon,* a critical-satirical monthly magazine, featured a thoughtful article about Charly Graf, a young black German who has also struggled his way up into a respectable career in sports—for a while, he was built up as Germany's "brown bomber"—but *his* fiancée was kicked out of her home when he formally came to call on her parents. Not because he was a boxer, no—but "black and white," said her father, was simply an *Unding,* "an impossibility."[27]

That year, a number of angry and intelligent women founded the IAF (*Interessengemeinschaft der mit Ausländern verheirateten Frauen,* an association of German women married to foreigners) in order to provide a sorely needed support system, legal and otherwise, for the growing number of binational and biracial families in the Federal Republic—many of them with a black partner, of course. Threats of violence by phone and mail (the dominant theme was "racial pollution") and abusive treatment at the hands of public officials and, incidentally, not a few physicians had rapidly increased during the preceding years. And meanwhile in a Frankfurt suburb—we are still in 1972—an object lesson was presented in how to teach racist images at an early age. During a school festival under the motto "All the World's Children," the fourth graders had a special treat for their parents: dressed in black tights and sporting big signs with the legend *Schwarzer Neger,* they offered a *Kannibalenimbiß* ("cannibal lunch") from a huge papier maché kettle in the middle of their class room. As they say in the song—"you've got to be carefully taught." That cannibal cartoons and grotesque advertising *Neger* were still around goes without saying.

In 1961, the Eyferth study on *Colored Children in Germany* had come to the following conclusion:

> There is no doubt that the German public is still incapable of assuming an attitude, a way of life, that is free of prejudice....Only a long-range, consistent, and conscious process of education will be able to dissolve that tradition which still lets us believe in the superior worth of our own race.[28]

Today, it must be conceded that this long-range, systematic teaching and learning process has not taken place. The West German establishment culture, which controls most of the institutions, has more or less practiced a hands-off policy in matters of racial discrimination—in part, because the total number of blacks living in Germany (African, American, and German) is estimated to be only about 250,000. That racism is an all-pervasive learned behavior mechanism which needs to be unlearned regardless of whether there be a single member of a discriminated minority in the country: that sort of thinking has never entered into state level curriculum planning, for example.

But since the end of the 1960s, in part as a spin-off from the APO, the so-called extraparliamentary opposition, a kind of "alternative" culture has emerged where a teaching process at the grass-roots level (and admittedly, in bits and pieces) is taking place: in the form of workshops, seminars, and publications for teachers, for the mediators of information, for concerned citizens. In Frankfurt, for example, there exists a standing committee for *Parents of Black Children* sponsored by the Ecumenical Center; a Center for Social Psychology (directed by an African psychologist) tries to take care of the needs of an increasing number of people coming from Third World countries, some of them political asylum seekers; the GEW (*Gewerkschaft Erziehung und Wissenschaft,* a teacher's union) is beginning to hold small workshops dealing with curriculum and teaching materials at various levels—a particularly important area, it seems to me; the IAF mentioned above has been getting more frequent exposure in national newspapers; and of the churches, the "progressive wing" of the EKD, the Protestant Church of Germany, has been extremely supportive—often standing against its own establishment superstructure.

The functioning principle in much of this is still time-tested CR, that is, consciousness-raising; but beyond that—and depending on the target group—there has been a fair amount of critical analysis and theory as to the origins, the function, and the political ramifications of racist imagery and racial discrimination. Important initial impulses for the activities within this "alternative" culture (I am using the term hesitantly for want of a better one) came out of the realm of pedagogy and sociology and, specifically, out of research on the content of schoolbooks and children's and young people's literature—both being vitally important socialization media as well as traditionally neglected areas of criticism—research that unearthed incredible amounts of outdated colonialist misinformation and racist stereotypes and clichés. The two authoritative works are Fohrbeck, Wiesand, and Zahar's *Heile Welt und Dritte Welt,*[29] a detailed analysis of the representation of the Third World in West German geography textbooks, and Jörg Becker's *Alltäglicher Rassismus,* an analysis of children's and young people's literature of compendium scope.[30] Both works (published in 1971 and 1977, respectively) still serve as basic source material for many of the workshops conducted today. And the former, at any rate, is beginning to show some effect on publishing policies. With cautious optimism, we can say that at least in West Germany's 'alternative' culture there appears to be a slow but steady progression from socialization theories toward social action.

It is the artifacts and everyday manifestations of popular culture that tell us most about a society's attitudes and prejudices, because they tend to confirm majority beliefs and values, traditionally quite undisturbed by critical attention.[31] And a close look at blacks in that context reveals that in German everyday popular culture, black is not very beautiful, alas.

1 Eva Windmöller, "Mein Schwiegersohn, der Neger," *Stern* (1972), nos. 33–39. All translations are mine.

2 Quotations from *Stern,* nos. 33 and 34.

3 Hermann Ebeling, "Zum Problem der deutschen Besatzungskinder," *Bildung und Erziehung* 7, no. 10 (1954): 612–30.

4 Keith L. Nelson, " 'The Black Horror on the Rhine': Race as a Factor in Post–World War I Diplomacy," *Journal of Modern History* 42, no. 4 (1970): 606–27.

5 Ibid., p. 616.

6 Martha Mamozai, *Herrenmenschen: Frauen im deutschen Kolonialismus* (Reinbek, 1982), p. 292.

7 Henry T. Allen, *Die Besetzung des Rheinlandes* (Berlin, 1927) and Nelson, p. 616.

8 Rheinische Frauenliga, *Farbige Franzosen am Rhein: Ein Notschrei der deutschen Frauen* (Berlin, 1923).

9 Reiner Pommerin, *Sterilisierung der Rheinlandbastarde: Das Schicksal einer farbigen deutschen Minderheit* (Düsseldorf, 1979).

10 Ibid., p. 24.

11 *Constanze* (1950), no. 17.

12 *Das Parlament* (1951), no. 12.

13 Klaus Eyferth, Ursula Brandt, and Wolfgang Hawel, *Farbige Kinder in Deutschland* (München, 1960). For more details and bibliographical data, see Rosemarie K. Lester, *Trivialneger: Das Bild des Schwarzen im westdeutschen Illustriertenroman* (Stuttgart, 1982), pp. 90–99.

14 Rudolf Sieg, "Häufung von Hautaffektionen bei Mischlingen in Kinderheimen," *Praxis der Kinderpsychologie und Kinderpsychiatrie: Zeitschrift für analytische Kinderpsychologie* (1961): 179–80.

15 The longest series: *Deutsche Illustrierte* (1953), nos. 26–32.

16 For historical details and media analysis, see my *Trivialneger,* pp. 180–273.

17 *Frankfurter Allgemeine Zeitung,* 12 August 1961.

18 Quoted from the television documentary "Mischlinge in Deutschland," televised on 26 December 1971 over ZDF.

19 From an interview with Frau Dr. Lotte Schiffler (former city councillor, and foster mother to seven racially mixed children) conducted in Frankfurt in 1978.

20 The title page of *Jasmin* (1970), no. 21, featured that headline, illustrated by a bare-bosomed young black woman in the embrace of a (half visible) white male.

21 Ursula Schaake, *Meine schwarze Schwester,* in *Revue* (1960), no. 52; (1961), nos. 1–15. Paperback edition (München, 1967). A third edition was published with same company in 1977, under the pseudonym Alexandra Cordes. Stefan Doerner, *Mach mich weiß, Mutti,* in *Quick* (1963), nos. 16–27. Book under the title *Die braune Rose* (Bayreuth, 1963).

22 Cf. the trial report in *Deutsche Illustrierte* (1956), nos. 38–40.

23 Berthold Roedern, *Mischlingsmädchen Billie,* in *Praline* (1971), no. 12 to (1972) no. 8. Numbers in parentheses indicate the issue in which the quotes occurred.

24 Cf. notes 6 and 17 above.

25 As reported in *Das Parlament* of 12 November 1977, Strauß declared in a parliamentary debate on 27 October 1977: "You can say what you want: SWAPO and Patriotic Front are terror organizations and not liberation movements."

26 Richard Kraft (pen name for a team of writers), *Verbotene Liebe,* in *Bunte* (1972), nos. 24–41.

27 Helmut Fritz, "Charly Graf boxt sich nicht durch," *Pardon* (Sept. 1972).

28 Eyferth et al., p. 109.

29 Jörg Becker, *Alltäglicher Rassismus: Die afro-amerikanischen Rassenkonflikte im Kinder- und Jugendbuch der Bundesrepublik* (Frankfurt, 1977).

30 Karla Fohrbeck, Andreas J. Wiesand, and Renate Zahar, *Heile Welt und Dritte Welt: Medien und politischer Unterricht I. Schulbuchanalyse* (Opladen, 1971).

31 Bernard Berelson and Patricia J. Salter, "Majority and Minority Americans: An Analysis of Magazine Fiction," *Public Opinion Quarterly* (Summer 1946): 168–190.

"The Theater of the White Revolution Is Over": The Third World in the Works of Peter Weiss and Heiner Müller

DAVID BATHRICK

The August 1966 issue of the West German periodical *Kursbuch* contained an article by the writer Peter Weiss in which he attacked its editor Hans Magnus Enzensberger for the latter's equivocating stance toward revolutionary struggles in the Third World. In a piece entitled "European Periphery," Enzensberger had set forth an argument which from our vantage point today has become a cliché of global politics. The supposed two-block system dividing the world between East and West, or socialist and capitalist, has given way to a struggle between rich nations and poor, Enzensberger said. European and North American left-wing intellectuals had better realize that their Manichaean notions of international proletarianism no longer grasp the realities of world politics—a world where *all* industrial powers are vying for colonialist gain and spheres of influence, regardless of any ideological pronouncements they might make about fighting for socialism or protecting the Free World. The Third World is the center and Europe now the periphery of the struggles for the future.[1]

Weiss rejected such views as passive and fatalistic. Reaffirming the continued split between the socialist and capitalist camp, he called on Enzensberger to leave his ivory tower of doubt, and to join the proletarian struggle: "I have a question for Enzensberger: when will he . . . be ready to take some risks and state explicitly: I am in solidarity with the oppressed and as an author shall seek all means to support them in their struggle, which is also my struggle."[2] Never one to be outdone in the arena of hyperbole and rhetoric, Enzensberger was quick to excoriate Weiss:

> Unlike the rest of us, Peter Weiss and consorts no longer have anything to do with the society in which they live. They have pulled out. They are standing shoulder to shoulder with the black laborer in the copper mines of Transvaal, with the Asian rice peasants in the fields of Vietnam, with the Peruvian Indian in the Vanadium mine works. But I ask you gentlemen, take a good look in the mirror before you open your mouths again. Is it really a black mine worker who is sitting shoulder to shoulder with you as you swig your beer?[3]

Let us forget for a moment the simplifications and bravado in both men's positions. Beyond the personal, stylistic, and even generational differ-

ences between the ironic *enfant terrible* Enzensberger and the older, more serious Weiss, this clash stands indeed as paradigmatic for the shifts occurring
among many West German intellectuals at that time. The building of the
Berlin Wall in August of 1961, temporarily decathecting East-West confrontation; the increasing self-scrutiny of a younger critical generation because
of the Eichmann trial; and, finally, the emergence of Third World concerns,
first, around Algeria, then, around Vietnam—all served to challenge Western and, in particular, American moral and political hegemony, and led to a
realignment of the basic binary oppositions of postwar thought. Where
once the givens of cold-war Europe had clearly narrowed the framework of
political debate to an unquestioned acceptance of the divisions of Yalta, intellectuals were now led to test such suppositions by questioning the role of
the Federal Republic as part of a larger imperialist alliance. The
Enzensberger-Weiss exchange is perhaps most significant as an example of
two rather apolitical—some might say, esoteric—poets being drawn into the
orbit of world politics at a time of crisis.

Yet let it be emphasized that we are not simply talking about analytical
strategies or political *Weltanschauungen.* Enzensberger's use of the "mirror
image" metaphor, regardless of any conscious Freudian or even Lacanian
implications, raises the much more intriguing question concerning the relation of the Third World as the locus of a new—in some cases, pristine— historical subject to the vital issue of an individual writer's own identity: of
political and national, but also of psychological and aesthetic identity as
well. It is for this reason significant that a number of Germany's most radical playwrights from the East and West have written key plays about, and
centered in, the Third World, and that in each instance the implications of
their choice of subject matter have meant an important political and aesthetic "re-locating" for the writer's development as a whole. Weiss's *The
Song of the Lusitanian Bogey* and *Vietnam Discourse,* Enzensberger's *Hear-
ing in Havana,* Volker Braun's *Che Guevara* and Heiner Müller's *The Mission*
are some of the most important examples that come to mind.

Certainly the central theme in Weiss's early fiction and autobiographical writings is the obsession with identity and homelessness. Born outside
Potsdam in 1916, the son of a Czech-Jewish textile manufacturer, he grew up
in Berlin and Bremen until 1933, after which he began to flee. The family
first emigrated to London, where he studied photography; then to Prague,
where he took up painting; and, finally, via Switzerland on to Stockholm,
where he was to spend the rest of his life as a writer, resident, and citizen—
but, as he himself was often to emphasize, never at home.

Weiss's autobiographical novels *Abschied von den Eltern* ("Departure
from My Parents") and *Fluchtpunkt* ("Vanishing Point") were written in the
early 1960s and dealt with his years in exile up through his thirty-first birthday in 1947. What becomes clear in these works is that exile for him does not

begin with his banishment from Germany; that is, it is not simply a matter of national identity. It is there in his Jewishness, emerges in his tortured relations to his parents, is a constituent part of his outsiderness as an artist. What is also clear is the extent to which his struggle to overcome this sense of alienation and exile is connected to writing and his finding of a language. In a revealing passage of his *Notizbücher,* Weiss describes his first return to Germany in 1947. At this time, he visited the publisher Peter Suhrkamp, interviewing him in German, but taking notes in Swedish. Suddenly, says Weiss, it didn't work anymore. "I was no longer a reporter, I was in a conversation. And all at once it was easier for me to speak German than Swedish. It was easier, although I stumbled, often had to search for words. The sounds were bound up with terror, but also with discoveries. My earliest concepts were a part of these sounds."[4] While Weiss is willing to acknowledge here the connection of the German language to his unconscious and to the deeper reaches of an unexplored past, he was also to emphasize repeatedly how much the discovery of language meant a freedom from commitment and location. In the final pages of *Vanishing Point,* he stresses the joy at finding a language which he had learned at the beginning of his life, but which was not bound to any country: "I could live in Paris or Stockholm, in London or New York and I carried this language as the lightest of baggage."[5]

These two views of language contradict one another and point to the ambivalences and paradoxes in Weiss's own early views of himself as a German. On the one hand, the "mother tongue" puts him in touch with a repressed past, the world of childhood and the inner self. It is also connected to what he has described as his bifurcated national identity: "When I think of Germany, a split is touched within myself. With language, the most concrete and at the same time most seductive of all means of expression, standing as it does in close relationship to this double Germany, I constantly feel myself forced to take a stand, to make a decision."[6] In the novel *Vanishing Point*, on the other hand, Weiss's discovery of the German language on a bridge in Paris in 1947 is seen by the later self as a moment of liberation from having to be at home in one place, and as the terms of his cosmopolitanism as a writer. In this light, it is not surprising that Weiss's early aesthetic models were drawn from the international avant-garde—such artists as Buñuel, Jarry, Breton, Rimbaud, Knut Hamsun, Henry Miller; from the least political of the Surrealist and Dada movements; or from those exile German writers, like Hermann Hesse and Franz Kafka, who were most profoundly dislocated from any national experience. Avant-gardism and cosmopolitanism were linked in Weiss's world view, if not consciously then structurally. Both were ways of maintaining one's individualism, one's freedom from commitment—also one's integrity.

Weiss's attitude toward his national, political, and aesthetic location in the world underwent another shift in the mid-1960s. In an essay appropriately entitled "Meine Ortschaft" ("My Location"), we find him once more reflecting upon his life as a person in exile. "They were places of transit," Weiss wrote of his changing locales, "cities in which I resided, in whose houses I lived, on whose streets I walked, with whose inhabitants I spoke, but which have no particular contours—they flowed one into the other, they were parts of a single, changing, earthly outer world . . . And only this one location, of which I had long known but only saw much later, is real for me. It is a location for which I was meant and from which I escaped. I myself never experienced anything in this place. I have no relation to it other than that my name was on a list of those who were to have been located there forever."[7]

Weiss, of course, is speaking of Auschwitz, which he visited as a tourist. And while his designation of it as "my location" is clearly provocative it also tells us much about the emerging connection in his thinking between world view and being at home, about his growing identification with those who suffer—his search for a moral center and political certitude. The essay was written in 1964, shortly after the international success of his *Marat/Sade*, when he was working on his play about Auschwitz, *Die Ermittlung* ("The Investigation"). Seen in retrospect, this whole period clearly marked an important turning point in Weiss's thinking: one which began with a shift to a drama about a political stand-off between collectivism (Marat) and individualism (Sade), and which evolved further into what he himself described at the 1966 Princeton meeting of the Group 47 as the moment when "I Come out of My Hiding Place" (the title of his controversial talk at that conference). In all of his writing from this time of upheaval during the 1960s, but particularly in his "10 Working Points of an Author in a Divided World," Weiss strives to assert to self and other, to self *as* other, that he no longer is what he was. "For years I believed that my work as an artist could provide me with an independence which would open the world to me. Today I realize that such a lack of connection for art is an illusion, in light of the fact that the jails of those countries in which differences of race and class are maintained by force, are filled with the tortured fighters of a future world."[8] Weiss's struggle to walk the path between an insistently asserted, painfully experienced cosmopolitanism and the claims of identity embedded in the reaches of language clearly began to resolve itself, first, in the discovery of Auschwitz as his "location," then, of Angola and Vietnam—"the tortured fighters." And this discovery of a locus (geographical, political, moral) had important implications for his writing as well. Whereas antinationhood had initially expressed itself in neutrality and unconnectedness vis-à-vis the rest of the world; whereas the cautious figure of the outsider without a home gave voice aesthetically to fragmented, carefully executed stories and autobiographical first-person narratives, Weiss now looked to larger social themes—to the political writings of Marx, Lenin, Fanon, Malcom X—but also to the epic-dramatic structures of Mass and agit-prop drama as a means to overcome his political and intellectual isolation.

In *The Investigation*, Weiss continued to broaden his commitment and perspective. This dramatization of the 1964 War Crime Trials in Frankfurt, which premiered simultaneously in seventeen theaters in East and West Germany, not only re-created with austerity the horror of the camps, but sought to link the fate of Jewish extermination beyond Nazi atrocities to structures of the capitalist system itself. While such an emphasis ran the risk of trivializing the enormity of specifically Nazi policies, it did highlight the relationship between the Third Reich capitalists who had helped Hitler come to power and their continued existence in the Federal Republic. More important for Weiss himself, his political perspective gave him an Archimedean point from which to structure his Jewish experience, and to explain what had been previously an inchoate world. But this did not solve the problem. He could explain the past—but what about the future? Is there a conceivable world in which injustice can be eliminated?

Weiss's next play, *Gesang vom Lusitanischen Popanz* ("Song of the Lusitanian Bogey"), was one attempt to answer that question. In his aforementioned reply to Enzensberger, Weiss had called upon Western intellectuals to engage themselves in the struggles of the Third World by "providing enough knowledge of the conditions in the lands most sorely oppressed by the 'rich' [so that] we can draw these lands close to us and develop our solidarity with them."[9] The essay itself had actually included many of the data which Weiss was to use in his play. *Lusitanian Bogey* is a "musical in two acts" about Western exploitation of Angola and the uprising by the blacks against their Portuguese oppressors in March of 1961. Borrowing numerous techniques from the agit-prop theater of the Weimar period, Weiss employs pantomime, chorus, cabaret, reportage, and puppet theater to present his sweeping condemnation of colonialism.

In his oratorio, *The Investigation*, he had divided the 11 cantos into three parts, in analogy to the 33 cantos of the *Inferno*, the *Purgatorio* and the *Paradiso* of Dante's *Divine Comedy*. In his *Lusitanian Bogey*, he repeats the structure by having each of the 11 scenes broken down into three voices: first, those of the oppressors—the Bogey, the bishop, the general, and the colonialists—who speak for the most part in unrhythmic prose; then, the chorus, who is African and speaks in lyric free verse; and, finally, the epic narrators, who primarily use rhymed couplets. The presence of the Bogey— a giant doll constructed of junk, which will be put together and taken apart before our eyes—dominates the stage both physically and allegorically, symbolizing collective oppression (by church, state, military) as well as the personage of Mr. Salazar himself.

But the Bogey is more than a symbol. As stage presence, it serves as source and demystification of official ideology: the central organizing object around which the fragments of the play cohere. For instance, many of the oppressors' speeches are read through the gaping, traplike mouth of the Bogey, whose preposterous appearance estranges the utterances into the lies they really are. On the other hand, as the target of critical attack, it seems to change before our eyes: at once imposing yet vulnerable, defeatable. And viewed in relation to the lyric beauty of African folk song—for instance, the haunting ballad in scene 2, "The earth it rips open, it tears open, it heaves open"—the Bogey metamorphoses once again into all that is decadent: the garbage disposal of Western culture. Thus Weiss brilliantly uses a stage object to lend unity and coherence to the disparate litany of imperialist misdeed and revolutionary struggle, which he unfolds before us. The five-hundred-year history of colonial rule, the system of economic exploitation, the practices of torture and forced labor, the system of elites and assimilation, the destruction of native culture, the role of NATO and Western capital, the growing revolt and revolution—all swirl around and gain meaning in relation to this central object. They become, as it were, linked within the total Lusitanian system.

But what of Weiss's portrayal of the Third World and, more specifically, blacks in this play? And how is such a depiction related in turn to his "political and aesthetic re-location" as a writer? Significantly, Weiss's stage directions suggest that the cast be limited to four women and three men, and that the actors, "regardless of the color of their skin, speak alternately for Europeans and Africans."[10] As with many aspects of this play, the interchanging of parts from black to white carries multiple meanings. At the level of content and ideology, its semiotic message serves to minimize the dimension of racial oppression in favor of a class analysis. The Lusitanian system as a whole is a capitalist one, it seems to say; the colony is just one more manifestation of that. Not surprisingly, the East German production of the play done in Rostock by Hans-Anselm Perten emphasized this point, which has textual support as well. For instance, scene 1 takes place not in Africa but in Lusitania-Portugal and has as its centerpiece the dramatization of a typical liberal home life in the motherland. The so-called progressive husband and modern wife describe their enlightened values while at the same time exploiting their white maid Juana. After Juana describes in detail the misery of her daily chores, the scene concludes with a three-way dialogue between husband (5)–wife (1)–maid (4):

> 1: I think our Juana has a very nice sleeping place
>   and had she not, it would be a disgrace.
> 4: It may not be much larger than a coffin
>   but I've given my thanks for it very often.
> 1: Our Juana knows perfectly well her probable fate
>   had we not taken her up to live within our gate.
> 5: And our Juana boastfully can say
>   200 escudos are her monthly pay.

    4: Not a bit of it can I save, yet I cannot shirk
        from adding I rejoice to have regular work.
    5: It's gotten so anything turns these people's heads around
        Nowadays every sort of propaganda is found.[11]

The follow-up lines of the Bogey make clear the connection between home-land and colonies: "The conspiratorial activities of the enemy are aimed particularly at our black citizens in the oversea provinces who because of their immaturity are vulnerable to attempts to incite them by those elements which are out to destroy our ideals."[12] This initial linkage between black and white, colonial and home experience is reinforced throughout the work. Repeatedly, the multifigured speeches of the monster-Bogey underscore an interlocking web of ideological and economic oppression, just as the African and narrator voices stress agitationally the need for a common struggle.

    But let us be clear on one point. Weiss does not minimize race conflict or cultural difference in this play. On the contrary, he demonstrates clearly how white paternalism functions to hold down African wages and to deny blacks their most fundamental legal, social, and cultural rights. However, underlying all this is the epic Marxist voice of historical truth, informing us of common *material* interests between blacks and whites which transcend the problems of racial, national, or cultural difference, and lead inexorably to socialist revolution. For instance, the black choral song about white workers earning six times more in wages than black ones ends with the hopeful lines, "the white workers in our land still do not realize who determines these differences and who gains the most from them."[13] The phrase "still do not realize" bespeaks an optimism about the coalescence of black and white revolution which tells us more about European intellectuals in the 1960s than it does about the historical realities of Third and First World politics.

    In this light, it is interesting to compare Weiss's play with the one other contemporary German drama that has dealt extensively with the race question and the Third World—namely, the East German Heiner Müller's play entitled *The Mission*. Like Weiss, Müller had reached a crisis in his work. His preceding "history" plays *Cement, Germania Death in Berlin, Life of Gundling Frederick the Great Lessing's Sleep Dream Scream* had increasingly questioned the possibility of history as drama and, finally, even of authorship itself. His short "anti-drama" *Hamletmachine*, written in 1977, is a text (at best a text) in which the writing subject self-destructs into a series of monologic identities: Shakespeare, Ophelia, Hamlet, father, mother, whore, and son. It has been described as the "self-reflection of the Marxist intellectual mirrored in the Hamlet tragedy."[14] I would only add, at the end of his creative rope. The rest, Müller seems wont to say, is authorial silence.

    And again like Weiss, Müller has looked to the Third World as one way out of the dilemma of solipsism, and as a means for him to renegotiate the link between history and drama. But here the tenuous similarities end. *The Mission*, subtitled "remembrance of a revolution," deals with the failure of revolution, not its incipient realization. And it is Müller's confrontation, indeed his poetic assertion, of that failure which has propelled him to write again. In stark contrast to Weiss's unequivocating submersion of authorial persona into the epic perspective of collective black Africa, and his reabsorption of that voice through the strictures of Marxist epistemology, Müller's *The Mission* is *explicitly* about white First and Second World intellectuals.

Briefly, then, the context (I purposely avoid the use of the term plot): Three emissaries of the French revolutionary government of 1789 are sent to the British colony of Jamaica in an unsuccessful attempt to organize an uprising of the slaves for the French Republic. The play, based on a short story by Anna Seghers,[15] begins with the reading of a letter from the peasant Galloudec—one of the three—to Antoine, the man who contracted them in the name of the Convent to do the mission, and who is now in hiding because Napoleon has come to power. In the letter, Galloudec cancels the mission and reports that his black comrade Sasportas has been hanged, and that the third revolutionary, a white named Debuisson, has betrayed the cause. Müller's ensuing, fragmentary and illusive, treatment of this material is less a representation of events, but rather a mixture of pantomime, abbreviated dialogue, surrealist dream sequence, poetic chant, and long, unbroken prose monologue—all of which address in various ways the portentous utterance of Sasportas that THE THEATER OF WHITE REVOLUTION IS OVER. The line, of course, can and should be read in two ways: one stressing the end of white revolution, the other, of its theatrical representation. In the interactions of the three revolutionaries with each other and with the mother country, Müller plays out black-white relations on both a geo-political and personal scale. The not so veiled analogies between Napoleon and Stalin, postrevolutionary France and post-Leninist Russia mark the different stages of "white" revolution as the return of a paradigm vis-à-vis the colonies. In this sense, Müller's play could be seen as a somewhat negative answer to Weiss's more optimistic vision of Socialist–Third World solidarity. Written from within the East Bloc and during a considerably sober time of world politics at the end of the 1970s, Müller's allegorical "broken contract/mission" (the German title *Der Auftrag* contains both those meanings) resonates with implications concerning national self-interest and betrayal of the Third World—implications which seem to challenge not only ideological shibboleths of Soviet foreign policy, but the very infrastructure of Marxist historiography as well.

But surely such an allegorical reading is far too simple. For Müller's play does not present a thesis, and in that sense is not primarily "about" the failure of socialist solidarity with the Third World. Much more in the spirit of a Brechtian "Learning Play,"[16] it, like *Hamletmachine*, seeks rather to explore a crisis of consciousness among left-wing intellectuals. Thus, if indeed it is an answer to Weiss, then only to the extent that Müller dramatizes his own severe inner doubts, much in the way Weiss did in his play *Marat/Sade*. It is also in this regard that *The Mission* has been compared to two other plays about white revolution, Georg Büchner's *Danton's Death* and Bertolt Brecht's *The Measures Taken*. For example, when the three emissaries arrive in Jamaica, they are masked, just as the comrades in Brecht's play are when they arrive in China, and for similar reasons. However, whereas for Brecht this is mainly a tactical maneuver, Müller uses masks to explore dimensions of identity. The white intellectual Debuisson, for instance, returns to Jamaica masked as himself. "I am who I was," he says upon arrival, "Debuisson, son of a slaveholder in Jamaica, heir to a plantation with four hundred slaves. I have returned home into the lap of my family . . . after the horrors of the revolution have opened my eyes to the eternal truth that everything old is better than anything new."[17] Are mask and self identical? Debuisson will struggle with that question and answer it finally in the affirmative. The black Sasportas, "masked" as a slave, does not have that privilege. Although he also is two selves, revolutionary and slave, both must lead inexorably to a kind of death. Revolution is not a choice, it is a condition of his blackness. As Galloudec says: "I know, Sasportas, that you play the most difficult role, it is written onto your body."[18] The race question, not the class question, is central here. But the race question is not just skin-deep, and this is where Büchner comes in.

Hans-Thies Lehmann has shown well the parallels between Büchner's Danton and Müller's Debuisson,[19] both caught, as they are, between a commitment to revolutionary action, on the one hand, and a melancholic compulsion toward sexual fulfillment, loss of self, and, in Debuisson's case, literally a crawl back into the womb, on the other. Upon arrival at his "home" court, Debuisson is greeted by his former lover, "Firstlove" (*Erste-Liebe*), who tells a story about freed slaves crawling back to their former plantation owner, begging to be reinstated as slaves: "Behold the human being: his first home is the mother, a prisonhouse." At this point, servant slaves raise Debuisson's mother's skirts high above her head for all to see. "Here it lies, gaping wide, the homeland," Firstlove continues, "here it yawns, that lap of the family. Just say one word if you want to return and she'll stuff you back in, the idiot, the eternal mother."[20]

Müller's images and fantasies as well as his juxtaposition of bodily and historical truth remind us not only of Büchner's *Danton*, but again of Weiss's *Marat/Sade*. Yet where the dualism between sexual and political freedom for Büchner and the pre-Marxist Weiss remains constituted as the dilemma of the European Enlightenment—the aporia of white revolution—Müller posits in black Sasportas an alternative. Not Sasportas as a figure—this would be a dialectical-dramatic and representational resolution. But Sasportas as the externalized and internalized "other," as an absolute negation. He is there in all the speeches, is as much a projected "actor" in the *Traumarbeit/Traumspiel* of Debuisson (as mentioned, the play is subtitled a "remembrance") as he is an objectively constituted, ontologically centered dramatic character.

For example, following Debuisson's arrival at the court, he is placed upon the throne (with Firstlove as his footstool) and told that "the theater of revolution has opened." What ensues is a nonsensical pantomime-play, part Beckett part Büchner, featuring "SasportasRobespierre" and "GalloudecDanton" and acted *out* by the "masked" blacks and peasants themselves (the plays within the play and displaced/inverted identities are legion here). The grand theater of revolution reveals itself as nothing but an absurdist farce in which the two revolutionaries play football with decapitated masked heads and ridicule each other as the hapless, vice-riddled clowns of a failed revolution:

> GALLOUDECDANTON: The theater of revolution has opened. Attraction: the man with the missing genitals. Maximilian the Great. Moralmax. The chairfarter. The masturbator from Arras. The bloody Robespierre.[21]

At the conclusion of the "play," Sasportas replaces Debuisson on the throne, to utter the epic summation of the now accumulating levels of reference: "The theater of white revolution is over. We condemn you to death, Victor Debuisson. Because your skin is white. Because your thoughts are white. Because your eyes have seen the beauty of our sisters . . . The trouble with all of you is, you can't die. And for that reason you kill everything around you. For your dead ordered world in which intoxication has no place. For your revolution without sex."[22] Sasportas' double "role" is an important one. As a player in *The Mission* and as Sasportas/Robespierre in the farce, he is but one of the equally flawed components of a flawed revolution. But replacing Debuisson as "spectator" of his own play, he then voices Debuisson/Müller's self-reflections concerning the larger questions. It is the theater of *white* revolution that is over, thematically and formally: impaled upon the immutable dualities of the white revolutionary intellectual; reduced from the epic grandeur of historical tragedy (*Danton's Death*) to an absurdist nonrepresentational farce (*Waiting for Godot*). Yet the black revolutionary Sasportas can and does die, regardless of any moral strength or failing as character. Unlike Debuisson's, *his* body and history are one. And it is from the configuration of meanings he generates in this play that any future revolutionary theater must emerge.

But let us return to Weiss's *Lusitanian Bogey*, and let us do it fairly. The point is not to compare these plays ideologically or aesthetically in order to find one of them wanting. Müller and Weiss, both temperamentally and even aesthetically, come from very different directions—and are writing at different times. Clearly, for Weiss the Third World meant a watershed for his aesthetic development. During his first trip to Havana in June of 1966, he took part in a collective mural painting, an experience which he compared to being a part of the Soviet avant-garde in 1917:

> a totality of action
> openness for all possibilities and
> "joie de vivre"
> something of this must have been felt
> when the Russian Revolution was young
> when art was part of life.[23]

Art and life. If Peter Bürger believes that in capitalist society the historical avant-garde has failed in its effort to eliminate the distance between art and life, becoming instead a part of the commercial market,[24] Peter Weiss discovers the possibility for its renewal in the Cuban revolution and the Third World. Certainly his Angolan play was written in this spirit.

The *Lusitanian Bogey* has often been described as the most politically assertive of Weiss's plays. And as Reinhard Baumgart has pointed out, herein lies its aesthetic paradox.[25] Although written from a position of utmost political and moral conviction, it is the least moralizing and heavy-handed of all his political dramas in its artistic realization. A mixture of musical review and political agit-prop, this liturgical *Gesamtkunstwerk* dispenses effortlessly with plot, character, and psychological conflict, to paint in broad, dazzling strokes five hundred years of colonial history and the beginnings of its resolution. Its language is openly tendentious and propagandistic—it makes no bones about that—and the naïve way it spouts its message is ironically also its source of success as a play of estrangement. More important, its montage of African folk poetry, music, and body rhythms and its dynamic, creative use of theatric space combine the sexual energies of *Marat/Sade* with a portrayal of history and politics in a way that Weiss was never to achieve again on the stage.[26]

But our comparison with Müller also points to a paradox in Weiss's appropriation of black Africa, an inherent ambiguity of self-location registered at the very level of aesthetic form. His discovery of a political-aesthetic identity, grounded philosophically in the writings of the Marxian classics, experientially in the living or imagined destiny of Third World peoples, meant within his own work a freedom to experiment aggressively and imaginatively with avant-garde theater—to push the possibilities of revolutionary theater to their limits. But at a price. What he does not incorporate, in a way that Müller does, is the reality of contradiction inherent in black-white solidarity; is an aesthetic and political location of self as a white, First World intellectual vis-à-vis black revolution.

One could, of course, argue that Müller's *The Mission* is not in any way an agit-prop play, and that it is unfair to demand of Weiss what the genre itself must refuse to deliver. And yet I would still maintain that Weiss's refashioning of 1920s agit-prop theater for the anti-imperialist struggles of the 1960s recapitulates at the level of aesthetics (sentimental and simplistic figural representation, absence of internal contradiction) a notion about political interests and human behavior which even at that earlier pre-Stalinist time represented a historical-aesthetic simplification as well as a removal of self. For instance, the difference between Bertolt Brecht and the myriad of other left-wing playwrights from the Weimar period surely lies in the fact that even in Brecht's most emphatically agitational plays we find at their formal and political center the problematicization rather than harmonization of relationships. His revolutionary play *The Mother* as well as his *Lehrstück* as a genre were notable for their inclusion of characters (the teacher/intellectual) and problems (the necessity of violence, individual vs. collective) which, regardless of where Brecht finally ended up politically, were clearly a part of his own unresolved relationship to communism at this period, and which necessitated formal innovation (estrangement) to render them dramatically. Weiss, on the other hand, buries himself with his new self, smooths out the edges, replaces the authorial "I" with an uncontested "we" of revolutionary history.

What becomes clear both from *The Song of the Lusitanian Bogey* and from Weiss's essays and notes from this period is the importance of the Third World for his political and moral bearings during a time of political change. It was the colonialist exploitation by the West as evidenced by events in Cuba, Angola, and Vietnam which underscored his belief that "the principles of socialism were the only valid truth,"[27] just as it was the suffering and struggle of the Vietnamese people against that oppression which proved for him once and for all the revolutionary and moral superiority of the Socialist Bloc as a whole. "Personally, I would prefer to call the 'Third World' the First World, as it is the revolutionary world of our time," wrote Weiss in 1967. "In Vietnam, the people created a society which realizes the dignity of man. In comparison to Vietnam, the U.S. society is atavistic, reactionary, anti-humanitarian."[28] Weiss's outrage toward the United States was to grow during this period in direct proportion to the increased bombing of North Vietnam. It finally led him in 1970 to speak of the United States as an imperialist-fascist society, where there is total thought control, where dissenters are beaten down in the streets and threatened with gas chambers, a society, "where the general deformation of human thought and action are taking on drastic dimensions."[29] Weiss's thinking is apocalyptic here, as was the case with many of us, and the projection of his own fearful experiences during fascism onto the American scene explains why he conceived of the world at this point much in terms of a Divine Comedy. In an essay entitled "Preliminary Exercise for the Tripartite Drama *Divina Commedia*," Weiss sketches out his plan for a "purgatorio, with jazz insertions and with dancing, in the style of a musical."[30] Although this "World Theater" never materialized, it is clear from the *Notizbücher* that the antipodes of good and evil were skewed between Nazism-Imperialism as the inferno, on the one hand, and such figures as Lumumba, Malcom X, Che, Fanon, etc., residing in paradise, on the other.[31]

We also see in his notes that the privileging of the Third World as the locus of suffering and struggle, hope and the future was accompanied by intermittent disillusionment with the established socialist societies. The invasion of Czechoslovakia by the Warsaw Pact troops in August of 1968, but particularly the repressive cultural policies and control of the arts, especially as experienced in the GDR, brought forth constant expressions of disappointment. The most obvious example of conflict for Weiss developed around the play he wrote about the renegade Leon Trotsky, entitled *Trotsky in Exile*. It was presented to the world in 1970, the 100th anniversary of Lenin's birth, in the naïve belief that the Eastern authorities were ready for open and critical discussion of this subject. The attacks and even temporary banishment of Weiss from East Germany were to disabuse him of any more illusions along that line. Yet it should also be mentioned that, despite differences around individual policies, Weiss was to maintain his allegiance to the Socialist Bloc as a whole, and to view the contradictions in it as resulting from what he called "human weakness," rather than from any structural flaw.

Which all brings us back to our original discussion of the debate in *Kursbuch*. Weiss's subordination of Third World struggles to the Manichaean paradigm of socialism vs. capitalism clearly finds him parting ways with Enzensberger and the New Left, who were as critical of Soviet imperialist practices as they were of capitalist ones. This position was of course strengthened by the Soviet invasion of Prague in 1968, but it was there also from the beginning. And it is for this reason that Enzensberger would have to characterize Weiss's assertion—namely, that the "differences between the Soviet Union and China (simply because they are both socialist) are much more likely to be resolved than the differences between either one and the U.S."[32]—as the empty idealism that history has proven it to be.

Conversely, however, Weiss's portrayal of colonialist and imperialist histories and structures in both his Vietnam and African plays, clearly shows him attentive to the complicated ways that class structures from the capitalist world reproduce themselves in the colonialist one, and to the role of outside capital and the internalization of ideology in the maintenance of the system. Here Enzensberger's absolute dichotomy of rich and poor nations and his occasional romanticization of China and Cuba fall into the same uncritical stance as that of Weiss.[33] Indeed, like many left-wing intellectuals in the 1960s, both Weiss and Enzensberger generalize abstractly about the Third World as a monolith—whether rich vs. poor, white vs. black, or socialist vs. capitalist—in a way that tells us as much about their own political struggles as it does about those parts of the world.

But that, of course, is precisely the point. Weiss's confrontation with the Third World was most significant as a relocation of his political-aesthetic self. Certainly his affirmation of a socialist avant-garde, felt first and most in his visits to Cuba and Vietnam, was an important further step in his being able to place himself positively within Germany, and specifically within the history and traditions of German socialism. And, in a sense, his three-volume opus *Die Ästhetik des Widerstands* ("The Aesthetics of Resistance"), an autobiographical history of that tradition completed at the end of his life, is really the story of Peter Weiss finally coming home.

1   Hans Magnus Enzensberger, "Europäische Peripherie," *Kursbuch* 2 (August 1965): 154–73.
2   Peter Weiss, "Enzensbergers Illusionen," *Kursbuch* 6 (July 1966): 170.
3   Enzensberger, "Peter Weiss und andere," *Kursbuch* 6 (July 1966): 175.
4   Weiss, *Notizbücher 1971–1980*, vol. 2 (Frankfurt, 1981), p. 679.
5   Weiss, *Fluchtpunkt* (Frankfurt, 1962), p. 306.
6   Weiss, *Notizbücher 1971–1980*, p. 690.
7   Weiss, "Meine Ortschaft," in his *Rapporte* (Frankfurt, 1968), p. 114.
8   Weiss, "10 Arbeitspunkte eines Autors in der geteilten Welt," in his *Rapporte 2* (Frankfurt, 1971), p. 23.
9   Weiss, "Enzensbergers Illusionen," p. 168.
10 Weiss, *Gesang vom Lusitanischen Popanz* (Berlin, 1967), p. 5.
11 Ibid., pp. 15–16.
12 Ibid., p. 16.
13 Ibid., p. 39.
14 Genia Schulz, *Heiner Müller* (Stuttgart, 1980), p. 149.
15 Anna Seghers, "Das Licht auf dem Galgen," in her *Karibische Geschichten* (Berlin, 1962), pp. 121–238.
16 See Frank Hörnigk, "Erinnerungen an Revolutionen: Zu Entwicklungstendenzen in der Dramatik Heiner Müllers, Peter Hacks' und Volker Brauns am Ende der siebziger Jahre," in *Tendenzen und Beispiele: Zur DDR-Literatur in den siebziger Jahren*, ed. by Hans Kaufmann (Leipzig, 1981), p. 115. Hörnigk emphasizes the importance of this work as a learning play also for an East German audience, "whose willingness to join in the production of meaning is assumed."
17 Heiner Müller, "Der Auftrag," in his *Der Auftrag Der Bau Herakles 5 Todesanzeige* (Berlin, 1981), p. 16.
18 Ibid., p. 17.
19 Hans-Thies Lehmann, "Dramatische Form und Revolution in Georg Büchners *Dantons Tod* und Heiner Müllers *Der Auftrag*," in *Georg Büchner: Dantons Tod. Die Trauerarbeit im Schönen*, ed. by Direktorium Schauspielhaus Frankfurt (Frankfurt 1980). I am indebted to Lehmann for a number of central points in my discussion of this play.
20 Müller, "Der Auftrag," p. 19.
21 Ibid., p. 22.
22 Ibid., p. 23
23 Weiss, *Notizbücher 1960–1971*, vol. 2 (Frankfurt, 1982), p. 543.
24 Peter Bürger, *Theorie der Avantgarde* (Frankfurt, 1974).

25 Reinhard Baumgart, "In die Moral entwischt," *Text und Kritik* 37 (1982): 47–57.
26 See Rüdiger Sareika, *Die Dritte Welt in der westdeutschen Literatur der sechziger Jahre* (Frankfurt, 1980), p. 209. Sareika reports that the play was put on in Montevideo, Skopje, Buenos Aires, Cairo, Bagdad, and Alexandria, in addition to its European productions.
27 Weiss, "10 Arbeitspunkte eines Autors in der geteilten Welt," p. 22.
28 Weiss, *Notizbücher 1960–1971,* p. 549.
29 Weiss, "Die Luftangriffe der USA am 21.11.1970 auf die Demokratische Republik Vietnam," in his *Rapporte 2,* p. 140.
30 Weiss, "Vorübung zum dreiteiligen Drama Divina Commedia," ibid., pp. 125–41.
31 Weiss, *Notizbücher 1960–1971,* p. 613.
32 Weiss, "Enzensbergers Illusionen," p. 167.
33 For a discussion of Enzensberger's position from the perspective of the Third World, see Amadou Booker Sadji, "Hans Magnus Enzensberger und die 'Dritte Welt,' " in *Hans Magnus Enzensberger,* ed. by Reinhold Grimm (Frankfurt, 1984), pp. 258–75.

Germans, Blacks, and Jews; or
Is There a German Blackness of Its Own?

REINHOLD GRIMM

In his definitive study of 1978, *Toward the Final Solution: A History of European Racism,* George L. Mosse states with his usual succinctness:

> Historically, Jews and blacks have always played the outsider, the villain who threatens the tribe. Who knows but that 6 million Jews might not have been joined by as many blacks had these lived in the midst of the peoples of Europe.

"From the eighteenth century onwards," Mosse repeats and explains, and not merely with regard to the Germans, "the [racial] ideal-type and counter-type would not vary much for the next century and a half, nor would it matter fundamentally whether the inferior race was black or Jewish."[1]

These are no isolated insights and judgments. As early as 1937, in what might be termed a classic of its kind, Sterling Brown, the author of *Negro Poetry and Drama* and *The Negro in American Fiction,* noted laconically, referring to the treatment of blacks in the United States, thus to the history of American racism: "The Jew has been treated similarly by his persecutors."[2] Indeed, even the comparison with the genocide committed by the Nazis was made in this country before—not, to be sure, by a scholar looking back in gloom and anger, but by a revolutionary looking ahead in anguish and wrath. It was none other than Malcolm X who, addressing a black audience, exclaimed:

> I tell you, they'll be building gas chambers and gas ovens pretty soon...[and] ...you'll be in one of them, just like the Jews ended up in gas ovens over there in Germany. You're in a society that's just as capable of building gas ovens for black people as Hitler's society was...[3]

As to the Germanist investigating the reflections of that joint racist "counter-type" in literature, the logical conclusion to be drawn seems to be clear. There must obtain a double image of blacks and Jews: namely, a negative one in the eyes of the others, those by whom they have been oppressed and persecuted, and a positive one in their own eyes, that is, their own self-understanding and mutual evaluation and esteem. Blacks and Jews, it appears to follow, must feel and betray a profound solidarity, both in their common suffering from the others' stereotyping and all it has caused, and in their common struggle against such prejudices and what they still are able to bring about. Accordingly, the former aspect was stressed only recently by Sander L. Gilman in his important volume *On Blackness without Blacks: Essays on the Image of the Black in Germany,* especially where he comments on "this interconnection... in twentieth-century Germany" effected by Nazism, or where he opens up the somber perspective that even nowadays "the Black remains a mythic figure in German thought, joined [after the Holocaust] by another figure that exists, for the Germans, only in the world of myth: the Jew."[4] But the brighter aspect was likewise emphasized very recently—in 1983, to be precise, and in the newly founded journal, or yearbook, *Etudes germano-africaines*—by Uta Sadji, whose seminal article on the decline of the West and the rise of a black era, as pictured in post–World War I utopian literature written in German, culminates in the confident assurance that the Jew is the "natural ally" of the black African as well as the black American: "Der Schwarzafrikaner beziehungsweise -amerikaner und sein natürlicher Verbündeter, der Jude..."[5]

While there is a great deal of truth in most of the statements and contentions just quoted, I hold they have to be supplemented and, in part, corrected nevertheless. For one thing, the Jewish-black relationship in this country can hardly be said to constitute an *entente cordiale;* rather, it presents itself as highly contradictory. Stokely Carmichael, who talked to a similar crowd as Malcolm X, did not affirm or propound an alliance in the least, quite to the contrary, and bluntly refused to see any resemblance between his people and Jewry, let alone the State of Israel.[6] On the other hand, Leslie A. Fiedler, in a review of James Baldwin's *Notes of a Native Son,* was at considerable pains to come to grips with his situation, for all his eloquence and verve. "We are strangers both, outsiders in some senses forever," he confessed, "but we are outsiders with a difference." His piece of uneasy soul-searching titled "Negro and Jew: Encounter in America" does speak, granted, of their "fraternity"; still, he couldn't but concede that such a "yoking" (as he also put it) was felt by either to be "improbable and unwanted." In fact, not only was Fiedler compelled to realize a growing "black anti-Semitism," but he was even forced to perceive and admit a lingering Jewish "hatred" of blacks as well. Hence, unable to voice his contentment with any existing solidarity, he entered an impassioned though, perhaps, itself not altogether unquestionable plea for creating and maintaining one:

> For the Jew, the Negro is his shadow, his improbable caricature, whom he hates only at the price of hating himself; and he learns quickly (unless he allows rage to blind him) that for this reason his own human dignity depends not only theoretically but in terrible actuality upon that of the Negro. No Jew can selflessly dedicate himself to the fight for the equality of the Negro; when he pretends that he is not also fighting for himself, he is pretending that he is indistinguishable from a *goy.*[7]

So much (without any claim to conclusiveness whatsoever, nor to any competence on my part) for the parallel problem of blacks, Jews, and Americans.

Concerning, then, the situation in Germany—or, at any rate, its reflections in her literature—I venture to submit that it is, or has been, of a comparable intricacy indeed; actually, it may well turn out to present itself, despite appearances, and its many and patent divergences notwithstanding, as even more complex and contradictory. A few citations and brief quotations will suffice to illustrate this for the time being. Of course, that blacks and Jews were lumped together by Nazi writers and ideologues, with all the heinous consequences ensuing from that, is well known; prime examples can be found both in Hitler's own report *Mein Kampf* and in what has been called the "ideological bible" of the movement, Alfred Rosenberg's *Der Mythus des 20. Jahrhunderts* ("The Myth of the 20th Century").[8] However, less known though surely not surprising at all is another fact: to wit, the proclamation of a Jewish-black unity in suffering and hope by the great German poet, Heinrich Heine. What is, Heine asked as early as 1828, the task and mission of our age? And he answered:

> Es ist die Emanzipation. Nicht bloß die der Irländer, Griechen, Frankfurter Juden, westindischen Schwarzen und dergleichen gedrückten Volkes, sondern es ist die Emanzipation der ganzen Welt...[9]

Not just the Irish exploited by the British, and the Greeks fighting against the Turks—a much publicized event during those years—were placed side by side under Heine's progressive aegis of a global emancipation, but precisely the German Jews from Frankfurt, who had been confined to their ghetto, and the black Afro-Americans from the West Indies, the victims of slavery. (It will be remembered, I trust, not only that Heine composed the fierce and powerful accusatory ballad "Das Sklavenschiff" ["The Slave Ship"], but that it was also he who hailed America bitterly as "that enormous as well as monstrous prison of freedom" [*dieses ungeheure Freiheitsgefängnis*—neither the ambiguity of the adjective nor the oxymoronic poignancy of the noun can be rendered with any degree of adequateness].)[10] Yet between these two clear-cut opposites marked, on the one hand, by the Nazis and Hitler himself, the German if Austrian-born exterminator of European Jewry, and, on the other, by Heine, the emancipated German Jew and herald of the liberation of all the wretched of the earth, i.e., between the plainly negative and the purely positive manifestations of the dual "counter-type"—to borrow Mosse's terminology—of blacks and Jews, there extends a vast and multifarious and, above all, most complicated spectrum of stereotyping, mythmaking, and imagery that has hitherto, at least as far as I have been able to ascertain, scarcely been touched upon, much less surveyed in its entirety. In German letters of the 20th century in particular, such "double-types" occur and recur in sizable numbers, both in the racists' and emancipationists' veins as well as, paradoxical though it may sound, in combinations thereof; and they are in no way restricted to trivial literature or magazines.[11] Nor are, as one might be tempted to expect, the negative images the sole prerogative of Nazis and anti-Semites and, conversely, the positive ones that of Jewish authors (black writers have not yet emerged in Germany, to my knowledge). As a matter of fact, racial prejudices of the grossest sort and of outrageous dimensions can be encountered even in the realm of progressive German liberalism, in the camp of German proponents of democracy, indeed among German antifascists who were themselves destined to end in a Nazi concentration camp! This is almost unbelievable, and the language employed with regard to blacks, downright unbearable; but, nonetheless, I have to tender evidence.

A typical case in point is the derogatory term "Vernegerung" (i.e., "Negroization"), again from Hitler's *Mein Kampf*.[12] That a man like Hitler should conceive it is certainly no great surprise; what is really upsetting and truly inconceivable is its adoption and, worse yet, adaptation by a man like Friedrich Percyval Reck-Malleczewen. Unconditionally opposed to Nazism, Reck died in Dachau in 1944, but for about a decade had kept a diary that shows him virtually foaming with hatred and contempt for Hitler and Hitler's henchmen, and which was published posthumously under the title, *Tagebuch eines Verzweifelten* ("Diary of a Desperate Man"). I shan't go into many details; suffice it to say that one of this antifascist's favorite words for contemptuously denouncing the most hateful debasement imaginable was "Verniggerung," and that such was, in his opinion, precisely that which the Nazis had brought down upon Germany and Europe! Literally, Reck equated the "accomplishments" of Nazism "mit der systematischen Ertötung des Geistigen und der vollendeten Verniggerung der Massen" and pilloried German bomber pilots and brutalized young soldiers as "diese weißen Nigger";[13] incessantly, while crying out against Nazi atrocities, he made use of those and similar terms... And he was, alas, not the only one. No less a literary worthy than Ernst Jünger, the recent if quite controversial Goethe Prize laureate of the City of Frankfurt, also adopted Hitler's word and concept, however much he despised and ridiculed him. The instances Jünger furnishes—I shall once more select merely two—are, in effect, even more revealing. Both stem from his notes and diaries which deal with the latter half of the Second World War, *Strahlungen* ("Radiances") of 1949. In them, this erstwhile ace of World War I and internationally renowned author, himself an officer in Hitler's army, tells the story of a German colonel who, when asked how the Eastern extermination camps made possible by him and his likes (i.e., the ignominies of the "final solution of the Jewish question," as the Nazis had it) were compatible with his being a soldier, with carrying arms and wearing high decorations, was not ashamed to declare: "Das trägt vielleicht einmal meine jüngste Tochter in einem Negerbordell ab" ("One day, perhaps, my youngest daughter will pay for that in a Negro brothel").[14] Admittedly, Jünger's entry, dating from 13 May 1943, relates an incident he observed, and words spoken to him. Yet he reports them approvingly, as it were; moreover, less than a year thereafter, on 3 April 1944, he unmistakably fell into the very same repugnant lingo, weirdly echoing Hitler to boot. Thus, commenting on the brutalities Germans were then committing in Poland and Russia, Jünger asked himself "how this cannibal way of thinking, how this...rapid and overall negroization [could] be explained":

> Ich frage mich, wie diese kannibalische Gesinnung, wie dieses...rasche und allgemeine Vernegern sich erklärt.[15]

As I said, this man served under Hitler, but he was opposed to Nazism all the same; he has always been associated with the so-called inner emigration. And still, Jünger, just like Reck, decried the utmost horrors of racism in the most racist of vocabularies.

It is true, research of things black and German has increased dramatically over the past lustrum or so, forming already an impressive array of critical contributions. Even if we disregard the respective articles and numerous papers—naturally, there have also been a few scattered attempts in earlier decades or years[16]—at least a dozen independent studies have been produced during that short span of time, both monographs and dissertations as well as volumes of essays by various hands, plus an edition of pertinent documents. Scholars from East and West Germany, from Belgium and the United States, but likewise, significantly, from several African countries have devoted themselves, writing in German, English, or French, to the topic of "blacks and German culture, art, and literature" in its manifold ramifications. To name but those whose work has come out in book form,[17] they are: Sander L. Gilman,[18] Amadou Booker Sadji (founder and editor of *Etudes germano-africaines*), Georg M. Gugelberger, Beverly Harris-Schenz, Kouamé Kouassi, Rosemarie K. Lester, E. C. Nwezeh, Uta Sadji, Martin Steins, Joachim Warmbold, and Vernessa C. White.[19] Inasmuch as is known and accessible to me, what all their findings and demonstrations have in common is the irrefutable proof that German literature, even though it be characterized by a "Blackness without Blacks," does partake of the general attitude towards blacks that has permeated Western history and culture, in Europe as in America, and that it also shares the widespread black images thereby engendered (such as the noble savage or the tortured slave, the exotic or the devilish figures, etc.). But the question arises nevertheless—and is both implied and implicitly answered in Gilman's pithy title—as to whether there might not obtain, in excess of such conformities, a specific, perhaps unique, German relationship to blacks as reflected in art and letters. Or as I myself have phrased it: Is there a German blackness of its own? That mine, too, is a rhetorical question of sorts, hence, that I am also inclined to answer in the affirmative, ought to be obvious; in fact, I did so reply explicitly, if in broad outlines, in an unpublished lecture delivered at Howard University

(Washington, D.C.) in 1978. Yet unlike Gilman, who has broached this German-black specificity more than any other student in the field, I tend to think that it can neither be adequately defined nor fully exhausted by the mere historical absence of blacks on German soil—an absence which has never been absolute, anyhow, either in Germany herself or in the greater German-speaking community.

Also, let us not forget that there once was, in German culture and art, a black saint—actually, the foremost saint of the Holy Roman Empire—and that he had a mundane half brother in German letters of near equal proportions. To both has been ascribed, by scholars in Europe and Africa alike, a uniqueness and brilliance unmatched not only in the Middle Ages but in all Western art and literature. (And the same holds true for the iconography of the black Wise Man in German Adorations of the Magi.)[20] However, I hasten to add that if indeed medieval Germany can pride herself on Wolfram von Eschenbach's Feirefiz, the epitome of black[21] knightliness, valor, and magnanimity in what is perhaps her most typical courtly epic, *Parzival*; and if indeed she can be proud of her Saint Maurice, the wielder of the imperial Holy Lance and epitome of black sanctity, glorification, and Christian knighthood (as witness his marvelous statue in the Cathedral of Magdeburg, or his depictions in the paintings of Matthias Grünewald, Hans Baldung Grien, Hans von Kulmbach, and others); then, I am afraid, the constellations of the double imagery of blacks and Jews in modern, especially post-18th-century, Germany and their reflections in her literature are, for the most part, anything but flattering, and some are outright shocking. As singular as they may be, they are, on the whole, exceedingly ambiguous, and only in a few isolated cases might be said to be satisfactory or, in any event, fairly tolerable.

The following remarks will try to unfold, however fleetingly, this interrelationship and interaction. All in all, five authors, each with at least one work of fiction, will be discussed in them: to wit, Gustav Meyrink (1868–1932), Bruno Frank (1887–1945), Anna Seghers (1900–1983), Wolfgang Koeppen (born in 1906), and Gerd Gaiser (1908–1976). Of these five—all of whom are surely not trashy, nor even minor, writers—Seghers and Koeppen present the positive version of the racial "counter-type," whereas Frank and Gaiser, albeit in a strikingly different manner, provide instances of the negative one; Meyrink, an enigmatic author to begin with, occupies a position in between. It should further be noted that two of them, Seghers and Frank, were Jewish, Koeppen and Gaiser being what Fiedler would label as *goyim*, or goys; as for Meyrink once more, I can merely say that, on the one hand, he is listed as a "Jewish storyteller" *(jüdischer Erzähler)* in the new reference work, *Lexikon der phantastischen Literatur,* but that, on the other hand, he reportedly sued a journalist for slander and "for accusing him of being Jewish."[22] All that seems to be safe to say is that Gustav Meyrink—which was his pen name—was born the illegitimate son of a sixty-year-old nobleman and prominent diplomat, the Foreign Minister of the then Kingdom of Wurttemberg, Freiherr Karl von Varnbüler, and the young Viennese actress, Maria Wilhelmine Adelaïde Meyer.[23] Be that as it may, Meyrink's novel in question, *Das grüne Gesicht* ("The Green Face") of 1916, is a strange and adventurous narrative related, in many ways, to his most famous novel, *Der Golem* ("The Golem") of the preceding year. Originally, according to the manuscript variants now at Yale's Rare Book Library,[24] he even intended to call it "Der Ewige Jude"; and, clearly, the legendary figure of the Wandering Jew, above all when viewed in our context, does play a momentous role in it. Situated, though, not in Prague, as is *Der Golem,*[25] but in a half real, half fantastic Amsterdam and its ghetto, *Das grüne Gesicht* also introduces a black African as a protagonist. He is a Zulu by name of Usibepu—or, to be more precise, a Zulu king—and Meyrink describes him thus:

> Es war ein riesenhafter Zulukaffer mit schwarzem, krausem Bart und wulstigen Lippen, nur mit einem karierten Regenmantel bekleidet, einen roten Ring um den Hals und das von Hammeltalg triefende Haar kunstvoll in die Höhe gebürstet, so daß es aussah, als trüge er eine Schüssel aus Ebenholz auf dem Kopfe.
> In der Hand trug er einen Speer.[26]

This grotesque caricature—naked under a "checkered raincoat," his "hair dripping with tallow," and looking like a "tureen of ebony"—who, moreover, prostitutes his primeval magic power in taverns and a cheap circus, is nonetheless taken quite seriously by the author, particularly as Usibepu confronts the incarnation of the Wandering Jew, the old cobbler and mystic, Klinkherbogk, whom "the horrid Negro" *(der grauenhafte Neger)*[27] kills and robs. His victim, having himself just sacrificed his granddaughter, stabbing her with a shoemaker's awl in a fit of trancelike postfiguration of Abra-(ha)m's story from the Old Testament, awaits the black murderer with a "transfigured smile," arms stretched forth in yearning, as if welcoming, verbatim, "the Savior":

> Einen Augenblick sah Klinkherbogk einen schmalen, roten Streifen unter den Wolken im Osten;—wie ein Blitz kam ihm die Erinnerung wieder an seinen Traum, und er breitete sehnsüchtig die Arme nach Usibepu aus wie nach dem Erlöser.
> Der Neger prallte entsetzt zurück, als er das verklärte Lächeln in Klinkerbogks Zügen bemerkte, dann sprang er auf ihn zu, faßte ihn am Hals und brach ihm das Genick.[28]

The "dream" referred to is the cobbler's earlier vision of Usibepu as the Black Magus offering myrrh to the infant in the manger; and myrrh being an ointment for corpses, hence a symbol of death and mortality yet, in the New Testament, also of resurrection (cf. John 19:39),[29] Klinkherbogk aptly prophesied that the black Wise Man (literally, "the King from the Moors' Land" *[der König aus dem Mohrenland]*) will bring him, through death, "the other life" (*das andere Leben,* or afterlife).[30]

Whatever cryptic message may be shrouded in these happenings, imbued as they are with a syncretistic mysticism of Hasidic and cabalistic as well as of Christian and Eastern provenance, one thing is beyond dispute: the close connection in *Das grüne Gesicht* between blackness and Jewishness, both on a realistic and an allegorical level. That the "savage" (*Wilder,* as he will be apostrophized presently) is perceived as the "redeemer" *(Erlöser)* cannot be gainsaid; besides, the bonds so mysteriously tying the Jew to the black are reinforced, to all intents and purposes, by yet another Jewish figure, Lazarus Eidotter. Blissfully, as it were, he gives himself up to the authorities, claiming that it was he who killed Klinkherbogk, and thus tries to redeem, so to speak, the African in turn. Eidotter envisions his vicarious death for Usibepu—it does not come to pass, incidentally—as nothing short of a "gift" *(Geschenk).*[31] And why? Because the Zulu, though certainly not Jewish, belongs to the Jews all the same, as Eidotter points out. To him, the black is "one of our people." Eidotter iterates persistently:

> "Und dann...is der Mörder aner von ünsere [*sic*] Leut!—Nicht ä Jud,...aber doch aner von unsere Leut!...Er is ä Wilder und hat sein Glauben; Gott soll hüten, daß viele so än gräßlichen Glauben haben wie er, aber sei Glauben is ächt und lebendig. Das sind unsere Leut', die wo än Glauben haben, der im Feuer Gottes nicht schmilzt...Was is Jud, was is Christ, was is ä Heide? Ä Name für die, wo ä Religion haben statt än Glauben."[32]

The content and hidden meaning of the "lurid faith" here evoked are, once again, highly unclear; what is all the more manifest, however, is the intensity of this black-Jewish certitude, its being "genuine" and "alive." Indeed it is proof against the very "fire of God"! I need not dwell on the sinister overtones such images have taken on in the meantime—nor elaborate, for that matter, on the stereotyping ever so often betrayed by Meyrink's text. Do I have to state expressly that Usibepu attempts to rape the blond heroine of the novel, but, wondrous enough, fails? Still, for all his stereotypical and ludicrous features, he is portrayed not with hostility, but rather with an uncanny awe and even admiration. There exists no conscious racist attitude towards the black in this book; instead, we sense a remarkable empathy on the part of its author (which applies, of course, to the many Jewish characters as well, be they Sephardim or Ashkenazim; in fact, Meyrink proves to be one of the very few German writers that have succeeded in picturing both divisions of Jewry in a single work). To repeat, then: *Das grüne Gesicht* and its author are serious. And to top it off, the constellation of Jewishness and blackness as developed by Meyrink in this utopian novel—for it long presupposes, in 1916, the end and disastrous results of World War I—seems to foreshadow, somehow or other, the ultimate doom and destruction of a ravaged West drained of its physical and spiritual energies. Consequently, the finale is eschatological. An apocalyptic tempest sweeps across Amsterdam, Holland, and Europe at large; European culture and civilization are totally (I have to resort to my native tongue) *weggefegt,* and the whole decadent continent is *leergefegt,* indeed *reingefegt* of any and all of their remnants.[33]

Compared with Meyrink's strange and fantastic novel, the triptych of novellas by the late Anna Seghers, *Karibische Geschichten* ("Tales of the Caribbean") of 1962, reveals itself as utterly clear, sober, straightforward, and unequivocally progressive. The following stories are comprised within her collection: "Die Hochzeit von Haiti" ("The Wedding in Haiti"), "Wiedereinführung der Sklaverei in Guadeloupe" ("Reestablishment of Slavery in Guadeloupe"), both first published in 1949, and "Das Licht auf dem Galgen" ("The Light on the Gallows"), which first appeared in 1960. Netty Radvanyi née Reiling, an accomplished art historian who derived her *nom de guerre* from her field, was, in addition to being herself a great writer, an expert in, and lover and emulator of, realist narrative prose and, specifically, the tales of Heinrich von Kleist, as well as a firmly convinced socialist and committed member of the Communist Party: all of which indelibly shaped not only her career and her work in general, but also, in two of her *Karibische Geschichten,* her joint portrayals of blacks and Jews in particular. Already the title of her "Die Hochzeit von Haiti" harks back to one of Kleist's stories, his "Die Verlobung in St. Domingo" ("The Engagement in Santo Domingo") of 1811, which constitutes, in all likelihood, both the earliest and most widely debated as well as, I daresay, boldest and most personal treatment of a turning point in black American history that has intrigued and inspired the German mind for over a century and a half.[34] Time permitting, I could analyze an entire series of examples, both of the impact of Kleist's tale and of the influence exerted by its place and subject matter; and either would issue not merely from literature but from music, too.[35] Let me recite but a modicum of names, dates, and facts: The year 1812 saw Theodor Körner's dramatization of the Kleistian novella and, especially, its heroine, *Toni.* In 1836, a six-volume novel entitled *Die Kreolin und der Neger* ("The Creole Girl and the Negro") was at once brought out by a man writing under the pseudonym Emerentius Scävola.[36] The expressionist turned objectivist, Karl Otten, penned a volume which dates from 1931 and bears the somewhat ironical heading, *Der schwarze Napoleon* ("Black Napoleon"), given its reference to Toussaint Louverture, the father of Haitian liberty so treacherously caught and put to death precisely by Bonaparte. And since 1976, the year Hans Christoph Buch published his documentary *Die Scheidung von San Domingo* ("The Separation of Santo Domingo"—the title is a pun alluding to both Kleist and Seghers, for "Scheidung" also means "divorce"), no fewer than three new literary works dealing with the selfsame topic have come out: in 1979, Heiner Müller's forceful play *Der Auftrag* ("The Mission"), which demonstrably draws upon two of the Seghers stories; in 1980, the latter's own second triad of pertinent tales, *Drei Frauen aus Haiti* ("Three Women from Haiti"); and, in 1984, Buch's second contribution, his ambitious if controversial novel *Die Hochzeit von Port-au-Prince* ("The Wedding in Port-au-Prince"), which is likewise indebted to Seghers as well as Kleist. Nor has this vogue as yet abated, at least not insofar as the prolific Buch is concerned. His third production of the genre, a booklet of reportages containing, among other things, his Haitian diary, has already been announced; its title will run, so we hear, *Karibische Kaltluft* ("Cold Air from the Caribbean").

With which we are back at Seghers' *Karibische Geschichten*. But let me quote Buch one more time, because his first publication is subtitled, "Wie die Negersklaven von Haiti Robespierre beim Wort nahmen" ("How the Negro Slaves of Haiti Took Robespierre at His Word"); and that, combined with what has already been hinted at in respect to Napoleon and Toussaint Louverture, pretty much sums up the purport of the aforesaid historical turning point and, thereby, the hub of Seghers' book. For not only are the three tales assembled in it located in the West Indies, but they also cover the same period: the years around 1802 and shortly afterwards, when Bonaparte revoked the liberation of blacks and the abolition of slavery once mandated and carried through by the French Revolution, and set out to reestablish the status quo—successfully, alas, in most cases—by force of arms. Both slavery itself and the slave trade, he decreed, were to be restored in concordance with the rules and regulations that had been in effect prior to 1789:

> L'esclavage sera maintenu conformément aux lois et règlements antérieurs à 1789...La traite des noirs et leur importation dans les...colonies auront lieu conformément [*etc.*][37]

In other words, the man who was about to emancipate, notably in Germany, large segments of European Jewry, which earned him the lifelong affection of a Heine who revered him as "My Emperor" and declared as late as 1852: "I have gone through every phasis of modern thought and feeling...but I have never swerved from my faith in the Emperor"[38]—this man was simultaneously bent on subjugating and debasing, oppressing and exploiting an entire branch of humankind, in Africa no less than in America. Indeed, so angry was Bonaparte at a liberty, equality, and fraternity which had created black officers wearing epaulets and medals, and even black generals such as Toussaint Louverture or Dessalines, that he could hardly wait to see these rights abolished, or reabolished, throughout the so-called colonies, and these upright men, in the most brutal sense of the term, degraded. His brother-in-law, the commander in chief of the army the white racist in Paris sent to what then was still considered France's possession, Saint-Domingue, but soon became known as the first modern black state, Haiti, received the curt instruction: "Pray rid us of those gilt Africans" *(Défaites-nous de ces Africains dorés)!*[39]

This chilling Napoleonic backlash, or jarring contrast in Bonaparte's attitude towards the Jews, on the one hand, and the blacks, on the other, prompted Seghers' portrayal of the dual "counter-type" in her Caribbean tales "Die Hochzeit von Haiti" and "Das Licht auf dem Galgen." Whether, in composing them, the progressive author succumbed herself to some unwitting stereotyping is a problem of its own the solution of which I shall readily leave to the specialists; from what I can judge, they are soundly divided on the question. The professional African Germanist Maguèye Kassé heaps lavish and unrestrained praise upon Seghers[40] while the black American scholar Marian E. Musgrave takes her to task, if only in part. "Seghers' depiction of the status of mulattoes and Jews...is valuable," Musgrave admits in an unpublished paper she kindly made available to me; but Seghers' depiction of blacks, she concludes, "show[s] how ancient emotional attitudes can persist even in intelligent persons dedicated to socialism and the classless society."[41] That which is decisive here, though, is the simple fact that blacks, Jews, and mulattoes are depicted together, and that their joint portrayal is meant to bespeak and symbolize the unity of all the wretched of the earth, regardless of race or color. It is the same unity invoked and demonstrated by friends and comrades of Seghers such as Bertolt Brecht and Erich Arendt: for instance, in the former's "Solidaritätslied" ("Song of Solidarity," with its rousing appeal, "Schwarzer, Weißer, Brauner, Gelber!")[42] or in the latter's impressive (and, as it seems, still undiscovered) cycle of near thirty poems on the toil and hardships of blacks in Colombia, "Tolú," a cycle framed, most tellingly, by two equally impressive texts on the similar lot of the Columbian Indios.[43] Clearly, Brecht's and Arendt's ideas are unambiguous—but so are those of Seghers, for, in both her stories, it is a Jew who either joins hands with, or even assays to lead, the blacks in their struggle for freedom. In "Die Hochzeit von Haiti," he is the young Michael Nathan who not only marries a black girl but also—which is far more important—indefatigably serves Toussaint Louverture; in "Das Licht auf dem Galgen," he is Jean Sasportas who stirs the slaves in Jamaica to their rebellion which, although it proves to be abortive, signals the future liberation of blacks from British bondage. This pronounced message of an overall, indeed global, solidarity and the perspective it opens up of hope and defiance fully come to the fore at the end of each tale, when the Jewish protagonist pines away (as does Nathan) or is hanged by the oppressors (as is Sasportas). As a matter of fact, Toussaint Louverture in his icy dungeon in France and Nathan, who has managed to escape, die, suggestively enough, "at about the same time" *(ungefähr um dieselbe Zeit);* and the narrator comments:

> Bei diesen zwei Toten fallen einem die Bäume ein, die, längs der Heerstraßen quer durch Europa gepflanzt, zusammen krank werden und verkommen. Ihr Tod, gleichzeitig an verschiedenen Enden der Welt [!], erscheint einem weniger rätselhaft, wenn man weiß, daß sie derselben Aussaat entstammen.[44]

The roads all over Europe along which the trees wither and die together because they were sown or planted together are the highroads of the French Revolution and what it stands for; there is scarcely much of an enigma, but plenty of symbolism, about these trees and their "simultaneous deaths." Nor can there be any doubt as to the ending of Seghers' other black-Jewish story and its significance. Sasportas, when being led to the gallows, and asked, one last time, who were his "accomplices," replies, pointing to the hundreds of newly enslaved blacks that have been herded together by their masters and are forced to watch his execution: "Ich sehe hier viele meiner Komplicen, sie stehen hier, sie stehen dort." And when the hangman finally ties the noose around his neck, Sasportas shouts: "Ihr Neger, macht es wie die in Haiti!"[45] Which is to say that the blacks of all the world are, or ought to be, not just his comrades but also their mutual companions; that the oppressed, as it were, are all children of one people, and should think and act and fight accordingly. "To Anna Seghers," it has been observed, "the Haitian upheaval was a dress rehearsal for the world revolution..."[46] Yet what had happened in Haiti was not a mere rehearsal but a historical event in its own right, and what Seghers actually conveys is, I believe, better expressed by Müller's poignant and laconic variation, in his aforecited play, on the Marxian "Proletarians of all countries": namely, "the Negroes of all races" *(die Neger aller Rassen)*.[47] Here as elsewhere, in literature as in politics, "the fact that German left-wing intellectuals were predominantly of Jewish origin cannot be ignored," to quote Mosse[48] again.

Sasportas' corpse, thrown to the bottom of the bay to be eaten up by the shark, disappeared like a stone, Seghers tells us; to those watching, however, it was "as if a light shone from the top of the gallows" *(als leuchte ein Licht von der Spitze des Galgens)*.[49] In Wolfgang Koeppen's novel *Tauben im Gras* ("Pigeons in the Grass," from a line by Gertrude Stein) of 1951, there is no such comforting symbol and little, if any, defiance or hope; rather, what he opens up is the bleak outlook on a disheartening recurrence of the same age-old prejudices and persecutions. Or should that be too pessimistic an interpretation of Koeppen's decidedly positive vision, though critically negative version, of the dual "counter-type" of blacks and Jews? At any rate, like all of the numerous actions of *Tauben im Gras*—its whole plot and structure are formed after Joyce's *Ulysses* and the novels of Dos Passos, *Manhattan Transfer* in particular—these two strands run parallel to each other and, moreover, intersect at one point only, in a juncture of realism, symbolism, and authorial commentary; and both the remembrance of Jewishness and its union with the experience of blackness have been dealt with convincingly by Nancy A. Lauckner, first, in her dissertation of 1971, then, in an article on the "Surrogate Jew" *(Ersatzjude)* based on it.[50] The latter term is ominous indeed, but fittingly characterizes the role of the two black protagonists (American soldiers by name of Washington Price and Odysseus[51] Cotton, respectively) whose doings and sufferings during one hectic day in a postwar German city (a thinly veiled Munich in 1949 or 1950) Koeppen relates, and ruminates upon, in his book. On the symbolic plane,[52] Price, Cotton, and their black fellow GI's represent the Jews; yet likewise, in dire reality, they live and reflect the plight of the minority to which they themselves belong. Their treatment by the German populace exposes the perpetuation of anti-Semitism as well as the existence of a racist attitude towards blacks. The analogy between both groups is amply established by the similar reactions they provoke: both are regarded as inferior by the Germans, and both are charged with *Rassenschande* in their sexual relationships with German women. However, their strongest identification is provided by a pogrom scene in which the black soldiers serve as scapegoats who are virtually being stoned, after one of them has killed an old German porter by accident, and stereotyping associates them all with the crime. Koeppen consciously and unmistakably modeled the assault upon the black GI Club on the events of the infamous *Reichskristallnacht* of 1938, for even the mob recognizes the similarity between the two attacks:

> Die Älteren fühlten sich an etwas erinnert; sie fühlten sich an eine andere Blindheit, an eine frühere Aktion, an andere Scherben erinnert.[53]

But there are more memories yet. Not without reason, the incident is also connected by Koeppen, through his subtle evocation in the thoughts of the people involved, with the stationing of black French troops in the Rhineland in the aftermath of World War I, that is, with the so-called Black Horror, or Ignominy *(Schwarze Schmach),* which their presence signified for racist Germans...and, I might add, Englishmen and Americans as well:

> Die Neger in Uniform, ihr Club, ihre Mädchen, waren sie nicht ein schwarzes Symbol der Niederlage, der Schmach des Besiegtseins, waren sie nicht das Zeichen der Erniedrigung und der Schande?[54]

All this is laid bare and branded by Koeppen with the admirable verve and indignation but, even more so, the familiar resignation and sadness of what has been nicknamed "the melancholic Left." Perhaps he discerned a faint glimmer of hope in the closeness and determination of Washington and his pregnant friend, Carla, and in the innocence, despite appearances, of the love between Odysseus and Susanne;[55] otherwise, gloom and despair prevail. As if summarizing *Tauben im Gras* and the mood it imparts, Wolf Wondratschek noted as late as 1969 that the Germans hadn't learned anything; they had simply found different Jews: "Sie haben nichts dazu gelernt. Sie haben andere Juden gefunden."[56] Or as Carla's mother has it in the novel itself, "whether Negro or Jew, it was the same" *(ob Neger oder Jude, es war dasselbe).*[57]

Surely one of those who had not learned anything was Gerd Gaiser, the author of the 1958 novel and best-seller *Schlußball: Aus den schönen Tagen der Stadt Neu-Spuhl (The Final Ball*—Gaiser's subtitle, with its disdainful allusion[58] to the "economic miracle" in West Germany, the *Wirtschaftswunder,* was dropped in the American edition). The eerie reminiscences exuding from the English title are, it must be said in all fairness, accidental;[59] unfortunately, however, they are not unjustified. For Gaiser's is not only an unabashedly negative, but a *volkish* and fascist version of the black-Jewish "counter-type," indeed of the stereotype *par excellence* of an inferior race— inferior, that is, to the Teutonic or Aryan "ideal-type." He may not have been a major literary figure; yet he was certainly a skillful and effective narrator who enjoyed considerable fame, both in his country and abroad, between the end of World War II and the early 1960s until, in a spectacular and sovereign piece of criticism, Marcel Reich-Ranicki unmasked and dethroned him for good. The gist of the matter can be summed up by the experts' general observations. "Most racists," writes Mosse in *Toward the Final Solution,* "endowed inferior races whether black or Jewish with several identical properties such as lack of beauty, and charged them with the lack of. . . middle-class virtues, and finally with lack of any metaphysical depth."[60] And Gilman chimes in, adding that "one of the qualities ascribed by anti-Semites to the Jews (as well as to the Gypsies) was their 'blackness,' a quality of the world of the stereotype rather than of reality."[61] What we are faced with in Gaiser's book is indeed a blackness without blacks, but also a Jewishness without Jews; still, it constitutes one of the worst and most despicable instances of that double racial stereotyping.

*Schlußball'*s main plot is centered on the "dark" *(dunkel)* and "dangerous" *(gefährlich)*[62] Rakitsch, a youngster who hails from somewhere in the East, and on the most indigenous girl, Diemut Andernoth, whose unblemished purity, chastity, and blond braid make her the prototype of a German Gretchen figure and, therefore, the natural prey such an unwanted foreign creature lusts for. Her very name is revealing, both in terms of her innate Germanism, or *Deutschtum,* and of the threat hovering about her. As to her Christian name, Diemut, it not only suggests "humility" (*Demut,* as opposed to Rakitsch's impudence)[63] but likewise, if surreptitiously, a *volkish* mind, for Middle High German "diet" (*Volk,* which has the selfsame etymological root as *deutsch*) and "muot" (which designates, among other things, *Gemüt* and *Gesinnung*) may, and perhaps are to, be combined to read 'Die[t]mut.' The symbolic qualities of her surname are downright blatant, with its twofold suggestion of "another emergency" *(ander[e] Not),* on the one hand, which it is "necessary" (*not*wendig) and "high time" (*an der* Zeit) to contravene, on the other. However, far more important is the portrait, gradually taking shape under Gaiser's mean pen, of Rakitsch, "that fellow"—as he is repeatedly referred to[64] with a scornful gesture—from Eastern Europe. Little, if any, commentary will be needed,[65] I am afraid, as we proceed from his facial features to his mental traits and, at last, his deeds and misdeeds, all of which are equally "repulsive" *(widerwärtig).*[66] For example, Rakitsch's "etwas zu volle Lippen" ("rather overful [i.e., thick, or pouting] lips")[67] or the concomitant emphasis on the "lower part" of his face, implying, it goes without saying, the "typical" protruding jaw to which the no less "typical" low forehead corresponds, clearly implied in turn in Gaiser's remark that Rakitsch's "Stirn war auffallend durch eine einzige tiefe, waagrechte Falte geteilt" ("his forehead was conspicuously divided by a single deep horizontal wrinkle").[68] And not only is Rakitsch equipped, *tout court,* with a "black face" *(schwarzes Gesicht),*[69] but he can boast, at least in an earlier and even more outspoken version,[70] of a "dark accent" *(dunkler Akzent).* Indeed, one of the characters in *Schlußball* muses, again in its earlier version:

> Ich habe mich manchmal gefragt, warum Rakitsch so schwarz wirkte. Betrachtete man ihn genau, so waren seine Haare nicht einmal tiefschwarz, sie waren nur sehr dunkel und sehr dicht, auch seine Brauen; das ganze Untergesicht [!] hatte diesen dunklen Anflug.

> (I've sometimes asked myself why Rakitsch conveyed such an impression of blackness. If you looked at him well, his hair was not jet black, it was only very dark and thick; so were his eyebrows. The whole lower part of his face had this air of darkness.)[71]

What kind of a mentality can you expect to reside in so base a head? Accordingly, Rakitsch is both "very polite" *(sehr höflich)* and "insidious," even "malicious" (for this is what *hinterhältig,* rendered as "cunning" in the American edition, really means);[72] his manners are a mixture of servility and stubbornness[73]—Gaiser goes so far as to call them "dunkelfarbig und geschmeidig" (i.e., not just "dark" but, literally, "dark-colored" or "-skinned," and "supple").[74] Or compare yet another telling variant from that passage the author thought best to change:

> Rakitsch aber mit seinem dunklen Akzent hatte die Verkehrsart eines Stammes, der gewohnt war, sich zu biegen, um am Ende oben zu sein.

> (But Rakitsch, with his dark accent, had the mode of behavior of a breed accustomed to bowing down [literally: to bending] in order to finish on top.)[75]

As befits the member of such a "breed" or "tribe"—one could scarcely have been more explicit in post-Nazi Germany—Rakitsch has no culture, either, nor any sense of understanding cultural achievements,[76] for, as Mosse informs us, the racial characteristics of the Jews included, in the eyes of German anti-Semites, a "lack of [genuine] culture."[77] Small wonder, then, if the people of Neu-Spuhl never feel "comfortable" in Rakitsch's presence,[78] and nobody wants to have anything to do with him.[79] Soon, they even suspect him, questionable *nouveaux riches* and properly poor and modest Germans alike, of being capable of committing murder![80] Yet isn't this, once more, but logical, in view of his being both bestial and mad? "His approach was sometimes that of a simpleton," we read in the American translation;[81] however, the German original runs: "Manches sah er so simpel an wie ein Schwach-sinniger [i.e., a half wit, or imbecile]."[82] As a result, Rakitsch is solidly placed, if only for a few weeks, "in a mental institution *[Heilstätte]* for ob-servation."[83] And not sometimes, but time after time, almost throughout the whole book, he is classified as a "mad dog" *(verrückter Hund)*[84]—which is not a mere figure of speech, nor a current invective or term of abuse, but an intentional equation, on the part of the author, with insanity as well as ani-mality, indeed beastliness. Just ponder the shrewd rhetoric with which Gaiser juxtaposes, hence implicitly equalizes, the attack of a real dog, re-lated at great length in a previous chapter, with the advances of Rakitsch to Diemut, whose teacher reflects: "...ich versuchte, sie vor einem Hund zu schützen und später vor diesem Rakitsch" ("[I tried] to protect her first from a dog and then from that [fellow,] Rakitsch").[85] Alternately, the latter is likened to a "poisonous spider" *(eine Spinne, die giftig ist)* in a "thick black [!] forest,"[86] to a beast of prey "lying in wait," its "claw *[Kralle]* raised,"[87] and to a "reptile" *(Reptil)* that even kindhearted people are tempted to do away with:[88] that is, Rakitsch is equated with either a murder-ous predator which has to be killed, or a disgusting and harmful vermin which has to be exterminated. The last literary step to be taken—and Gaiser does take it—is the switch from figurative speech, or the residue thereof, to direct wishful thinking and, consequently, blunt and uninhibited abomina-tions:

> Ich weiß nicht, warum es Menschen wie diesen Rakitsch überhaupt geben soll. Und wenn es sie gibt, weiß ich nicht, warum sie frei herumlaufen...Am be-sten, der Kerl wäre tot.

> (I don't know why people like Rakitsch should exist at all. And if they must I don't know why they should run about loose.... It would be best if the fellow *were* dead.)[89]

At the end of the novel, he is. Having in vain pursued and molested pure, chaste, blond Diemut over some two hundred pages, he decides to snare the girl with a loop of piano wire, in order to subdue and rape her, but in the rainy night mistakenly attacks her mother, the equally pure, chaste, blond widow of a German officer missing in action: she pushes him back against an iron fence, and, losing his balance, he hits the slippery pavement and breaks his neck. Whereupon Mrs. Andernoth spends a long, long time washing and rinsing her hands....

To conclude: Rakitsch the Easterner is in every respect, physically as well as mentally, an amalgam of what the Nazis considered the salient fea-tures of inferior races, not only in blacks and Jews but also in Slavs and Gypsies, though in the former two primarily; and the same applies to the opposition of this lustful, beastly, and "idiotic" *(schwachsinnig)*[90] "counter-type" to the "ideal-type" embodied, no less saliently, by Diemut and her mother. As if the endless repetitions and variations of such traits were still not sufficient proof, both of Rakitsch's preponderant blackness and Jewishness in disguise, he is even said, with a grotesque turnabout, to be a talented musician albeit so stupid as to produce, "doggedly," and "with a terrifying infernal persistence," nothing but one single "outcry forty and fifty times over, nagging, howling like a dog" *(hechelnd, hündisch klagend)*.[91] Which is exactly the way Nazism conceived of jazz, that depraved kind of music; and while jazz is or was, at least in Germany, stereotypical of blacks—as was (or is) madness chiefly in this country, according to Gilman[92]—Rakitsch's twisted and distorted German grammar is a replica of the Nazi conception of Yiddish, thus stereotypical of Jews. For example, instead of saying, "Ich möchte mit Ihrer Tochter gehen dürfen," Rakitsch says, "Ich möchte gehen dürfen mit Ihrer Tochter" ("I should like to be permitted to go with your daughter");[93] or he stutters:

> Ich komme immer, wenn Sie werden wollen.... Vielleicht ist für mich gut, wenn Unruhe.

> (I shall always come when you wish it.... Perhaps for me it is good, anxiety.)[94]

The anxiety is all ours, as is the revulsion. Justly, Reich-Ranicki, without even noticing the black implications, has pronounced the devastating and lapidary verdict on Gaiser: "His work does not serve the truth" *(Sein Werk dient nicht der Wahrheit)*.[95]

Incidentally, should anyone have qualms as to the legitimacy of the foregoing reading and its conclusions, I recommend the perusal, however cursory, of a slim volume of very mediocre poetry entitled *Reiter am Himmel* ("Riders in the Sky"). It was published by Gerd Gaiser in 1941, and everything racist, fascist, indeed Nazi which I have laid to his charge is more than borne out by this collection. Paying express homage to "Der Führer" in a like-named poem,[96] and celebrating, over and over, the Aryan race, and the Teutons, Germans, and Swabians in particular,[97] it reveals itself as a specimen of *Blut und Boden* scribble of the vilest persuasion. Concerning the Jews, who are pictured as hissing snakelike instigators, having "hetzend uns unter den eigenen Sohlen angezischt," Gaiser puts forth the assertion, veritably macabre in view of the "final solution" it coldly anticipates:

> Als der Führer das unerbittliche
> Auge auf euch geheftet,
> Gewichen seid ihr den Blicken der Helden, schrittweis taumelnd,
> In Dämmer verlöschend, ins Nichtsein, in schale Vergessenheit.[98]

The "inexorable" stare of the *Führer* brings about, by means of such questionable "heroes" as mentioned in Jünger's *Strahlungen,* a virtual "twilight" of the Jews and, literally, their "extinction," their "nonexistence" and final "oblivion"! Yet conversely, in the adulatory poem on Hitler, one of them, "ein Hebräer" ("a Hebrew") in Gaiser's wording, even has the *chutz-pah* of leading and commanding Germany's enemies! Again, though, we cannot but shudder when realizing what ensues:

> Einer Schlachtsau Leben wird einstmals das eure gelten,
> Stickig und fett.

> (Your lives will be counted as those of swine to be slaughtered,
> Sticky and fat.)[99]

Blacks, it is true, emerge only once, as far as I am aware; but the lengthy poem, "Unheil, ihr weißen Völker" ("Danger [or Disaster], Ye White Nations"), one of the longest and most elaborate verses of the entire collection, is all the more telling. Namely, it amounts to a thoroughly racist and Pan-Germanic exhortation, a warning urging the Europeans to be on their guard, under enforced Nazi leadership, against the impending Black menace; for although Gaiser merely talks, summarily, of "colored people" *(die Farbigen)* he clearly points to Africa and the Africans in the main. The following lines, replete with racial as well as political supremacism, speak for themselves:

> Waffen, ihr Völker. Sollen die Farbigen
> Eure Söhne morgen vom Wege fegen?
> Auf euer Weiß und Blond
> Wie auf Vogelscheuchen
> Ihre Kinder kreischend mit Fingern deuten?
> Soll denn versinken,
> Was eure eisernen Reiter erstritten, was sie
> Brennend von Gift und Durst
> Fiebernden Hirnes erschaut,
> Euch vererbend die reisige
> Vorhand über die ganze Welt?

> Denn es lauern die andern. Einstens
> Waren sie laut, in verschnörkelten
> Tänzen kindisch die Hüften drehend,
> Von ihren Inseln
> Scholl ihr närrisches [!] Schellengeklingel.
> Stumm geworden nun sind sie.
> Drohender schweigt,
> Als sie ehemals rief gegen den Nachbarstamm,
> In den Wäldern die Fehdetrommel.
> Tief holen sie Atem.
> Euch zu ersticken, langen sie lautlos aus.
> Ihr gabt ihnen Waffen.
> Schweigsam äugt über seine Fibel das Zambokind.
> Eure schnellen Maschinen
> Steuert der Farbige ebenso gut wie ihr,

Und entschlossener noch, des Todes
Weniger achtsam.
Unerschöpflich an Zahl,
Schiert ihn kein Leben.

Having noted in passing that, indeed, the concept of innate black craziness
is not confined to the United States, and readily lends itself to utterances like
these, we hear the author addressing the "white nations" afresh, as he goes
on:

Und ihr zerfleischt euch.
In euren Brudermord,
Da vom erwürgenden Neid
Schwimmt der verdunkelte Blick,
Wird, euch begrabend, der Aufruhr schlagen.

Gaiser's text culminates in the unconditional justification of Hitler's war:

Darum tritt du, mein Volk,
Du dieses Erdteils
Altes Gewissen, die Führung an.
Aus den Händen
Schlage das Schwert den Verblendeten.
Mit bewaffneter Faust
Schirm dies helldunkele Land.
Schlichte die Marken.
Weise die Stätte an allen Bewohnenden.
Laß ohne Neid und Furcht,
Selbstgenügsam und streng
Aneinander geschart,
In gerüstetem Frieden
Weiß und Gelb und Rot ihre Wohnstatt haben.[100]

Whites—with the exclusion of Jews, naturally—and people of yellow or red
skin may live in peace under the German dominance taken for granted in
that imperialist and colonialist poem. Conspicuously absent from Gaiser's
pax nazista, in spite of its ecumenical claim, are the blacks.[101]

Turning to Bruno Frank, ought we not to expect something unequivocally antiracist from a man who was an antifascist, after all, and a fellow exile and intimate friend of Thomas Mann, and who, moreover, closely
modeled his tale in question on the latter's *Death in Venice*? Unfortunately,
Frank's ideas about blacks and, especially, black Africans as expressed in his
Politische Novelle ("Political Novella") of 1928 do not in the least diverge
from the Nazi lore ground out and disseminated in *Reiter am Himmel,* or
from the stereotypical blackness within the crypto-racism pervading
Schlußball—whereas his image of Jewry is totally different from Gaiser's,

even diametrically opposed to it. What is also remarkable is the fact that this (I hate to say) well-wrought story, which appeared in American translation under the allusive title *The Persians Are Coming,* has gone wholly unheeded so far in pertinent criticism[102] although it is a most revelatory piece of writing indeed. Frank's tale is a *livre à clef,* the famous event underlying it being the *Gespräch von Thoiry* ("Conversation at Thoiry," a small village near Geneva)[103] between the French politician Aristide Briand and his German counterpart Gustav Stresemann, then the two leading European statesmen. They had met there secretly on 17 September 1926 in order to work out, after the signing of the Locarno Treaties, further steps toward appeasement in Europe and, above all, a lasting reconciliation of Germany with France. But if the meeting as such was quite congenial and cordial, and bade fair, its results proved to be disappointing nonetheless; and both the proverbial "silver lining on the horizon" and its quick disappearance are reflected in Frank's fictionalized account, the ending of which, fraught with symbolism, is marked by the German protagonist's violent "death in Marseilles."[104]

Two aspects are of crucial importance in *Politische Novelle:* first, Frank's political creed as it manifests itself in the thought and talks and entire behavior of Carmer alias Stresemann and Dorval alias Briand, as well as in the agreement they reach and in the fatal outcome for one of them all the same; and, second, Frank's conception of Jewishness as it can be gleaned from the encounter and heated debate yet, likewise, sudden and ultimate harmony between another pair of Franco-German characters, Dr. Erlanger and Monsieur François Bloch, the Jewish secretaries of Carmer and Dorval, whom they respectfully address as "Meister" or "Maître," and who in turn are united with their young aids and colleagues in "brotherly" *(brüderlich)* sympathy and understanding.[105] In either instance, the images and/or realities of Africa, indeed of blacks at large and the "dark world" *(dunkle Welt)*[106] in general, supply the hateful and hostile foil to the views propounded or insinuated by the author, and to the hopes and fears he nourishes with regard to his beloved Europe, which he praises, extols, nay boundlessly adulates. For what is at stake here is not, as in the case of Gaiser's poem, a chauvinistic Germany, let alone her Nazi hegemony over the world, but precisely Europe or, to be more specific yet, Europe's heartland and innermost core represented by both France and Germany, the discordant heirs to the once universal monarchy of Charlemagne. (Belgium and the Netherlands are of course included in it, as are Switzerland, Austria, and Italy.) Not just Charlemagne, whose name is duly invoked,[107] but a wealth of similar invocations serve to underscore Frank's Eurocentric—and, for its part, chauvinistic enough—notion of a supreme and superior Occident, or *Abendland,* that has thriven and bloomed ever since Greek antiquity, and brought forth all the paramount cultural achievements on this globe, but which had also to be defended against the incessant thrust of all sorts of barbarians from the days of Marathon and Salamis onwards. In earlier centuries, though, the attacks of such uncouth and inferior races came from one flank only—namely, the vast plains of Russia and the steppes extending beyond—whereas the latter-day Huns and Mongols, Turks and Tatars (to use Gaiser's apposite list)[108] are now coming, according to Frank, from no fewer than three sides at one and the same time: to wit, the Asian East, the American West (which is, in effect, a pseudo-West as it is infected with blackness), and, last but surely not least, the African South. Threatening the pure and genuine West—i.e., occidental and continental Europe—or already assailing and invading it in their attempts at causing its downfall and ignominious decline, are the barbarized Bolsheviks, on the one hand, and the uncivilized plutocrats, on the other. The most dangerous and, in the long run, disastrous onslaught, however, is that of "the African Persians" (as Frank explicitly labels the blacks from Africa)[109] who, having succeeded in making a breach on the Mediterranean shores of France, are pouring in through the very harbor of Marseilles where Carmer, in a way clearly reminiscent of the events at Thermopylae, will die at the hands of a traitor. While the "huge wave of collectivist uniformity" *(ungeheure Woge kollektivischer Uniformität)*[110] swelling up in the East, Russian Communism, is discarded lightly and speedily by the author, he spends an enormous amount of space and effort on depicting, in grotesque and gruesome detail, the dual black menace: first, the one from America, palpably typified by Josephine Baker (whose name here is Becky Floyd) and a jazz band; then, the one from Africa, most tangibly concretized by what Dorval sarcastically refers to as "our glorious colonial army" *(unsere glorreiche Kolonialarmee),*[111] that is, the actual presence of black troops in European lands. Both these depictions would easily yield a couple of studies of their own—a comparison, for example, with the portrayal of *Josephine* in Dieter Kühn's recent book[112] would be particularly interesting—and both also abound with reckless stereotyping. Suffice it, therefore, simply to record that the "howling" nonmusic of jazz is performed by "grinning [black] devil[s]," that Becky's dancing boils down to an orgy of "primitive paroxysms" (literally, *Urwaldraserei*), and that, once more, none other than Dorval himself calls the African soldiers "thick-lipped gentry" (literally, *diese Wulstmäuler*) and even "that herd of grey-skinned cattle they are training so that one day it can destroy Europe" *(diese Herde von grauhäutigem Vieh, das man dressiert, damit es einst Europa vernichten kann).*[113] The ending is melodramatic: Carmer, lured into the brothel district of the old Marseilles harbor quarter, finds himself irresistibly attracted by a beautiful girl from Madagascar, fifteen years of age and, as one will guess, not really black but a Hova, and of royal lineage at that. Frank explains:

> Ihr gemischtes Blut machte diese schön. Es war wenig vom Neger an ihr und viel vom Malayen.

(It was the mingled blood that made her lovely. She had little of the Negro and much of the Malay.)[114]

Alas, this embodiment of blissful ecstasy and "sensual sweetness" *(sinnliche Süße)*[115] is but the decoy of a gigantic black, hideous and tattooed, who brandishes a monstrous dagger and intends to rob and, if necessary, kill Carmer. Yet lo and behold, the latter—hardly very Stresemann-like—reveals himself as an experienced boxer and elegantly knocks the ogre out with a single uppercut. Only then, while finally embracing the lovely one, is he stabbed to death from behind—not by his felled assailant who lies "still dazed" *(in Betäubung),*[116] nor by any other of the black Africans populating the district, but, most significantly, by a member of the white rabble associated with them. The scene is well worth quoting:

> Carmer...wandte sich um. Sie war da. Sie bot sich ihm hin, anders als zuvor. Sie blickte ihn wohlig von unten an, mit wohlig leicht geöffnetem Mund. Ein Duft stieg auf von ihr wie von Mandel oder seltenen Hölzern, bitter und zart. Ihre starre, starke Brust drängte ihm zu. Da schlug er die Arme um sie und beugte sich nieder und suchte den dunklen Mund und verging. Und in diesem Kusse starb Carmer.
>
> Sein Mörder war leise hervorgekommen. Er stolperte fast über die Beine des Geschlagenen, hielt sich noch und raffte das Messer auf, das jenem entfallen war.
>
> Er trat hinter die umschlungen Dastehenden und maß Carmers Rücken.
>
> Er zielte mit feigem Bedacht und stieß ihm mit voller Gewalt die Flammenklinge unter das linke Schulterblatt.
>
> Der Getroffene bäumte sich auf aus dem Kuß, hob weit seine Arme, kreiste schwankend um sich und fiel nieder auf das Pflaster, den Kopf zuhöchst.
>
> ...Der Mörder...stand zu Carmers Häupten, seinen letzten Atem erwartend, um ihn auszurauben und seinen Leichnam zu verbergen.
>
> Er war ein Weißer, ein junger Mensch mit einem breiten hellen Gesicht, mit stumpfblauen Augen und stumpfblondem Haar, das hervorquoll unter der Kokarde einer schirmlosen Soldatenmütze. Von dem einen Heer war diese Kokarde genommen, vom andern die blaue Zuavenjacke, vom dritten der Gurt. Er hielt das Urwaldmesser in seiner Hand, das er beim Stoß der Wunde entrissen hatte. Aber er selbst war nur ein Splitter der furchtbaren Waffe, mit der Europa seinen Selbstmord beging.

(Carmer...turned. She was there. She offered herself again but not as before, looking at him with an upward, appealing look, and parted lips. She gave out a faintly bitter fragrance, like almonds or exotic woods. Her firm bare breasts stood out. He flung his arms about her and bent and sought her dark mouth and was lost. In that kiss Carmer died.

His murderer had stolen forward; he almost stumbled over the Negro's legs, stooped, and snatched up the knife the other had let fall. He stepped behind the two standing there in their embrace and measured Carmer's back.

He aimed with cowardly deliberation and thrust the flame-shaped blade with all his strength under the left shoulder-blade.

His victim lifted himself from the embrace, flung up his arm, swung around, tottered, and fell head first to the ground.

. . .The murderer stood. . .at Carmer's head, waiting for his last breath to rob the body and hide it.

He was a white man, and young, with a broad, fair face, dull blue eyes, and a shock of dull blond hair beneath the cockade of a peakless soldier's cap. The cap he had from one army, his blue zouave jacket from another, from a third his belt. He held the primeval knife in his hand, he had torn it out of the wound upon the thrust. But he himself was only a splinter of [the] frightful weapon with which Europe was committing suicide.)[117]

Any commentary would be superfluous. Evidently, the ideology poeticized, more than a decade later, by Gaiser in his "Unheil, ihr weißen Völker" looms large in that scene and in the whole tale narrated so cleverly by the antifascist author, Frank. And such ideological contradictions are by no means isolated in his oeuvre.[118] Still, I must not omit mentioning that, on the other hand, and just one year after the text under consideration, Frank penned and published a second novella involving blacks, another *livre à clef*—this time, based on the life and work of the great Austrian director Max Reinhardt—and that the images of the Afro-American actors and actresses portrayed in *Der Magier* ("The Magician"), though certainly not without stereotyping, differ markedly from those, both of the black Americans and of the black Africans, contained in *Politische Novelle*. Conversely, however, Frank's concomitant image of the Jew remains, *mutatis mutandis,* the same.[119]

A chapter in a monograph devoted to American fiction bears the heading "The Black Siren" and arrives at the conclusion that it is almost invariably "the mulatto stereotype" which provides "the stock basis for the black temptress."[120] Frank's portrayal of the Hova girl perfectly fits this definition of a character closely akin to the so-called beautiful quadroon or octoroon. Yet the lovely one from Madagascar could likewise be shown to exemplify the German edition of that female stereotype—again, time permitting, I could digress into its history, which is one of true love and devotion as much as of enticement and lust, and trace it over the past two centuries. It would include not only Toni, the heroine of Kleist's "Verlobung in St. Domingo," but also Zambo-Maria, the heroine of a work totally neglected, to my knowledge, in our entire context: namely, Gottfried Keller's tale "Don Correa" from his cycle of novellas of 1882, *Das Sinngedicht* ("The Epigram"). Indeed it would take us back, in a way, to the ancient Ethiopians as deviating from the black Africans, at least in the European mind, and even to the Queen of Sheba, another venerable figure "blackened" (no pun intended) on medieval German soil,[121] not unlike her Biblical or Christian consorts, Saint Maurice and the youngest of the Magi, yet without becoming a real black. The missing link—that is, between antiquity and the Middle Ages, on the one hand, and the 19th century, on the other—might perhaps be found in Christoph Martin Wieland's *Geschichte der Abderiten* ("The Story of the People of Abder") of 1774, for he, too, differentiates the Africans inhabiting the tropics, who are "blacker than the ravens" *(schwärzer. . . als die Raben),* from those living on the fringes of Africa or nearby, especially toward the North, Northeast, and East, and who are "olive-colored" *(olivenfarb)* or "light brown" *(hellbraun),* such as the Ethiopians, the Egyptians, the legendary queen from Arabia, or, for that matter, an alleged Hova princess from Madagascar.[122] As is meet and proper for a man of the Enlightenment, though, Wieland proceeds in an ironical and critical vein, contrary to, say, Keller and the somewhat naïve and almost touching stereotyping he performs, despite all his humor, in "Don Correa." And while Wieland also concentrates on the idea of beauty, as do the others, he furthermore applies his observations to both sexes, since there has existed, from the beginning, a male counterpart of the female stereotype, penetrating to the lowest depths of triviality, as Lester's inventory proves.[123] Or as Michel Gneba Kokora argues, if only with regard to German literature between 1750 and 1884, the year of Bismarck's colonial conference: Germany cherished "a dualistic concept" *(une idée dualiste)* of the African continent, as well as of everything pertaining to it. The Germans perceived, in sum, two Africas, one of which they esteemed while the other was questioned by them:

> 1) l'Afrique ancienne (l'Egypte, Carthage, etc.) intimement liée à leur fonds culturel et qui, dans les lettres de l'époque, avait une image respectable;
> b) l'Afrique Noire dont la respectabilité constituait un point de litige dans le monde intellectuel de l'Allemagne d'alors.[124]

Nevertheless, as must be obvious by now, this double standard seems to have been considerably more complex or, at any rate, far more persistent than is assumed by the African scholar.

But let us return to Messrs. Bloch and Erlanger and their initial meeting, which is described as follows:

> In der Vorhalle des Hotels erhob sich aus seinem Sessel Herr François Bloch. . . Er war nicht älter als Doktor Erlanger. Im Gegensatz zu ihm war er zierlichen Leibes und beinahe blond, nur ihre engstehenden Augen glichen sich überraschend und blickten gleich klug, gleich freundlich, gleich traurig. Sie schauten einander an, als man sie vorstellte; ein mehrtausendjähriges gleiches Schicksal grüßte sich selber in diesem Blick.

> (Herr François Bloch. . .rose out of his chair in the vestibule of the hotel. He was no older than Dr. Erlanger, but by contrast delicately built and almost fair. Only their eyes were surprisingly alike, close-lying, shrewd and friendly and sad all at once. These eyes met as they were introduced; and in their gaze spoke thousands of years of identical destiny.)[125]

Earlier, it was specified with equal care by the narrator that Erlanger is "tall, young, brunette, with strikingly close-set eyes" *(jung, groß, sehr brünett, mit auffallend engstehenden Augen);*[126] and while those eyes—note that Frank employs exactly the same word each time—may or may not be interpreted as a subtle though firm revaluation of the Mossean "countertype," the complete absence of any of the stereotypical features commonly associated with Jewishness is beyond dispute.[127] Instead, by purposely mixing the traits usually attributed to the French and German stereotypes (delicately built and brunette vs. tall and blond), and by evenly but crosswise dividing them among Bloch and Erlanger, the author aims at conveying the impression of a kind of Pan-European, indeed occidental, or *abendländisch,* unity wherein the Jewish heritage has been sublated, as it were, but doubtless not lost. This strong suggestion of an ethnic and, by implication, both linguistic and literary as well as overall cultural oneness is also imparted by what happens subsequently, and it is carefully corroborated by way of authorial commentary. Thus we are alerted, for instance, to the neighborly resemblance between the pronunciation of the French vocable, "Maître," and that of its German equivalent, "Meister":

> . . .es [i.e., the word] klang auf Französisch ein wenig anders, aber eben nur so, wie in dem einen Gebirgstal die Leute anders reden als im nächsten.
>
> (The word sounded a little different in French, but not more so than the speech of peasants in one mountain valley does from the speech of peasants in the next.)[128]

In the personal sphere, too, a responsive chord is immediately struck as Bloch, a dilettante in criticism yet who has just been published in the famed *Nouvelle Revue Française,* learns to his delight that not only is Erlanger a kindred spirit and fellow connoisseur of belles lettres, but that he has even read and studied his recent piece. And so they sit down "in a nook among orange and laurel," under the starlit sky, and briskly embark on a long and lively conversation, its point of departure being Bloch's essay and his truly European subject, or subjects: namely, the joint Franco-German cultural contribution of the great symbolist poets, Stéphane Mallarmé and Stefan George.[129] On all levels, from the humblest to the most sublime, the union of France and Germany—and, thereby, the very essence of Frank's beloved Europe—appears to be safely established, if only symbolically, through its brilliant incorporation by these two young Jewish intellectuals.

However, when the narrator, after having focused for a while on Dorval's and Carmer's discussion, switches back to their erudite secretaries, Bloch's and Erlanger's previous harmony and friendly exchange of ideas has suddenly turned into a dissonant confrontation and ever more heated debate. The topic is now a comparison between French and German, the inherent virtues or vices of both idioms, and the advantages or disadvantages they offer to their respective speakers. Bloch, "in ausgezeichnetem Deutsch" ("in faultless German"), defends and praises French while wittily attacking and denigrating his opponent's language; Erlanger, "in raschem Französisch" ("in rapid [i.e., equally fluent and flawless] French"), does the same with respect to his own and Bloch's native tongues.[130] This linguistic reversal, highly amusing in itself, is once more symbolic in that it further underpins said Pan-European oneness—albeit, ironically enough, as a unity in discord. But the mutual quips and gibes go on, more rapidly yet, affecting the two literatures as conceived and executed on either side of the Rhine, the two ways of thinking and reasoning and their manifestations in philosophy, and, finally, the two national characters of the French and Germans as such. For both Erlanger and Bloch are, their erudition notwithstanding, quite serious, and the narrator does not fail expressly to observe that "solcher Chauvinismus in das...Staatliche übersetzt, hätte ungefähr bei jeder Wendung Gefahr und Kriegsfall bedeutet" ("Chauvinism like that, translated into the affairs of...states, would have meant danger of war at almost every turn").[131] The weightiest comment, though, put forth by the narrator is the following:

> Seltsam zu denken, daß dies nun 'Gäste' waren in ihren Völkern, Fremde anstößigerweise unter denen, deren Wort und Dichtung sie so verzehrend liebten, Unechte, Störer, Geduldete. Hätte sie einer gehört, die Erwägung hätte ihm kommen können, ob nicht der innige Anteil am Worte, am Laut werdenden Erinnerungsschatz eines Volkes Zugehörigkeit tiefer begründe, als manche fragwürdige Blutsverwandtschaft.

> (And these two, strange to say, were 'guests' among their nations, strangers on sufferance among those whose language and poesy they so burningly loved—spurious nationals, barely tolerated, often trouble-makers. A listener might have speculated whether such profound sympathy for a language—its store of common memories made vocal—is not rooted deeper than a mere equivocal blood-relationship is.)[132]

Yet, with the sadness he has himself evoked previously, Frank cannot but add the melancholic question:

> Vielleicht aber, wer will da schwören, hätten sich einem strengen Hörer die Streitenden nur vollends verdächtig gemacht. Der hätte vielleicht gefunden, daß jeder von ihnen allzu vollkommen die Sprache des andern rede.

> (On the other hand, who knows but the two antagonists might only have made themselves utterly suspect to a listener's ear? Each of them spoke far too well the other's speech.)[133]

These renditions are scarcely always faithful, much less perfect, but Frank's message does come through. Even though he was not at all unaware of what might be termed the dialectics of assimilation—sovereign assimilation, mind you, five years before Hitler's rise to power and the systematic genocide that ensued—Frank nonetheless portrayed and openly propagated his ideal and ultimate solution: Not only are the Jews (the liberal bourgeois Jewish intellectuals, that is) on the same footing with their French and German coequals, but they are in fact the better Frenchmen or Germans, more deeply rooted in "their" peoples, more profoundly committed to "their" cultures, than the mere "natives." Indeed they are the better Europeans, precisely in that bold and precarious sense espoused by Frank.

If, as Mosse states on several occasions,[134] "the Jew was the outsider" and "eternal foreigner," and was so considered by Germans and Frenchmen alike, and if, as a consequence, "culture was closed to him," all the more so since he would never learn how "to speak the national language properly," then this image has not only been completely refuted but absolutely reversed in Frank's *Politische Novelle*. In it, if anywhere, "the outsider [is] the insider," to reiterate Peter Gay's well-known formula.[135] Of necessity, therefore, the harmony between Bloch and Erlanger must be restored by the author. Reconciliation and, as before, European sublation must reign supreme. And Frank accomplishes both, I concede, with superb craftsmanship. In a scene which occupies the very center of the whole tale, he has his Erlanger simply relate a little story:

> 'Ich werde Ihnen etwas erzählen, Herr Bloch. Etwas erzählen ist immer das Beste. Eine kleine Geschichte, sie stammt aus einem französischen Buch, einer Biographie...Sie müssen sich in den Norden Ihres Vaterlandes versetzen, in die Normandie, nach Rouen. Dort gibt es oder gab es am linken Ufer der Seine eine Allee, eine schöne Allee mit hohen Bäumen. Jenseits sieht man die Stadt mit ihren Türmen. Man schreibt 1837 oder 38. Es ist ein schöner Frühlingsnachmittag und zwar Ostersamstag. Über den Fluß herüber kommt ein junger Mensch. Er kommt aus seinem Gymnasium, eben war Schulschluß. Es ist der junge Flaubert. Er hat keinen Hut auf seinem halblangen prächtigen Haar, bekleidet ist er mit einem gelben Rock, der viel zu leicht ist für die Jahreszeit, und mit einer weiten, hellblauen Hose. In der Hand trägt er ein Buch. Er setzt sich auf eine Bank dort am Ufer und beginnt zu lesen. Sein Gesicht verändert sich, er wird blaß, mit dem Handrücken muß er sich Tränen fortwischen. Er liest. Die Sonne ist beinahe hinunter. Da fangen vom jenseitigen Ufer her die Glocken zu läuten an, die das Fest verkündigen. Aber das ist zu viel für den jungen Menschen, der Zusammenklang übermannt ihn, ihn schwindelt vor Glück der übermächtigen Schönheit, das Buch entfällt seiner Hand, die Augen werden ihm dunkel, ohnmächtig sinkt er hernieder an seiner Bank. Hinzukommende bringen ihn heim.'
>
> 'Der Faust?' fragte Herr Marcel [*sic*] Bloch leise, 'welche Stelle? Der Osterspaziergang?'
>
> 'Der zweite Monolog. Flaubert hat es erzählt. Aber denken Sie doch, daß er ihn auf Französisch las! Das ist kaum dasselbe, nicht wahr. "Annoncez-vous déjà, cloches profondes, la première heure du jour de Pâques...cantiques célestes, puissants et doux, pourquoi me cherchez-vous dans la poussière?" Es heißt aber so...'
>
> 'Es heißt,' fiel Herr Bloch mit zuckenden Lippen ein, und er war bleich wie jener Gymnasiast, und sein Deutsch hatte fremdere Laute als sonst vor Erregung:

Welch tiefes Summen, welch ein heller Ton
Zieht mit Gewalt das Glas von meinem Munde,
Verkündiget ihr dumpfen Glocken schon
Des Osterfestes erste Feierstunde?
Was sucht ihr, mächtig und gelind,
Ihr Himmelstöne mich am Staube...

Die Himmelstöne! Besiegt und beglückt wäre er ihrer Stimme vielleicht lange gefolgt. Aber ein schriller Jubel zerschnitt sie. Es war der dämonenhafte Aufschrei jener Urwaldmusik, es war derselbe Triumph-Ruf der afrikanischen Perser, den man auch oben, in jenem Zimmer des zweiten Stockwerks [where Carmer and Dorval are conversing], so deutlich vernahm.

Herr François Bloch brach ab. Sie blickten sich an.

('I will tell you a story, Monsieur Bloch. A story is always best. A little story, out of a French biography. Listen... You must imagine yourself in the northern part of your own country, in Normandy, in Rouen. There, on the left bank of the Seine, there is, or was, a street, a fine avenue with lofty trees, and beyond it the town with its towers. The time is 1837 or 1838, on a beautiful spring afternoon, Easter Saturday, in fact. A young man comes across the river from his lycée, school having just closed. It is young Flaubert. The fine head of flowing hair is bare; he wears a yellow coat, much too thin for the season, and wide, light-blue trousers. In his hand he has a book. He sits down on a bench there by the river and begins to read. His features change, he grows pale, the tears come, he has to wipe them away with the back of his hand. He reads on. The sun is almost down. Then from across the river comes the sound of bells, ringing for Easter. And this is too much for the poor young man; he is overcome by the harmony of sound, giddy with the joy of this supreme beauty, the book falls from his hand, his eyes grow dim, he sinks down in a faint on his bench. They come up and carry him home.'

'*Faust*?' asked François Bloch, softly, 'What scene? The Easter Walk?'

'Second monologue. Flaubert tells the story himself. But remember, he read it in French—scarcely the same thing, is it: *"Annoncez-vous déjà, cloches profondes, la première heure du jour de Pâques... cantiques célestes, puissants et doux, pourquoi me cherchez-vous dans la poussière?"* No, it goes like this—'

'Like this,' broke in Bloch, his lips twitching; he was pale as the student Erlanger had described, and in his emotion his German pronunciation suffered:

Welch tiefes Summen, welch ein heller Ton
Zieht mit Gewalt das Glas von meinem Munde,
Verkündiget ihr dumpfen Glocken schon
Des Osterfestes erste Feierstunde?
Was sucht ihr, mächtig und gelind,
Ihr Himmelstöne mich am Staube...

Those 'heavenly accents'—he might have gone blissfully on repeating them, who knows how long? But a shrill outburst cut them short: the demoniac

shriek of that primitive music, the very same exultant yell of the Afric [*sic*] Persians which had burst in upon the conference in the upper room.
M. François Bloch broke off. They looked at each other.)[136]

Having recited Goethe with the lips of Flaubert, as it were, they now look at each other with those eyes of theirs which resemble each other so tellingly, and thus affirm and seal, one final time, the insoluble union of their Jewish *and* European, European *and* Jewish heritage,[137] as opposed to what Frank so indiscriminately lumps together as the barbarians from the East, the West, and, above all, the South. Yes, blacks and Jews *are* represented jointly in this novella; but no common bond whatsoever remains between them except alienation and utter hostility, both on the part of the latter and of the Europeans in general. In a manner of speaking, the redemption, indeed transfiguration, of the Jews *is* achieved here, shortly before the Holocaust; yet it is gained at the expense of the ruthless condemnation, indeed damnation, of all blacks, and of black Africans in particular.

Let me conclude on a more hopeful note, though. Today, at least as far as I can see, the joint black-Jewish "counter-type" has either vanished altogether from German literature, or it has been transformed almost beyond recognition. In Müller's play, based though it is on Seghers' novella, the erstwhile Jewish protagonist, Sasportas, is no longer a Jew who sides with the slaves, but himself a black who proudly affirms Third World unity and solidarity, proclaiming that he stands for Africa, Asia, and both Americas alike: "Ich, das ist Afrika. Ich, das ist Asien. Die beiden Amerika sind ich."[138] In Buch's novel *Die Hochzeit von Port-au-Prince,* the Nazis' racist stereotyping as epitomized, most execrably, in their dual slogan, "vernegert und verjudet," is conjured up only to be condemned, in scathing satire, once and for all;[139] and an author like Peter Schütt confesses in a 1979 poem entitled, precisely, "Bekenntnis" ("Confession"):

Ich weiß nicht, ob
in meinen Adern jüdisches Blut
fließt, aber alle Judenmörder
und Anwälte des Antisemitismus
hasse ich wie ein echter Jude.

In meinen Adern fließt
vermutlich kein afrikanisches Blut,
aber alle Sklavenhändler
und Verteidiger der Apartheit
hasse ich bis aufs Blut,
wie ein stolzer Schwarzer.[140]

I need not continue. This poet and critic from Germany is neither a black nor a Jew, but he feels and fights with both, as with all the oppressed, enslaved, and exploited. May he speak for many Germans.

A much abridged version of this essay was read at the colloquium "Images de l'Africain de la Renaissance au XXᵉ siècle" held in Brussels on the occasion of the 150th anniversary of the Université Libre de Bruxelles on September 13 and 14, 1984 and is included in its proceedings.

1 George L. Mosse, *Toward the Final Solution: A History of European Racism* (New York, 1978), pp. xi and 12. The first expressly to combine blacks and Jews in terms of such a negative "counter-type" seems to have been Christoph Meiners, "Über die Natur der Afrikanischen Neger und die davon abhangende Befreyung oder Einschränkung der Schwarzen," *Göttingisches historisches Magazin* 6 (1790): 385–456, espec. 386f.; cf. also Britta Rupp-Eisenreich, "Des Choses occultes en histoire des sciences humaines: Le Destin de la 'Science Nouvelle' de Christoph Meiners," *L'Ethnographie* 79, no. 2 (1983): 131–83.

2 Sterling Brown, *Negro Poetry and Drama* and *The Negro in American Fiction*, with a new preface by Robert Bone (New York, 1960), II, 1.

3 *Malcolm X Speaks: Selected Speeches and Statements.* Ed. by George Breitman (New York, 1966), p. 168. In a fragmentary letter dated January 11, 1964, the Black American playwright Lorraine Hansberry (1930–1965) wrote: "I have...learned that it is difficult for the American mind to adjust to the realization that the Rhetts and Scarletts [from *Gone with the Wind,* i.e. the Southern slaveholders] were as much monsters as the keepers of Buchenwald—they just dressed more attractively and their accents are softer. (I *know* I switched tenses.)" Quoted in *Les Blancs: The Collected Last Plays of Lorraine Hansberry.* Ed., with critical background, by Robert Nemiroff. Introduction by Julius Lester (New York, 1972), p. 196.

4 Sander L. Gilman, *On Blackness without Blacks: Essays on the Image of the Black in Germany* (Boston, 1982), pp. xiv and 128.

5 Uta Sadji, "Visionen eines schwarzafrikanischen Zeitalters: Der Untergang des Abendlandes in der deutschsprachigen Literatur zwischen den Weltkriegen," *Etudes germano-africaines* 1 (1983): 72–92; here p. 92.

6 See *Stokely Speaks: Black Power Back to Pan-Africanism* (New York, 1971), pp. 161f.

7 Leslie A. Fiedler, *No! in Thunder: Essays on Myth and Literature* (Boston, 1960), pp. 234, 239f., 242, and 250. For an interesting statement by an outsider from the German-speaking countries, see Stefan Zweig, "Zwei Bilder aus Amerika 1939," *Monatshefte* 76 (1984): 345–52; here pp. 350ff. ("Negerfrage"). For more information see Lenwood G. Davis, *Black-Jewish Relations in the United States, 1752–1984: A Selected Bibliography* (Westport, Conn., 1984).

8 Compare Gilman, p. xiv; for details, see Keith L. Nelson, "The 'Black Horror on the Rhine': Race as a Factor in Post–World War I Diplomacy," *Journal of Modern History* 42 (1970): 606–28.

9 *Heinrich Heines Sämtliche Werke.* Edited by Ernst Elster (Leipzig und Wien, n.d. [= 1887ff.]), III, 275 (from his "Reise von München nach Genua"). Of similar significance is the fact that, almost a century thereafter, the Jewish writer and critic Carl Einstein published the first German treatise on African art, his famous *Negerplastik* ("Negro Sculpture") of 1915.

10 See *Heines Sämtliche Werke,* II, 117ff. (the poem dates from 1854) and VII, 44 (from *Ludwig Börne: Eine Denkschrift* of 1840).

11 Cf. Rosemarie K. Lester, *Trivialneger: Das Bild des Schwarzen im westdeutschen Illustriertenroman* (Stuttgart, 1982), p. 277 *et pass.*—On the other hand, even a decidedly antifascist work such as Klaus Mann's satirical *roman à clef* of 1936, *Mephisto,* which exposes the collaborative career of the famous director Gustaf Gründgens, must be relegated to trivial literature, at least as far as its portrayal of the German mulatta Juliette Martens is concerned, and although the Nazis' dual racism is summed up as follows: "Eine Schwarze: das war mindestens ebenso arg wie eine Jüdin. Es war ganz genau das, was man jetzt allgemein 'Rassenschande' nannte und äußerst verwerflich fand"; cf. Klaus Mann, *Mephisto: Roman einer Karriere* (Berlin, 1956), p. 265. See also below.

12 See Paul Valentin, "Histoire du nom de l'Africain en allemand," in *Négritude et Germanité: L'Afrique Noire dans la littérature d'expression allemande* (Dakar, 1983), pp. 25–36; here p. 33.

13 Friedrich Percyval Reck-Malleczewen, *Tagebuch eines Verzweifelten.* Mit einem Vorwort von Klaus Harpprecht (Stuttgart, 1966), pp. 46 and 110.

14 Ernst Jünger, *Strahlungen* (Tübingen, 3d ed. 1949), p. 330.

15 Ibid., p. 499.

16 The only monograph among those early contributions seems to be Leroy H. Woodson, *American Negro Slavery in the Works of Friedrich Strubberg, Friedrich Gerstäcker and Otto Ruppius* (Washington, 1949).

17 Maguèye Kassé's "Le personnage du Noir dans la littérature allemande de 1870 à 1939" (Thèse Paris VIII, 1980), which I have not been able to consult, appears to be a type-written dissertation.

18 See his aforementioned collection *On Blackness without Blacks;* also, compare his *Wahnsinn, Text und Kontext: Die historischen Wechselbeziehungen der Literatur, Kunst und Psychiatrie* (Frankfurt/Bern, 1981), pp. 33ff. *et pass.*

19 Cf. *Nama/Namibia: Diary and Letters of Nama Chief Hendrik Witbooi, 1884-1894.* Ed. by Georg M. Gugelberger (Boston, 1984); Beverly Harris-Schenz, *Black Images in Eighteenth-Century German Literature* (Stuttgart, 1981); Kouamé Kouassi, *La Propagande Colonialiste dans la littérature allemande (De la Conférence de Berlin à la Deuxième Guerre Mondiale)* (Saarbrücken, 1981); Lester, *Trivialneger* (cf. n. 11 above); E. C. Nwezeh, *Africa in French and German Fiction (1911-1933)* (Ile-Ife, 1978); Uta Sadji, *Der Negermythos am Ende des 18. Jahrhunderts in Deutschland: Eine Analyse der Rezeption von Reiseliteratur über Schwarzafrika* (Frankfurt/Bern/Las Vegas, 1979); Martin Steins, *Das Bild des Schwarzen in der europäischen Kolonialliteratur 1870-1918: Ein Beitrag zur literarischen Imagologie* (Frankfurt, 1972); Joachim Warmbold, *"Ein Stückchen neudeutsche Erd'..."—Deutsche Kolonialliteratur: Aspekte ihrer Geschichte, Eigenart und Wirkung, dargestellt am Beispiel Afrikas* (Lübeck, 1982); Vernessa C. White, *Afro-American and East German Fiction: A Comparative Study of Alienation, Identity and the Development of Self* (New York/Berne/Frankfort on the Main, 1983). In the meantime, yet another important contribution has appeared: namely, Amadou Booker Sadji's *Das Bild des Negro-Afrikaners in der Deutschen Kolonialliteratur (1884-1945): Ein Beitrag zur literarischen Imagologie Schwarzafrikas* (Berlin, 1985).

20 See espec. vol. II/1, written and/or ed. by Jean Devisse, of the monumental work *The Image of the Black in Western Art* (New York, 1976ff.); also, compare Hans Joachim Kunst, *The African in European Art* (Bad Godesberg, 1967), as well as the two articles by Claude Sanchez, "Der Neger in der bildenden Kunst der deutschen Renaissance—seine Verherrlichung vor seinem Verfall," and Ulrich Müller, "Feirefiz Anschevin—Überlegungen zur Funktion einer Romangestalt Wolframs von Eschenbach," in *Négritude et Germanité,* pp. 49-57 and 37-48, respectively.

21 Technically speaking, he is of course a mulatto.

22 See Rein A. Zondergeld, *Lexikon der phantastischen Literatur* (Frankfurt, 1983), p. 169; "Chronologie," *L'Herne* 30 (1976): 15.

23 Cf. ibid., p. 13.

24 See Joseph Strelka, "Le Visage vert," ibid., pp. 59-65; here p. 60, fn. 5.

25 Cf. Sigrid Mayer, *Golem: Die literarische Rezeption eines Stoffes* (Bern und Frankfurt, 1975), espec. pp. 196ff.

26 Gustav Meyrink, *Das grüne Gesicht: Ein Roman* (München, 1916), p. 5.

27 Ibid., p. 173.

28 Ibid., p. 123.

29 Compare Sanchez, p. 50.

30 See Meyrink, p. 105; also, compare ibid., p. 287.

31 Ibid., p. 240.

32 Ibid., pp. 239f.

33 Compare also Werner M. Bauer, "Afrika und Afrikaner in der österreichischen Literatur des 18. und 19. Jahrhunderts," in *Négritude et Germanité,* pp. 111-24, espec. 122; Uta Sadji, "Visionen eines schwarzafrikanischen Zeitalters," espec. pp. 75ff., where she also discusses Franz Spunda's *Devachan* of 1921 and Güntsche's *Omu-Ssai: Die Königin von Afrika* of 1929 (the former author, by the way, became a follower of Hitler).

34 See Ruth K. Angress, "Kleist's Treatment of Imperialism: *Die Hermannsschlacht* and 'Die Verlobung in St. Domingo'," *Monatshefte* 69 (1977): 17-33; Gilman, *On Blackness without Blacks,* pp. 83ff.; Peter Horn, "Hatte Kleist Rassenvorurteile?", *Monatshefte* 67 (1975): 117-28; Maguèye Kassé, "Heinrich von Kleist et Anna Seghers: La Revolution française et le thème de la révolte dans les Antilles françaises," *Études germano-africaines* 1 (1983): 57-71. According to Uta Sadji, Kleist's novella was preceded only by a play of 1806 by the

Austrian dramatist F. Kratter, which seems to be almost irretrievable, though; compare her "La Traite des Noirs sur les scènes germanophones du XVIIIe siècle: Pièces à grand spectacle ou pièces politiques?" *Études germano-africaines* 2–3 (1984–85): 73–77.

35 Compare, for example, Werner Egk's opera, *Die Jungfrau von Port au Prince* ("The Virgin of Port-au-Prince") of 1963.

36 Gustav Nieritz, *Die Negersklaven und der Deutsche* ("The Negro Slaves and the German"; Berlin, 1841) has not been available to me. Scävola's novel was published in Frankfurt.

37 Quoted in Gaston-Martin, *L'Abolition de l'esclavage (27 avril 1848)* (Paris, 1948), p. 7; compare also Léon-François Hoffman, *Le Nègre romantique: Personnage littéraire et obsession collective* (Paris, 1973), p. 100.

38 *Dichter über ihre Dichtungen: Heinrich Heine.* Edited by Norbert Altenhofer (München, 1971), I, 169.

39 Quoted in Hans Christoph Buch, *Die Scheidung von San Domingo: Wie die Negersklaven von Haiti Robespierre beim Wort nahmen* (Berlin, 1976), p. 133.

40 Compare Maguèye, "Heinrich von Kleist et Anna Seghers," *pass.*

41 Marian E. Musgrave, "Anna Seghers's *Karibische Geschichten* and the Tradition of Slavery Literature" (paper read at the Annual Meeting of the American Association of Teachers of German in Bonn, June 27 to July 2, 1974; unpublished), pp. 2 and 9; for a brief summary, see id., "Anna Seghers's *Karibische Geschichten* and the Tradition of Slavery Literature," in *American Association of Teachers of German: Proceedings of the 42nd Annual Meeting,* ed. by Reinhold Grimm et al. (Philadelphia, 1975), pp. 70f.

42 Bertolt Brecht, *Gesammelte Werke in 20 Bänden* (Frankfurt, 1967), VIII, 369f. (the song dates from 1930/31).

43 See Erich Arendt, *Trug doch die Nacht den Albatros: Gedichte* (Berlin, 1951), pp. 93ff. (written in 1948–50).

44 Anna Seghers, *Karibische Geschichten* (Berlin, 1962), p. 60.

45 Ibid., p. 234.

46 Thus Willfried Feuser, "Slave to Proletarian: Images of the Black in German Literature," *German Life and Letters* (1978/79): 122–34; here, 127f.

47 Heiner Müller, "Der Auftrag: Erinnerung an eine Revolution," *Sinn und Form* 31 (1979): 1244–63; here, p. 1262.

48 See George L. Mosse, *Germans and Jews: The Right, the Left, and the Search for a "Third Force" in Pre-Nazi Germany* (New York, 1970), p. 204.

49 Seghers, p. 236.

50 Nancy A. Lauckner, "The Image of the Jew in the Postwar German Novel" (Diss. Wisconsin, 1971); id., "The Surrogate Jew in the Postwar German Novel," *Monatshefte* 66 (1974): 133–44.

51 Despite his first name, he is not to be confounded, however, with the stereotype described as the black Ulysses by Nancy M. Tischler, *Black Masks: Negro Characters in Modern Southern Fiction* (University Park and London, 1969), p. 55.

52 For these and the following remarks, compare Lauckner, "The Surrogate Jew," pp. 140f.

53 Wolfgang Koeppen, *Tauben im Gras: Roman* (Berlin-Grunewald, n.d.), p. 166.

54 Ibid., p. 160.

55 Compare ibid., p. 168: "sie [i.e., the stones] konnten den Traum [of Washington and Carla] nicht töten, der stärker als jeder Steinwurf ist" ("they couldn't kill the dream, which is stronger than any thrown stone"); ibid., p. 172: "weiß und schwarz, sie [i.e., Odysseus and Susanne making love] lagen...nackt und schön und wild, sie lagen unschuldig auf einem Floß das in die Unendlichkeit segelte" ("white and black, they were lying...naked and beautiful and wild, they were lying, innocent, upon a raft sailing into infinity"). The images of blacks in Koeppen's fiction, but also in his travelogues, deserve a study of their own.

56 Wolf Wondratschek, *Früher begann der Tag mit einer Schußwunde* (München, 1969), p. 19.

57 Koeppen, p. 108.

58 Neu-Spuhl recalls place names such as Neu-Ulm, with the twofold implication of *nouveaux riches* and vermin (cf. *Spulwürmer* = "mawworms"); "schön" is highly ironical.

59 Compare "final solution" and "final ball" vs. *Endlösung* and *Schlußball* (which is, in effect, a technical term for the festive event crowning a series of dancing lessons taken jointly by high school students).

60 Mosse, *Toward the Final Solution,* p. xii.

61 Gilman, *On Blackness without Blacks*, p. xiv.
62 See Gerd Gaiser, *Schlußball: Aus den schönen Tagen der Stadt Neu-Spuhl* (Frankfurt, 1961), pp. 87f., 94, *et pass.*; id., *The Final Ball* (New York, n.d.), pp. 107, 114, *et pass.*; also, compare Marcel Reich-Ranicki, *Deutsche Literatur in West und Ost: Prosa seit 1945* (München, 1963), pp. 55ff., who quotes and discusses some rather revealing variants from an earlier version of Gaiser's novel.
63 Cf. Gaiser, *Schlußball*, p. 89; id., *The Final Ball*, p. 109.
64 See id., *Schlußball*, p. 61 *et pass.*; id., *The Final Ball*, p. 77 *et pass.*
65 But compare Mosse, *Toward the Final Solution*, pp. 34ff. (plus illustrations).
66 Gaiser, *Schlußball*, p. 110; id., *The Final Ball*, p. 134.
67 Id., *Schlußball*, p. 123; id., *The Final Ball*, p. 150.
68 Id., *Schlußball*, p. 88; id., *The Final Ball*, p. 107.
69 Id., *Schlußball*, p. 100; id., *The Final Ball*, p. 121.
70 Quoted by Reich-Ranicki, p. 78.
71 Ibid.; cf. Gaiser, *The Final Ball*, p. 107.
72 Id., *Schlußball*, p. 94; id., *The Final Ball*, p. 114.
73 See id., *Schlußball*, p. 87; id., *The Final Ball*, p. 106.
74 Id., *Schlußball*, p. 94; id., *The Final Ball*, p. 114.
75 Quoted by Reich-Ranicki, p. 78; cf. Gaiser, *The Final Ball*, p. 107. Gaiser's later version reads: "Rakitsch aber mit seinem dunklen Akzent hatte eine Verkehrsart, die gewohnt war, sich zu biegen, um an ein Ziel zu gelangen"; cf. id., *Schlußball*, p. 87.
76 See ibid., pp. 88f.; id., *The Final Ball*, pp. 108f.
77 Mosse, *Germans and Jews*, p. 57.
78 See Gaiser, *The Final Ball*, p. 103; compare id., *Schlußball*, p. 84: "wenn ich Rakitsch sah, ist mir nie wohl geworden."
79 Compare id., *The Final Ball*, p. 108 and *Schlußball*, p. 88: "Aber niemand wollte mit Rakitsch zu tun haben."
80 See ibid., pp. 90 and 93; id., *The Final Ball*, pp. 110 and 114.
81 Ibid., p. 109.
82 Id., *Schlußball*, p. 89.
83 Ibid., p. 107; id., *The Final Ball*, p. 130.
84 Id., *Schlußball*, pp. 97, 100, *et pass.*; id., *The Final Ball*, pp. 117, 120, *et pass.*
85 Id., *Schlußball*, p. 74; id., *The Final Ball*, p. 91.
86 Id., *Schlußball*, p. 110; id., *The Final Ball*, p. 134.
87 Id., *Schlußball*, p. 196; id., *The Final Ball*, p. 234.
88 Id., *Schlußball*, p. 126; id., *The Final Ball*, p. 153.
89 Id., *Schlußball*, pp. 85 and 102; id., *The Final Ball*, pp. 104 and 123.
90 Id., *Schlußball*, p. 125; id., *The Final Ball*, p. 151.
91 See id., *Schlußball*, p. 86; id., *The Final Ball*, pp. 105f.
92 See Gilman's chapter, " 'The Nigger's Crazy': On the Nexus of Blackness and Madness," in his *On Blackness without Blacks*, pp. 1–18.
93 Gaiser, *Schlußball*, p. 95; id., *The Final Ball*, p. 115.
94 Id., *Schlußball*, p. 110; id., *The Final Ball*, pp. 134f.; also, note Gaiser's similar usage of *Rotwelsch* ("thieves' and gipsies' slang") in his novel of 1950, *Eine Stimme hebt an* ("A Voice Begins").
95 Reich-Ranicki, p. 80.
96 Gerd Gaiser, *Reiter am Himmel: Gedichte* (München, 1941), pp. 57f.
97 Compare poems such as "Die Ahnen," "Die Landnahme," "Wandergesang," "Vom eigenen Stamme," etc.; ibid., pp. 7ff.
98 See ibid., pp. 34f.
99 Ibid., p. 58.
100 See ibid., pp. 42ff.
101 Mention should also be made, if only in passing, of two postwar stories of Gaiser's involving blacks: to wit, "Der Forstmeister" ("The Head Forester") and "Die weiße Amsel und der Neger" ("The White Blackbird and the Negro"—in German, obviously, the oxymoron is only implicit). While free of overt racism, both tales still betray a feeling of superiority and, as a consequence, a condescending attitude on the part of the author; cf. Gerd Gaiser, *Gib acht in Domokosch: Erzählungen* (München, 1959), pp. 62ff. and 245ff., respectively, and compare Reich-Ranicki, *passim*.

102 Even the study that comes closest, Nwezeh's monograph of 1978 (cf. n. 19 above), remains entirely unaware of the existence of Frank's novella.

103 For a brief account, see *Lexikon der deutschen Geschichte: Personen · Ereignisse · Institutionen. Von der Zeitwende bis zum Ausgang des 2. Weltkrieges.* Unter Mitarbeit von Historikern und Archivaren hrsg. von Gerhard Taddey (Stuttgart, 1979), p. 1195.

104 Cf. Martin Gregor-Dellin's short essay, "Der Tod in Marseille," *Sammlung: Jahrbuch für antifaschistische Literatur und Kunst* 4 (1981): 4–7. I must confess that I wanted to use the very same title when, years ago, I planned a comprehensive study of Frank's novella; see my—perhaps all too lenient—portrait of its author, "Bruno Frank, Gentlemanschriftsteller," in *Views and Reviews of Modern German Literature: Festschrift for Adolf D. Klarmann,* ed. by Karl S. Weimar (München, 1974), pp. 121–32.

105 Bruno Frank, *Politische Novelle* (Berlin, 1928), pp. 74 and 14; id., *The Persians Are Coming* (New York, 1929), pp. 54f. and 7.

106 Id., *Politische Novelle,* p. 150. H. T. Lowe-Porter's rendition has "dark hordes" instead; cf. Frank, *The Persians Are Coming,* p. 116.

107 See id., *Politische Novelle,* p. 133; id., *The Persians Are Coming,* p. 86.

108 Cf. Gaiser, *Reiter am Himmel,* p. 34.

109 Frank, *Politische Novelle,* p. 105; id., *The Persians Are Coming,* p. 80 (literally, "the Afric Persians").

110 Id., *Politische Novelle,* p. 91; id., *The Persians Are Coming,* p. 68.

111 Id., *Politische Novelle,* p. 109; id., *The Persians Are Coming,* p. 83. It is interesting to note that, if only in retrospect, the most important representative of the idea of *négritude,* Sénégal's past President Senghor, likewise, and very similarly if in a thoroughly positive vein, refers to both jazz and Josephine Baker; cf. his introductory remarks to the volume, *Leo Frobenius: Une Anthologie.* Avec une préface de Léopold Sédar Senghor. Ed. Eike Haberland (Wiesbaden, 1973), pp. vii–xiii, espec. viii: "Mais, déjà, la trompette de Louis Armstrong avait retenti [in the 1920s and early 1930s] sur la capitale française, comme une condamnation, les hanches de Joséphine Baker secouaient rigoureusement tous ses murs" (the Biblical overtones are unmistakable; compare, above all, Joshua 6:20).

112 See Dieter Kühn, *Josephine: Aus der öffentlichen Biographie der Josephine Baker* (Frankfurt, 1980 [first published in 1976]), *passim.*

113 Frank, *Politische Novelle,* pp. 59, 72, and 109; id., *The Persians Are Coming,* pp. 42f., 53, and 83f.

114 Id., *Politische Novelle,* p. 175; id., *The Persians Are Coming,* p. 135.

115 Id., *Politische Novelle,* p. 176; id., *The Persians Are Coming,* p. 136.

116 Id., Politische *Novelle,* p. 179; id., *The Persians Are Coming,* p. 139.

117 Id., *Politische Novelle,* pp. 178ff.; id., *The Persians Are Coming,* pp. 138f.

118 See my "Vom sogenannten Widerstand gegen die Völkischen: Ein Nachtrag zum Thema 'Ritter, Tod und Teufel'," in Lawrence Baron et al., *Ideologiekritische Studien zur Literatur: Essays II* (Bern und Frankfurt, 1975), pp. 73–82.

119 See Bruno Frank, *Der Magier: Novelle* (Berlin, 1929), espec. pp. 78ff., where the joint portrayal of Jews and black Americans does in fact amount to an *entente cordiale;* black Africans, however, are excluded from it.

120 Compare Tischler's chapter on "Black Sirens," in her *Black Masks,* pp. 63–82; for the quotation, see ibid., p. 87.

121 Cf. *The Image of the Black in Western Art,* II/1, 129f. *et pass.*

122 Compare *C.M. Wielands sämmtliche Werke* (Leipzig, 1853ff.), XIII, 32: "Ich meine, daß die schönsten unter den Aethiopischen Nationen (nämlich diejenigen, die nach unserm Maßstabe die schönsten, das ist, uns die ähnlichsten sind) durchaus olivenfarb wie die Aegyptier, und diejenigen, welche tiefer im festen Lande und in den mittäglichsten Gegenden wohnen, vom Kopf bis zur Fußsohle so schwarz und noch ein wenig schwärzer sind als die Raben zu Abdera" ("I believe that the most beautiful among the Ethiopian people [namely, those whom we, according to our own criteria, view as the most beautiful, that is, those who are most like us] are olive-colored like the Egyptians, and that those who live farther in the continent and in the southernmost regions are black from head to foot, just as the ravens in Abder, indeed a trifle blacker"); the fact that Wieland, adhering to the ancient usage, applies the name of "Ethiopians" to all Africans alike is immaterial. As to Keller's Zambo-Maria, she is "light brown" *(hellbraun);* her hair is "not so woolly *(nicht so wollig)* as that of the Negroes," and all her features *(die Gesichtsbildung)* are "noble"

(edel) and, indeed, reminiscent of the ancient Egyptians *(an den Schnitt altägyptischer Frauengesichter erinnernd).* Also, she is not a native of Angola but came with her mother from the East *(von Sonnenaufgang her),* and the Jesuit priest in his sermon celebrating her baptism pictures her as "a last descendant of the wise Queen of Sheba" *(ein letzter Nachkomme der weisen Königin von Saba).* And so on and so forth; cf. *Gottfried Kellers gesammelte Werke in vier Bänden* (Leipzig, 1921), I, 703ff. (Frank singles out a "light brown" girl *[jene Schlanke, Junge, Hellbraune]* in his *Der Magier,* too; cf. ibid., p. 83.)

123 Compare Lester, pp. 84 and 176, where she notes that, above all, this stereotype doesn't look like a black man but rather like some handsome Southerner—an East Indian, at worst—or that he isn't black at all: "Vor allem sieht er nicht wie ein Neger aus, sondern gleicht...eher einem schönen Südländer, allenfalls einem Inder...[Er] ist eigentlich gar keiner [i.e., black]." Yet what holds true for fiction, whether trivial or sublime, holds also true for life; compare, for example, the biography of Angelo Soliman (1720–96), an erudite black married to an Austrian noblewoman, who was highly esteemed at the Imperial Court in Vienna: "Angelo war von mittlerer Größe, schlank und schön gebaut; seine Züge waren bey Weitem nicht so sehr von unseren Begriffen über Schönheit entfernt, als die Züge der Neger sonst zu seyn pflegen." Thus Karoline Pichler, *Sämtliche Werke* (Wien, 1820ff.), XXIV, 94; for more details—some of which are totally different, indeed almost incredible—see Bauer, pp. 114f. and 124, n. 13.

124 Michel Gneba Kokora, "L'Image de l'Afrique dans les lettres allemandes," *Annales de l'Université d'Abidjan,* série D, 8 (1975): 299–311; here p. 311. Compare also id., "La Satire et l'Afrique exotique dans la littérature allemande de 1750 à 1884," *Annales de l'Université d'Abidjan,* série D, 9 (1976): 509–19.

125 Frank, *Politische Novelle,* p. 73; id., *The Persians Are Coming,* p. 54.

126 Id., *Politische Novelle,* p. 12; id., *The Persians Are Coming,* p. 5.

127 Compare plate 1 (opposite p. 34) in Mosse's *Toward the Final Solution.*

128 Frank, *Politische Novelle,* p. 74; id., *The Persians Are Coming,* pp. 54f.

129 See id., *Politische Novelle,* p. 75; id., *The Persians Are Coming,* p. 55.

130 See id., *Politische Novelle,* p. 92; id., *The Persians Are Coming,* p. 69.

131 Id., *Politische Novelle,* pp. 94f.; id., *The Persians Are Coming,* p. 71.

132 Id., *Politische Novelle,* p. 95; id., *The Persians Are Coming,* p. 71.

133 Id., *Politische Novelle,* p. 95; id., *The Persians Are Coming,* pp. 71f.

134 See Mosse, *Germans and Jews,* p. 60; id., *Toward the Final Solution,* pp. 115 and 44.

135 Peter Gay, *Weimar Culture: The Outsider as Insider* (New York and Evanston, 1968). Ironically, Frank is not even mentioned in this influential book. Mosse, on the other hand, has only recently added the following observations: "Die Judenemanzipation [in Germany] führte zu einer neuen jüdischen Identität, die...von Juden übernommen wurde, die überwiegend aus der höheren Mittelklasse stammten und gebildet waren." And: "Der deutsch-jüdische Dialog hatte in diesen letzten Jahren vor Hitlers Machtergreifung die Tendenz, ein französisch-jüdisch-deutscher Dialog zu werden." Cf. George L. Mosse, "Gedanken zum deutsch-jüdischen Dialog," in *Chronik der Ludwig-Maximilians-Universität München* (München, n.d. [= 1984]), pp. 48–58 (the quotations are from pp. 55 and 54, respectively). Frank's Bloch and Erlanger—though not mentioned by Mosse—are perhaps the best example to bear out these contentions.

136 Frank, *Politische Novelle,* pp. 103ff.; id., *The Persians Are Coming,* pp. 78ff.

137 Precisely in Germany, such a union had been envisioned from the very beginning. The journal *Sulamith,* founded in order to speed up the process of Jewish emancipation, proclaimed as early as 1806 that Jews should, and could, "embrace Europe"; cf. *Sulamith* 1 (1806): 9 and George L. Mosse, *German Jews beyond Judaism* (Bloomington/Cincinnati, 1985), p. 7 *et pass.*

138 Heiner Müller, p. 1262.

139 See Hans Christoph Buch, *Die Hochzeit von Port-au-Prince: Roman* (Frankfurt, 1984), p. 256; also, compare ibid., p. 252.

140 Peter Schütt, *Zwei Kontinente: Gedichte von diesseits und jenseits des Ozeans* (Fischerhude, 1979), p. 8. Also quite noteworthy is the recent volume *Andenken an den Kolonialismus: Eine Ausstellung des Völkerkundlichen Instituts der Universität Tübingen.* Hrsg. von Volker Harms, in Zusammenarbeit mit Klaus Barthel, Sibylle Benninghoff-Lühl, *et al.* (Tübingen, 1984).